W9-AMQ-044

Looking for a Miracle

Weeping
Icons,
Relics,
Stigmata,
Visions &
Healing
Cures

Joe Nickell

Prometheus Books
59 John Glenn Drive
Amherst, NewYork 14228-2197

Published 1998 by Prometheus Books

Looking for a Miracle: Weeping Icons, Relics, Stigmata, Visions and Healing Cures.
Copyright © 1993 by Joe Nickell. All rights reserved. No part of this publication may
be reproduced, stored in a retrieval system, or transmitted in any form or by any
means, electronic, mechanical, photocopying, recording, or otherwise, without prior
written permission of the publisher, except in the case of brief quotations embodied
in critical articles and reviews. Inquiries should be addressed to Prometheus Books,
59 John Glenn Drive, Amherst, New York 14228–2197, 716–691–0133. FAX:
716–691–0137. WWW.PROMETHEUSBOOKS.COM

07 06 05 04 03   6 5 4 3 2

Library of Congress Cataloging-in-Publication Data

Nickell, Joe.
    Looking for a miracle : weeping icons, relics, stigmata, visions and healing cures.
/ Joe Nickell.
        p.   cm.
    Includes bibliographical references and index.
    ISBN 1–57392–680–9 (alk. paper)
    1. Miracles—Controversial literature. 2. Parapsychology—Controversial litera-
ture. 3. Occultism—Controversial literature. I. Title.
BT97.2.N53   1993
231.7'3—dc20   93–25322
                                                                          CIP

Printed in the United States of America on acid-free paper

Acknowledgments

Many people assisted with this book. I am especially grateful to Robert A. Baker (Lexington, Kentucky) and Bruce Mazet (Citrus Heights, California) for providing helpful suggestions and research materials. I am also grateful to Herbert G. Schapiro (Warren, New Jersey), whose generosity in providing me with his clipping service for the past several years has resulted in many important inclusions in this book.

I also wish to thank the staff members of the Margaret I. King Library, University of Kentucky, and the John F. Kennedy Memorial Library, West Liberty, Kentucky, for their assistance; the entire staff of the Committee for the Scientific Investigation of Claims of the Paranormal, including Paul Kurtz (Chairman), Barry Karr (Executive Director), Kendrick Frazier (Editor of the Committee's journal, *Skeptical Inquirer*), and the members of the executive council; and, as always, my mother, Ella T. Nickell, for typing the manuscript.

Finally, I extend my appreciation to forensic analyst John F. Fischer, friend and co-investigator of various "miracle" claims, who lent his expertise in many ways.

Contents

8   Contents

1

Introduction

We live in a time when rational thought and enlightened endeavor have given us wonders heretofore scarcely imaginable—ranging from such advancements in health and medicine as the conquering of dread diseases like smallpox and the ability to replace a defective heart, to such technological developments as the capability of instantly viewing important happenings around the world and of traveling to the moon and beyond. Elsewhere in the intellectual arena, we have replaced concepts of demon possession with psychological understanding and primitive authoritarianism with enlightened democracy.

Yet there are those whose beliefs and actions run counter to a rationalist ideal. Often seemingly contemptuous of science, or at best willing only grudgingly to acknowledge its benefits, they view the world in terms that hark back to the "Dark Ages," holding beliefs in myriad phenomena—from apparitions to weeping statues—that might generally be described as "miraculous."

The term *miracle* has been variously defined. According to *Webster's Third International Dictionary,* a miracle is "an extraordinary event taken to manifest the supernatural power of God fulfilling his purposes" or "an event or effect in the physical world deviating from the laws of nature."[1] The Anglican writer C. S. Lewis defined a miracle succinctly as "an interference with Nature by supernatural power."[2]

9

A term related to *miracle,* and thus one that may cause confusion, is *paranormal.* This refers to the supposed existence of things beyond the range of normal experience and nature—typically applied to such diverse phenomena as flying saucers, Bigfoot and other monsters, ghosts, spontaneous human combustion, and the like, as well as to certain alleged abilities such as levitation and extrasensory perception (ESP). The latter is typically subdivided into additional categories, including telepathy (thought transference or "mind reading"), clairvoyance (or "clear seeing," the alleged psychic ability to perceive things beyond the knowledge of one's senses), and psychokinesis (or "mind over matter," the reputed capability of influencing physical objects by mental power alone).

Paranormal is therefore a broad term inclusive of potentially natural phenomena. For instance, although it appears unlikely that Bigfoot exists, if it does it is assumed to be a physical creature like any other in nature. *Supernatural* is a more limited term, referring to a supposed existence beyond the natural world—whether applied to "occult" forces like witchcraft or satanism, or to "divine" manifestations, such as angels. The latter category—supernatural phenomena believed to have a divine origin—is generally referred to as *miraculous.*

The late D. Scott Rogo, a prominent researcher of reputedly paranormal phenomena, was careful to distinguish the broader category from the narrower one, although he did so in a way that skeptics are quick to take issue with. He believed (despite powerful evidence to the contrary) that the reality of paranormal phenomena such as telepathy and psychokinesis had been established in the laboratory.[3] That was his basis for stating: "Miracles are therefore events that are qualitatively different from those we can observe and which seem to indicate the intervention of some supernatural force into the affairs of human life."[4] But even if we question the "qualitative" aspect of Rogo's definition, we can nevertheless agree with the need to distinguish between types of phenomena.

Just such a distinction between the paranormal and the miraculous has long been made by the Catholic Church. In the 1730s Prospero Lambertini (later Pope Benedict XIV) addressed the issue in his *De canonizatione,* a treatise on miracles that still represents the Church's official view on the subject. Lambertini felt that it was necessary to separate the paranormal from the miraculous in order to determine whether an event was actually attributable to God. Lambertini therefore rejected not only such phenomena as clairvoyance, but he also disallowed most healings. In contrast, his definition of miraculous allowed the inclusion of certain nontraditional healings, as well as such additional phenomena as stigmata, levitation, wondrously appearing images of Christ, appearances of the Virgin Mary (if seen simultaneously by multiple witnesses), and the like.[5]

But is there proof of the actual occurrence of miracles? The philosopher David Hume thought not. In his treatise "Of Miracles" Hume stated:

> A miracle is a violation of the laws of nature; and as a firm and unalterable experience has established these laws, the proof against a miracle, from the very nature of the fact is as entire as any argument from experience can possibly be imagined . . . no testimony is sufficient to establish a miracle unless the testimony be of such a kind that its falsehood would be more miraculous than the fact which it endeavors to establish.[6]

Scott Rogo, on the other hand, answered in the affirmative. He stated, in response to Hume: "It is my hope to show . . . that the evidence authenticating the existence of miracles is indeed so strong that its collective falsehood would be, quite literally, miraculous."[7] Here, Rogo is following an approach that is popularly known as the "faggot theory." This "theory" holds that while one reported mystical occurrence may be discredited, just as a single stick may easily be broken, numerous reports withstand attack, just as a bundle of sticks (i.e., a faggot) resists breaking.

The problem with such a notion is readily apparent. If one case at a time can be disproved, or dismissed for lack of evidence (take an Elvis Presley sighting, for example), then the mere quantity of such cases means little if anything. (Often a rash of reports turns out to be nothing more than an original misperception or hoax, followed by what psychologists call "social contagion" or "mass hysteria.")

If Hume, then, is viewed as *a priori* dismissive, Rogo is to be faulted for the opposite extreme of being entirely too credulous. C. S. Lewis was pessimistic that the situation could ever be otherwise. Pointing out that our own experiences cannot be conclusive, since our senses are fallible (a "ghost," for example, may turn out to be "an illusion or a trick of the nerves"), Lewis states:

> If immediate experience cannot prove or disprove the miraculous, still less can history do so. Many people think one can decide whether a miracle occurred in the past by examining the evidence "according to the ordinary rules of historical inquiry." But the ordinary rules cannot be worked until we have decided whether miracles are possible, and if

so, how probable they are. For if they are impossible, then no amount of historical evidence will convince us. If they are possible but immensely improbable, then only mathematically demonstrative evidence will convince us: and since history never provides that degree of evidence for any event, history can never convince us that a miracle occurred. If, on the other hand, miracles are not intrinsically improbable, then the existing evidence will be sufficient to convince us that quite a number of miracles have occurred. The result of our historical enquiries thus depends on the philosophical views which we have been holding before we even began to look at the evidence. The philosophical question must therefore come first.[8]

But surely Lewis's position is a prescription for bias. W. I. B. Beveridge, in his treatise, *The Art of Scientific Investigation*, cautions against bias and urges the "intellectual discipline of subordinating ideas to facts." He quotes Claude Bernard, who stated: "Men who have excessive faith in their theories or ideas are not only ill-prepared for making discoveries; they also make poor observations." Warning that, "Unless observations and experiments are carried out with safeguards ensuring objectivity, the results may unconsciously be biased," Beveridge cites instances in which such bias occurred in science, including the experimental work of Gregor Mendel whose expectations colored his results. Beveridge adds:

> The best protection against these tendencies is to cultivate an intellectual habit of subordinating one's opinions and wishes to objective evidence and a reverence for things as they really are, and to keep constantly in mind that the hypothesis is only a supposition.[9]

So let us not put the cart before the horse by deciding, antecedent to inquiry, whether or not miracles exist. As with other mysteries, let us agree that they should neither be fostered nor dismissed, but rather that they should be approached in a rigorous, yet fair, manner—an investigative manner. The tools for such an approach come readily to hand.

The investigator begins by adopting a critical attitude toward the data he encounters. This helps insure that evidence is neither dismissed out of hand nor too readily accepted.

The investigation continues by following some accepted precepts. One is that the burden of proof lies on the asserter of fact, which protects the inquirer from the unfair requirement of trying to prove a negative. (Suppose, for instance, that instead of challenging someone to prove his or her assertion that there is an angel on the church roof, you attempt to *disprove* the claim. You go outside and point to the roof and the absence of any angelic form. But the contender may retort: "It flew away!" or "I can see it; why can't you?")

Another accepted precept concerns the standard of proof required when one is dealing with claims of the supernatural. It is expressed by the maxim that "extraordinary claims require extraordinary proof"—that is, that the level of proof that is requisite to establish a particular claim must be commensurate with the claim being made; the more remarkable the assertion, the higher must be the level of proof needed to confirm it.

Still another valuable precept is the principle known as "Occam's Razor" (after the fourteenth-century philosopher William of Occam), which is used to discriminate between competing hypotheses. Also referred to as "the maxim of parsimony," Occam's Razor postulates that the simplest tenable explanation—that is, the one with the fewest assumptions—is most likely to be correct and therefore is to be preferred.[10]

In addition, the investigator must be wary of a number of human limitations that can affect witnesses and belie a correct determination in a case. These include tricks of memory, the problems of perception, faulty reasoning, and similar factors.

For example, Elizabeth Loftus, in her book *Memory: Surprising New Insights Into How We Remember and Why We Forget*, explains:

> Memory is imperfect. This is because we often do not see things accurately in the first place. But even if we take in a reasonably accurate picture of some experience, it does not necessarily stay perfectly intact in memory. Another force is at work. The memory traces can actually undergo distortion. With the passage of time, with proper motivation, with the introduction of special kinds of interfering facts, the memory traces seem sometimes to change or become transformed. These distortions can be quite frightening, for they can cause us to have memories of things that never happened. Even in the most intelligent among us is memory thus malleable.[11]

As to perception, legal experts Leo Levin and Harold Cramer point out: "Eyewitness testimony is, at best, evidence of what the witness believes to have occurred. It may or may not tell what actually happened." The many problems that can plague accurate perception of people and events "all contribute to making honest testimony something less than completely credible."[12]

As already mentioned, bias is another problem for the investigator—not only his own, as we have seen, but also that of those offering evidence. For instance, theologian A. E. Garvie said of testimony in favor of saints' miracles that not only was the character of such miracles "such as to lack probability," but:

> Further, these records are imitative. As Christ and the apostles worked miracles, it is assumed that those who in the Church were distinguished for their sanctity would also work miracles; and there can be little doubt that the wish was often father to the thought.[13]

Faulty reasoning is another frequently encountered problem. For example, when one encounters the assertion that something is true because it cannot be proved untrue (an attempt to shift the burden of proof, as discussed earlier), the proper response is to point out the fallacy involved —that of an argument *ad ignorantiam* (i.e., literally an appeal "to ignorance"). Another common fallacy is the assumption that a cause-and-effect relationship has been proven before alternative possibilities have been fully considered. (For example, it would be fallacious to interpret moisture on a religious statue as evidence of miraculous "weeping," until the possibilities of condensation and outright hoaxing have been decisively eliminated.[14])

To illustrate how faulty recall, bias, and other factors can betray even the most credible and sincere witness, consider the case of Sir Edward Hornby, a Shanghai jurist. He related how, years before, he had been awakened one night by a newspaperman who had arrived belatedly to get the customary written judgment for the next day's edition. The man refused to be put off, and—looking "deadly pale"—sat on the bed. Eventually Judge Hornby gave a verbal summary, which the man took down in shorthand in his pocket notebook, whereupon he left. The judge then explained what had happened to Lady Hornby. The following day the judge learned that the reporter had died during the night and—more importantly—that his wife and servants were positive he had not left the house; yet with his body was discovered the notebook, containing a summary of Hornby's judgment!

This apparent proof of preternatural occurrences was reported by psychical researchers. However, the tale soon succumbed to the light of truth thrown on it by an investigator. As it happened, the reporter did not die at the time reported (about 1:00 A.M.) but much later—between 8:00 and 9:00 in the morning; the judge could not have told his wife about the events at the time since he was then between marriages; and, finally, although the story depends on a certain judgment that was to be delivered the following day, no such judgment was recorded.[15]

Confronted with this evidence of error, Judge Hornby admitted: "My vision must have followed the death (some three months earlier) instead of synchronizing with it. . . ." Bewildered by what had happened, he added: "If I had not believed, as I still believe, that every word of [the story] was accurate, and that my memory was to be relied on, I should not have ever told it as a personal experience."[16]

If the lapse of only a few months or years can so remarkably distort reported events, how much more potential is there for error in records that have filtered down from antiquity. For example, consider some of the miracles related in the Bible. Which version of the miracle of creation, if any, is correct: is it the one in Genesis 1:1–2:3, which relates how the earth and its creatures were created over six days, with fish being brought forth from the waters, and culminates with the creation of man; or is it the version in Genesis 2:4–25, which has creation compressed into a single day, with first man and the other creatures being formed out of dust?

The disparity comes as little surprise when we realize that Genesis is a composite work deriving in part from Babylonian and Persian creation myths.[17] That is why the story of Noah and his ark so closely resembles the much earlier Mesopotamian myth, related in the Babylonian *Epic of Gilgamesh* which is complete with a great flood sent by God as punishment for men's sins; a giant ark; a mountaintop landing; and birds sent out successively until one fails to return, thus signaling that it is safe to emerge from the ark. *Funk & Wagnalls Standard Dictionary of Folklore, Mythology and Legend,* commenting tactfully that the earlier flood tale is "strangely parallel to the Biblical version," observes that it was "evidently inspired by the phenomenon of seasonal floods which so frequently work havoc in Mesopotamia."[18] Not surprisingly, such stories entered Hebrew mythology at the end of the Babylonian Exile (about 500 B.C.).[19]

Similar problems arise when we look at accounts of the miracles of Jesus. For example, here is one commentator's plausible hypothesis for the miraculous calming of the storm (Matt. 8:23–27; Mark 4:35–41; Luke 8:22–25):

> The winds coming over the hills west of the Sea of Galilee sometimes swept down onto the surface stirring up sudden storms. The Valley of Doves acts like a funnel for the violent westerly winds and causes them

to swirl over the surface of the shallow water. This happens in summer or winter, and lasts only a short time. Jesus knew what to expect and watched the calm part of the sea. When the calm approached the ship, Jesus said something about it being peaceful and still. After [the story] was told and retold, Jesus was made to say, "Peace, be still."

Perfectly natural actions were misunderstood and turned into supernatural events. No miracle took place in the story.[20]

A complete critical look at biblical miracles lies beyond the scope of this book (and is left to other works already available on the subject[21]); however, the foregoing examples are, hopefully, sufficient to indicate the difficulty in citing ancient stories as evidence of the miraculous. It is the intent of this study, rather, to look at modern "miracles"—those which, by being more recent, can more successfully be investigated. The biblical or post-biblical background of certain alleged phenomena will occasionally be considered, but the main focus will always be on the question of whether or not miraculous events are part of the reality of today's world.

I have long been concerned with this question. As a former professional stage magician and private investigator for an internationally known detective agency, I have learned the importance of investigating magical claims. For over twenty years, I have seen how easily illusion can pass for reality—a harmless enough situation when mere entertainment is involved, but of serious import when relating to such profound possibilities as are represented by miraculous claims.

What are these claims? They begin with assertions treated in Chapter 2 concerning the Shroud of Turin (that it is tangible proof of Jesus' resurrection), the Image of Guadalupe (a supposedly miraculous self-portrait of the Virgin Mary), and other "miraculous" pictures; they continue in Chapter 3 with icons that supposedly weep, bleed, and are otherwise animated.

Chapter 4 examines "mystical relics" like the periodically liquefying blood of Saint Januarius, the reputedly "incorruptible" bodies of certain other pious figures, and additional relics that offer "evidence" of their efficacious powers and that supposedly prove the sanctity of saints.

In Chapter 5, we investigate certain "charismatic gifts of the spirit." Supposedly divinely bestowed, these powers include speaking in tongues, prophesying, and being impervious to serpents and other harmful things.

Chapter 6 explores faith healing—including the claims made for "miracle" cures at Lourdes—and examines how the "cures" actually work.

It also exposes the hype and even outright hoaxes that many so-called healers employ, sometimes with tragic results.

In Chapter 7 we take a close look at Marian apparitions—the claims that the Virgin Mary has appeared, often to peasant children, at such remote places as Fatima, Portugal, and Medjugorje, Yugoslavia.

And finally, in Chapter 8, we examine "sanctified powers," the supposed abilities of saints and mystics who—through allegedly divine sanction—may exhibit luminosity, levitation, bilocation, stigmata, inedia (the ability to go without food), the power to exorcise demons, and the production of "apports," that is, objects out of thin air.

In brief, we will look behind a myriad of claims of the miraculous (defined earlier as supernatural phenomena believed to have a divine origin), ranging from the philosophically challenging to the literally life-and-death aspects of faith healing. These are issues that must matter to all of us, and they must be approached in the serious, critical manner that they deserve.

Select Bibliography

Acquistapace, Fred. *Miracles that Never Were: Natural Explanations of the Bible's Supernatural Stories.* Santa Rosa, Calif.: Eye-Opener Books, 1991. A critical look at the more than 200 miracle stories of the Bible, organized by their order of appearance in the Old and New Testaments.

Baker, Robert A., and Joe Nickell. *Missing Pieces: How to Investigate Ghosts, UFOs, Psychics and Other Mysteries.* Buffalo, N.Y.: Prometheus Books, 1992. A handbook for investigators of the paranormal, explaining how to conduct investigations, interrogate witnesses, weigh evidence, and perform other tasks necessary to critically evaluate various mysterious anomalies.

Lewis, C. S. *Miracles: A Preliminary Study.* 1947; reprint Glasgow: Fontana Books, 1974. A classical defense of the reality of miracles by a major Roman Catholic writer.

Rogo, D. Scott. *Miracles: A Parascientific Inquiry into Wondrous Phenomena.* New York: Dial Press, 1982. An overly credulous view of allegedly supernatural phenomena by a partisan researcher in the field of parapsychology.

Notes

1. *Webster's Third International Dictionary* (Springfield, Mass.: G. & C. Merriam Co., 1966).

2. C. S. Lewis, *Miracles: A Preliminary Study* (1947; reprint Glasgow: Fontana Books, 1974).

3. D. Scott Rogo, *Miracles: A Parascientific Inquiry into Wondrous Phenomena* (New York: Dial Press, 1982), p. 8. For a contrary view, see C. E. M. Hansel, *ESP: A Scientific Evaluation* (New York: Scribner, 1966).

4. Rogo, *Miracles: A Parascientific Inquiry,* p. 8.

5. Ibid., pp. 8–9; see also Renee Haynes, *Philosopher King: The Humanist Pope Benedict XIV* (London: Nicolson and Weidenfeld, 1971).

6. Quoted in Rogo, *Miracles: A Parascientific Inquiry,* p. 9. Hume later retitled the treatise *An Inquiry Concerning Human Understanding* when he revised it in 1758.

7. Rogo, *Miracles: A Parascientific Inquiry,* p. 9.

8. Lewis, *Miracles: A Preliminary Study,* pp. 7–8.

9. W. I. B. Beveridge, *The Art of Scientific Investigation* (New York: Vintage, n.d.), pp. 67–68.

10. Ibid., pp. 115–116; Elie A. Schneour, "Occam's Razor," *Skeptical Inquirer* 10 (1986): 310–13.

11. Elizabeth Loftus, *Memory: Surprising New Insights into How We Remember and Why We Forget* (1980), p. 37.

12. A. Leo Levin and Harold Cramer, *Problems and Materials on Trial Advocacy* (Mineola, N.Y.: The Foundation Press, 1968), p. 269.

13. A. E. Garvie, "Miracle," *Encyclopaedia Britannica,* 1960 ed.

14. For a fuller discussion of logical fallacies, consult Ray Kytle, *Clear Thinking for Composition,* 5th ed. (New York: Random House, 1987), pp. 124–25.

15. Hansel, *ESP: A Scientific Evaluation,* pp. 186–89.

16. Quoted in Hansel, *ESP: A Scientific Evaluation,* pp. 188–89.

17. "Genesis," *Encyclopaedia Britannica,* 1960 ed.; Fred Aquistapace, *Miracles that Never Were: Natural Explanations of the Bible's Supernatural Stories* (Santa Rosa, Calif.: Eye-Opener Books, 1991), pp. 21–29.

18. Maria Leach, ed., *Funk & Wagnalls Standard Dictionary of Folklore, Mythology, and Legend* (New York: Harper & Row, 1984), pp. 992–93.

19. Acquistapace, *Miracles That Never Were,* pp. 21, 28.

20. Ibid., pp. 164–65.

21. In addition to Acquistapace's book (see n. 17), there are Lloyd M. Graham, *Deceptions and Myths of the Bible* (New York: Bell, 1979); Isaac Asimov, *Asimov's Guide to the Bible,* in two volumes (New York: Equinox Books, 1969); and many others.

2

Miraculous Pictures

An interesting class of reputed miracles consists of icons, divine portraits, or other images that are supposed to have been supernaturally produced. They include the Edessan Image, a reputed "self portrait" of Christ; the Holy Shroud of Turin, said to bear the miraculous imprint of Christ's crucified body; the image of Guadalupe, a likeness of the Virgin that many believe appeared spontaneously on a peasant's cloak; and many others, including magical images of Jesus or the Virgin Mary that have appeared in such unlikely forms as rust stains on a soybean-oil storage tank and skillet burns on a New Mexican tortilla.

The Edessan Image

As early as the sixth century there appeared certain images of Jesus that were reputed to be *acheiropoietoi,* or "not made with hands." There were different versions of these, and as many legends to explain their allegedly miraculous origin.

One such legend—concerning the "Image of Edessa"—is related in a mid-fourth-century Syriac manuscript known as *The Doctrine of Addai.*[1] This tells how King Abgar of Edessa (now Urfa, in southcentral Turkey), being afflicted with leprosy, supposedly wrote a letter to Jesus.[2] The king sent his "greetings to Jesus the Savior who has come to light as a good physician in the city of Jerusalem," and who, he had heard, "can make the blind see, the lame walk . . . heal those who are tortured by chronic illnesses, and . . . raise the dead." Acknowledging that Jesus must either be God or the son of God, Abgar entreated Him to "come to me and cure me of my disease." Further observing that he had heard of the Jews' plan to harm Jesus, Abgar stated: "I have a very small city, but it is stately and will be sufficient for us both to live in peace."

According to the story, Abgar instructed his messenger, Ananias, that if Jesus refused to accompany him to Edessa, he was at least to bring back a portrait. Jesus, who divined Ananias's mission and the contents of the letter he carried, replied with a missive of his own. He wrote, "Blessed are you, Abgar, in that you believed in me without having actually seen me." Although Jesus went on to explain that his mission on earth did not permit a visit, he promised that he would later send a disciple to cure Abgar's illness as well as to "also provide your city with a sufficient defense to keep all your enemies from taking it." Giving the letter to Ananias,

> The Savior then washed his face in water, wiped off the moisture that was left on the towel that was given to him, and in some divine and inexpressible manner had his own likeness impressed on it.[3]

In this version of the tale, Ananias is given the towel to present to the king as "consolation" for his disease.

However, there is another version of the story, given in an official account of the Image dating from the tenth century.[4] According to this version, the image was supposedly imprinted with Jesus' bloody sweat during his agony in the garden of Gethsemane (Luke 22:44):

> They say that when Christ was about to go voluntarily to death he was seen to reveal his human weakness, feel anguish, and pray. According to the Evangelist, sweat dropped from him like drops of blood. Then they say he took this piece of cloth which we see now from one of the disciples and wiped off the drops of sweat on it. At once the still-visible impression of that divine face was produced.[5]

Jesus gave the cloth to his disciple Thomas to be safeguarded until after Jesus had ascended to heaven, whereupon "the divine portrait of Christ's face" was to be taken by Thaddeus to King Abgar. Reputedly, upon receiving the magical cloth and touching it to the afflicted parts of his body, he was cured of his leprosy.

The distinguished historian, Sir Steven Runciman, denounces both versions of the story as apocryphal. As he states, "It is easy to show that the story of Abgar and Jesus as we now have it is untrue, that the letters contain phrases copied from the gospels and are framed according to the dictates of later theology."[6]

In fact, in one revealing fourth-century manuscript of *The Doctrine of Addai,* the Edessan Image is not even described as having a miraculous origin. Instead it is merely attributed to Ananias, who "took and painted a portrait of Jesus in choice paints, and brought it with him to his lord King Abgar."[7]

Yet another strain of the proliferating legend distinguishes the impressed cloth from the Image of Edessa (later called the Mandylion), terming it "Veronica's Veil." According to legend, Veronica was a pious woman of Jerusalem who so pitied Jesus struggling to carry his cross to Golgotha that she used her veil (or kerchief) to wipe his face. Thus she obtained a portrait of the Messiah imprinted with his bloody sweat.[8] (Variant tales have Veronica giving the veil to Jesus so that he can wipe his brow, and he—in return for her generosity—miraculously imprints the cloth with his holy visage.)[9]

It should come as no surprise that there were numerous such portrait veils, known, fittingly enough, as "Veronicas." (Some sources state, however, that the name may be a corruption of the words *Vera icon,* or "true image."[10] In what appears to be a further corruption, dating from the fifteenth century, the cloth is occasionally referred to as "the holy vernicle [*sic*] of Rome."[11]) According to Thomas Humber, these "veronicas" were "supposedly miraculous, but, in fact, painted."[12] Humber adds:

> Soon the popular demand for more copies representing the "true likeness" of Christ was such that selected artists were allowed or encouraged to make duplications. (There was, conveniently, another tradition supporting the copies: the Image could miraculously duplicate itself.)[13]

As to the belief that the Veronicas represented the "true likeness" of Jesus, we should take note of the fact that there is not a single clue to his appearance anywhere in the New Testament, and all that is said of the Messiah in the Old Testament is Isaiah's statement that "He hath no form nor comeliness" (Isa. 53:2), and the supposedly prophetic passage in Psalms (45:2) that "Thou are fairer than the children of men. . . ." Because of that, and no doubt partly due also to the Old Testament prohibition against making graven images, it is not until the mid-third century that we find the earliest known representation of Jesus: a fresco painting depicting him as youthful, beardless, and with cropped hair. From then on, there are varying conceptual portraits of Christ, yet none having any claim to accuracy.[14] So it was in the early fifth century that St. Augustine lamented, "We do not know of his external appearance, nor that of his mother."[15] Eventually, however, a Semitic representation prevailed as a matter of rigid artistic convention, and so it is that today people instantly recognize a portrait of Jesus, although the conceptual likeness is based on no more than a collective guess.

Therefore, any such depiction of Jesus as the Veronicas pretend to represent is *prima facie* suspect. Yet today controversy continues over just such a "self-portrait of Christ": the notorious "Holy Shroud."

The Shroud of Turin

Housed in a reliquary on the high altar in the Royal Chapel of the Cathedral of St. John the Baptist in Turin, Italy, is a fourteen-foot length of linen cloth known as the Shroud of Turin. Although some forty cloths have been reputed to be the Holy Shroud, the Turin cloth bears the front and back imprints of an apparently crucified man, leading many to believe it is the actual burial shroud of Jesus. At least, it does tap the same *acheiropoietos* tradition as the Edessan Image.

The earliest-known appearance of the "shroud" dates from the middle of the fourteenth century. About 1355, it turned up at a little collegiate church in Lirey, a town in the diocese of Troyes, in northcentral France. Its owner, a soldier of fortune named Geoffroy de Charney, claimed it was the true Holy Shroud, and it was depicted as such on a pilgrim's medallion of circa 1357. While pilgrims flocked to view the cloth—which was reputed to effect miraculous cures—a skeptical bishop named Henri de Poitiers launched an investigation of the "relic." As a consequence it was hidden away, only to resurface in 1389 to be reinvestigated—this time by Bishop Pierre d'Arcis and again with negative consequences (as we shall see presently).[16]

Eventually, the granddaughter of Geoffroy de Charney, Margaret, used a pretext to gain control of the shroud and took it on tour, where it met various challenges to its authenticity. Finally, in 1453, although she would be excommunicated for it, Margaret sold the cloth to the Royal House of Savoy (later the Italian monarchy). (Authenticity advocates like to say that Margaret "gave" the cloth to the duke and duchess, which is true if we note that in return they "gave" her the sum of two castles.)

The shroud was now reputed to have additional powers. According to Ian Wilson: "In the earliest days with the family it was carried about with them on their travels, like a holy charm to safeguard them against the dangers of a journey."[17] In later centuries the shroud would be reputed to provide protective powers over whatever city housed it; yet in the year 1532, came ample evidence that the shroud could not even protect itself: It was nearly destroyed in a chapel fire which resulted in burn marks and water stains that marred the image. In a shrewd political move to relocate the Savoy capital, the shroud was taken in 1578 to Turin, where it has remained ever since.

The cloth's modern history begins in 1898, when it was photographed for the first time by Secondo Pia. As he developed his glass plates, Pia was astonished to discover that the image's darks and lights were essentially reversed. Thus, although the shroud's history had suggested it was the handiwork of a medieval artist, proponents were now asking how it was possible that a mere medieval artist could have painted a *negative* image—centuries before photography was even conceived.

One possible explanation is known as the "contact theory," which suggests that the body was covered with oils and spices that naturally transferred to the cloth. The prominences would thus be imprinted while the recesses would remain blank; this would be the opposite of a positive image in which raised areas (such as cheekbones) are in highlight and the recessed ones (e.g., the hollows of the eyes) are in shadow. However, attempts to produce shroudlike images by imprinting from fully three-dimensional figures—bodies or statues—resulted in grotesque wraparound distortions, the results naturally expected due to the laws of geometry.

It was also soon recognized that not all of the features that imprinted would have been in contact with a simple draped cloth. Therefore, shroud proponent Paul Vignon concluded the imaging process must have acted across a distance—that is, it must somehow have been *projected*. Thus was born the "vaporography" concept—that body vapors (weak ammoniacal vapors from the fermented urea in sweat) interacted with spices on the cloth (which was likened to a sensitized photographic plate) to produce a vapor "photo." Unfortunately, vapors do not travel in perfectly straight (vertical) lines but instead diffuse and convect, and therefore—as shown by experiments I conducted in 1977—the result will simply be a blur.[18]

Undaunted, shroud proponents next suggested a miracle, although, of course, they tried to present it in scientific-sounding terms. Some members of the Shroud of Turin Research Project (STURP)—whose leaders served on the executive council of the Roman Catholic Holy Shroud Guild —proposed that the image resulted from "flash photolysis." This was described as a "short burst" of "radiant energy" such as Christ's body might have produced at the moment of resurrection. In brief, the image was hypothesized to be a "scorch picture." Yet one STURP scientist later admitted, "I incline toward the idea of a scorch, but I can't think how it was done." He added, "At this point, you either keep looking for the mechanism or start getting mystical."[19]

Reasons for doubting radiation-scorching as a mechanism are numerous. For one thing, real scorches on linen (such as those on the shroud resulting from the fire of 1532) exhibit a strong reddish fluorescence, while the shroud images do not fluoresce at all. In addition, examination of the cloth's threads show the image stain to be confined to the topmost fibrils, and there is no known radiation that—traveling various distances from body to cloth—would act uniformly superficially. Moreover, not only is there no natural source for any such radiation but, even if there were, there is no means by which it could have been *focused* to produce an image like that on the shroud.[20]

Just as claims that the shroud image was produced miraculously are untenable, so are claims that it is an authentic burial cloth. Take its iconography, for example. (*Iconography* refers to the study of artistic representation.) It is most suspicious that the shroud should turn up after thirteen centuries with its portrait looking just like more contemporary artistic representations of Jesus. Moreover, the shroud seems the culmination of a lengthy tradition of "not-made-with-hands" portraits: From the sixth century came images reputedly imprinted by the bloody sweat of the *living* Christ, and by the twelfth century there were accounts of Jesus having pressed "the length of his whole body" upon a cloth; already (by the eleventh century) artists had begun to represent a double-length (but non-imaged) shroud in paintings; and by the thirteenth century we find ceremonial shrouds bearing full-length images of Christ's body in death (even with the hands folded over the loins, an artistic motif dating from the eleventh century). Thus, from an iconographic point of view, these various traditions coalesce in the Shroud of Turin and suggest it is the work of an artist of the thirteenth century or later.[21]

Ian Wilson attempts to put the proverbial cart before the horse by suggesting the shroud and the ancient Edessan Image are one and the same! Although the latter bore only a facial image, Wilson supposes that it was really the shroud in disguise, folded in such a way that only the face showed! To explain how *both* an Edessan Image and a purported Holy Shroud are mentioned *separately* on certain twelfth- and thirteenth-century lists of relics, Wilson opines that the "other" Edessan cloth was a *copy*, made from the genuine—hypothetically folded—shroud!

In fact, the shroud's provenance (or historical record) tells against it. The New Testament makes no mention of Jesus's shroud being preserved. (Indeed, John's gospel describes multiple cloths, including a "napkin" over the face—a description that is incompatible with the shroud.) In fact, there is no mention of this particular "shroud" for some thirteen centuries; then a respected bishop reportedly uncovered an artist who confessed to having created it. In a letter of 1389 to Pope Clement VII, Bishop Pierre d'Arcis reported on an earlier investigation:

> The case, Holy Father, stands thus. Some time since in this diocese of Troyes the dean of a certain collegiate church, to wit, that of Lirey, falsely and deceitfully, being consumed with the passion of avarice, and not from any motive of devotion but only of gain, procured for his church a certain cloth cunningly painted, upon which by a clever sleight of hand was depicted the twofold image of one man, that is to say, the back and the front, he falsely declaring and pretending that this was the actual shroud in which our Savior Jesus Christ was enfolded in the tomb, and upon which the whole likeness of the Savior had remained thus impressed together with the wounds which He bore. This story was put about not only in the kingdom of France but, so to speak, throughout the world, so that from all parts people came together to view it. And further to attract the multitude so that money might cunningly be wrung from them, pretended miracles were worked, certain men being hired to represent themselves as healed at the moment of the exhibition of the shroud.

D'Arcis continued, speaking of the earlier bishop who conducted the investigation:

> Eventually, after diligent inquiry and examination, he discovered the fraud and how the said cloth had been cunningly painted, *the truth being attested*

by the artist who had painted it, to wit, that it was a work of human skill and not miraculously wrought or bestowed. (Emphasis added.)

In response, the shroud's owner, Geoffroy de Charney, was unable—or unwilling—to say how he had acquired the most significant relic in Christendom. As a consequence, Pope Clement judged the shroud an artist's "representation" and permitted it to be exhibited only as such. (As we have seen, however, de Charney's granddaughter would in later years ignore the prohibition, touring with and finally selling the "Holy Shroud" which she unfailingly misrepresented as genuine.[22])

Additional evidence against authenticity is found in the "blood" flows. While shroud proponents argue that they are amazingly accurate, there are critical, fundamental problems. For example, they are decidedly "picturelike," consistent with an artist's rendering. Dr. Michael Baden, a distinguished pathologist, pointed out that the "blood" had failed to mat the hair and instead flowed in rivulets on the outside of the locks. Another problem is that *dried* blood, as on the arms, should not have transferred to the cloth at all. Moreover, the stains are suspiciously still red, unlike real blood that blackens over time.

Anatomical details represent another category of flaws. For instance, the imprint of one leg shows it to be outstretched rather than bent at the knee as it would have to have been to produce the bloody footprint that is also depicted. In addition, the hair hangs down on either side of the face as if the figure were standing rather than reclining. Further, the physique is so unnaturally elongated (resembling the figures in gothic art) that one pro-shroud pathologist concluded that Jesus must have suffered from the rare disease known as Marfan's Syndrome (which is characterized by an excessive length of the extremities).

Among realistic details supposed to be beyond the knowledge of a medieval artist were flagellation marks on the body image (but medieval paintings depict contemporary flagellations), nail wounds in the wrists rather than the hands (but only one such wound shows and it seems clearly to be located in the base of the palm), and "Roman coins" over the eyes (the result of wishful imagining, say skeptics). "Pollen fossils"—which the late Max Frei claimed he found on tape samples he lifted from the shroud and which supposedly proved the cloth had been in Palestine—failed to appear on another set of tapes taken by STURP scientists, thus raising suspicions about Frei's work.[23]

Instead, what the STURP tapes did show were traces of paint pigments. After the pieces of special sticky tape were pressed to the shroud to remove fibers and other surface materials, they were then stuck to microscope slides and given to Walter C. McCrone, a world-famous microanalyst who served on the STURP team. McCrone conducted a "blind" study which separated the thirty-two tapes microscopically into two groups: one consisting of tapes with red pigment on the fibers, another of tapes without pigment. He discovered that the red pigment appeared on image ("body" and "blood") areas only, not on control tapes (from non-image areas), thus proving the pigment was a component of the image. He identified the pigment as red ocher.

McCrone also found in the "blood" (which had failed earlier forensic tests) the same red ocher, as well as small amounts of another red pigment, vermilion. He determined the "blood" was actually tempera paint. Two other STURP scientists, John Heller and Alan Adler, challenged McCrone's findings, but their claims were rebutted by forensic analyst John F. Fischer. At the 1983 conference of the International Association for Identification, Fischer explained how results similar to theirs could be obtained with tempera paint, and he demonstrated why spectral data were inconsistent with their claims.[24] As it happens, neither Heller nor Adler is a forensic serologist or a pigment expert, thus raising the question why they were chosen for such important work. Heller admitted that McCrone "had over two decades of experience with this kind of problem and a worldwide reputation. Adler and I, on the other hand, had never before tackled anything remotely like an artistic forgery."[25]

McCrone's work answered crucial questions but raised others. For example, he concluded that the image on the shroud was a painting, without explaining why the "body" image areas did not penetrate into the threads as the blood (which soaked through to the back of the cloth) had done. McCrone also discovered that another component of the shroud image is a straw-colored stain which he attributed to a tempera binder, but the samples were taken from him before he had completed his analyses. (McCrone alleges that he was "drummed out" of STURP.) Several scientists—both proponents and skeptics—thought the yellow stain might merely be the result of cellulose degradation caused by the presence of foreign substances.

As an alternative to the painting hypothesis, some two years before McCrone published his findings, I reported the results of my own successful experiments in creating shroudlike "negative" images. The technique involved wet-molding cloth to a bas-relief (used instead of a fully three-dimensional statue to minimize distortion), allowing it to dry, then rubbing on powdered pigment using a dauber—much as one would make a rubbing from a gravestone. This technique automatically yields "negative" images (or rather, just like the shroud, *quasi*-negative images, since the hair and beard are the opposite of what would be expected). It also produces numerous other shroudlike features, including minimal depth of penetration into the threads, encoded "3-D" information, and other similarities, some of which specifically pointed to some form of imprinting technique.[26] (See Figure 1.)

Final proof that the shroud dated not from the first century but from medieval times was reported on October 13, 1988, after samples from the cloth were carbon-dated. Postage-stamp-size samples were snipped from one end and transferred to laboratories at Oxford, England; Zurich, Switzerland; and the University of Arizona in the United States. Using accelerator mass spectrometry, the labs obtained dates in close agreement: The shroud dated from about 1260–1390, and the time span was given enhanced credibility by correct dates obtained from a variety of control swatches taken from ancient cloths of known date.[27]

But would shroud defenders accept such results? Of course not: they rushed to challenge the carbon-14 tests.

> They argued that the three labs had been given pieces of cloth taken from a much handled, much contaminated corner of the Shroud. Since only threads were needed, different parts of the Shroud could and should have been included, such as the "pristine" material next to the charred areas under the patches. Another major objection was that all three labs had agreed to use the same newly developed and relatively untested cleansing solvent. Since the contamination from centuries of handling is the most important obstacle to an accurate C-14 date, this procedure seemed to critics to be extremely careless.[28]

Or so it "seemed" to shroud devotees. Actually, their numerous criticisms of the carbon dating are little more than sour grapes, given the close proximity of the C-14 dates, the accuracy in dating the control swatches, the fact that the samples were thoroughly cleansed before testing, and other reasons—as I pointed out in an article commissioned by the prestigious science magazine, *Science et Vie*.[29]

Not surprisingly, some shroud adherents are again invoking the miraculous to rationalize the devastating results of the carbon-dating tests.

They suggest that the imagined burst of radiant energy at the moment of resurrection altered the carbon ratio! Will wonders never cease?

I say this response is not surprising because shroudologists have consistently begun with the desired answer and worked backward to the evidence. Lacking any viable hypothesis for the image formation, they offered one explanation for the lack of provenance (the cloth might have been hidden away), another for the forger's confession (the reporting bishop could have been mistaken), still another for the pigments (an artist copying the image could have splashed some on), and so forth.[30]

In contrast, investigators allowed the preponderance of *prima facie* evidence to lead them to the following conclusion: The "shroud" never held a body, and its image is the handiwork of a clever medieval artisan. The evidence is appropriately corroborative as well. For example, the confession is supported by the lack of prior record, the red "blood" and presence of pigments are consistent with artistry, and the carbon dating is consistent with the time frame indicated by the iconographic evidence. Indeed, skeptics had predicted the results of the carbon dating virtually to the year—a measure of the accuracy both of the collective evidence and of the technique of radiocarbon testing.

The Image of Guadalupe

Another supposedly miraculous portrait is Mexico's Image of Guadalupe, a sixteenth-century depiction of the Virgin Mary which—according to pious legend—miraculously appeared as a "sign" to a skeptical bishop as an inducement for him to build a shrine to her. "Yearly," according to Jody Brant Smith's *The Image of Guadalupe,* "an estimated ten million bow down before the mysterious Virgin, making the Mexico City church the most popular shrine in the Roman Catholic world next to the Vatican."[31]

This image of the Virgin is so popular that:

You will find every imaginable representation of her in the churches. . . . You may find her outlined in neon as part of a downtown spectacular, chalked into a hillside, on a throwaway advertising a mouthwash, pricked out in flowers in public parks; clowns and hucksters will distribute booklets about her as a preliminary to hawking patent medicines. . . . Bullfighters have her image woven into their parade capes; she is a popular tattoo subject; almost everyone wears her medal.[32]

Because the cloth was accompanied by a supposedly contemporary account of the "miracle," and because the image itself was amenable to analysis (if not made available for full scientific testing), John F. Fischer and I conducted a two-pronged investigation, as reported in full in our "The Image of Guadalupe: A Folkloristic and Iconographic Investigation."[33]

First we looked at the legend itself. It is related in the sixteenth-century *Nican Mopohua* ("an account"), written in the native Aztec language and sometimes called the "gospel of Guadalupe." According to this account, in early December of 1531 (some ten years after Cortez's defeat of the Aztec Empire), a recent Christian convert named Juan Diego supposedly left his village to attend Mass in another. As he passed the foot of a hill named Tepeyac, he heard birds singing, saw a bright light atop the hill, and heard a voice calling "Juanito."

The peasant climbed to the top of Tepeyac, where he encountered a young girl, radiant in golden mist, who identified herself as "the ever-virgin Holy Mary, mother of the True God." She said: "I wish that a temple be created here quickly, so I may therein exhibit and give all my love, compassion, help, and protection, because I am your merciful mother. . . ." She instructed Juan Diego to hasten to Father Juan de Zumarraga, bishop of Mexico, and tell him of her plans. The peasant complied, hastening to the bishop's palace and pleading to his servants for an audience. Finally, on bended knee, Juan Diego conveyed the message to the skeptical prelate and was then dismissed.

After reporting to the Virgin at Tepeyac, Juan Diego was again sent to the bishop, who now asked for a "sign" so that he might believe what he had been told. After a brief delay, caused by the illness of an uncle whom the Virgin then "cured," Juan Diego was instructed to gather flowers. Although it was not the season for them, they were blooming miraculously, and Juan Diego gathered them in his cloak to carry to the doubting bishop.

> He then unfolded his white cloth, where he had the flowers, and when they had scattered on the floor, all the different varieties of *rosas de Castilla,* suddenly there appeared the drawing of the precious Image of the ever-virgin Holy Mary, Mother of God, in the manner as she is today kept in the temple at Tepeyac, which is named Guadalupe. When the bishop saw the image, he and all who were present fell to their knees.

Convinced at last, Bishop Zumarraga placed the miraculous portrait in his private chapel "until the temple dedicated to the Queen of Tepeyac was erected where Juan Diego had seen her."[34] (See Figures 2 and 3.)

The alert reader will have noted in the legend a number of motifs from the Old and New Testament, including a divine command for the building of a place of worship (Exod. 25:8), miraculous blooms (Num. 17:8, Isa. 35:1), and an apparition's ultimate ability to convince a doubter with tangible "signs" (John 20:25–30). And when the Virgin tells Juan Diego to cease worrying about his sick uncle, saying, "Let not your heart be disturbed," she echoes Christ's words to his disciples in John 14:1.

Moreover, statements of specific religious dogma have been put in the mouth of the Virgin when—in the *Nican Mopohua*—she describes herself as "the ever-virgin Holy Mary." As Marcello Craveri explains in his *The Life of Jesus:*

> About the end of the fourth century, John Chrysostom proposed the definition of Mary's "perpetual virginity"; since her physical intactness had not been impaired by the birth of Jesus and she had maintained her virginity to the end of her life, she was to be called a virgin *ante partum, in partu, post partum* [before giving birth, while giving birth, after giving birth]. This formula was to become dogma at the Lateran Council of 649 and was to be confirmed by the Tolentino Council of 675, because not everyone had freely accepted it.[35]

The legend also incorporates *hyperdulia*—the ecclesiastical term for the special veneration given to the Virgin Mary. As Craveri points out, it was after the Council of Ephesus (in 431) that a cult of the Virgin originated, and Mary eventually "assumed the functions of divinity."[36] And so, in the legend it is the Virgin who appears to Juan Diego, the Virgin who is all-seeing and able to work miraculous cures, the Virgin to whom the temple is to be built, and the Virgin whose image appears for veneration. Christ is scarcely mentioned.

Indeed, the Guadalupan legend itself appears to have been borrowed. The very name Guadalupe (which had been given to the Tepeyac site by 1556, the date of the report of a formal investigation of the cloth) arouses suspicion. As historian Jacques La Faye observes, the Mexican tale is quite similar to an earlier Spanish legend in which the Virgin appeared to a shepherd and led him to discover a statue of her. The Spanish site was even on a river known as Guadalupe (that is, "hidden channel"), strongly suggesting that the Mexican tale was derived from the Spanish one.

Then there is the "not-made-with-hands" tradition of the miraculous portrait—a tradition of pious frauds. Even separated from the legend, the

Virgin of Guadalupe is linked to another tradition of "miraculous" representations of Mary. It is of the "dark-colored, ancient Greek Madonnas," which, says A. B. Jameson, "had all along the credit of being miraculous."[37] And Smith points out that the Mexicans have dubbed the Guadalupan Image "La Morena"—i.e., "the dark-complexioned woman"—because of the brownish flesh tones.[38]

To these disturbing elements in the legend—the familiar motifs; the suspiciously similar story and the transposed name, Guadalupe, together with the scandalous, "not-made-with-hands" portrait tradition and the blatant elements of religious dogma—we must add one further element that smacks of deliberate legend manufacture. As Smith states: "The Shrine which held the Image of Guadalupe had been erected on a hill directly in front of the spot where there had been an important temple dedicated to the Aztec Virgin goddess Tonantzin, 'Little Mother' of the Earth and Corn."[39] Thus the Christian tradition became grafted onto the Indian one (a process folklorists call *syncretism*).

Turning now from folkloristics to iconography, we again discover considerable borrowing. Even without knowing anything of the pious legend, one would at first sight recognize the image as a portrait of the Virgin Mary. That recognition factor is not without considerable significance, since—as St. Augustine observed in the fifth century—it is impossible to know what the Virgin actually looked like. We recognize her in a given picture because the likeness has been established by artistic convention.

In iconographic terms, the Image of Guadalupe is a devotional (as opposed to a narrative) portrait. The golden rays and crescent moon in the picture (see Figure 2) are motifs taken from Revelation 12:1, which many believe refer to the Virgin. Other standard artistic motifs that appear in the Image of Guadalupe are the mantle's forty-six stars, signifying the number of years required for building the temple of Jerusalem; gold fleur-de-lis designs that are symbolic of the Virgin Mother; an angel at the Lady's feet; a decorative tassel; and others, including a possible Aztec motif: a distinctive lower fold of the robe.

In fact, a Spanish painting, a Virgin of Mercy by Bonanat Zaortiza (now in the Museo de Arte de Cataluna in Barcelona), is said to be "of the exact form as the Virgin of Guadalupe" and even has "a similar brooch at the throat," according to Philip Serna Callahan, who terms it "strikingly imitative of the Virgin of Guadalupe"[40]—although it preceded the latter picture by nearly a century!

Defenders of the image's authenticity hold that all the motifs mentioned thus far are later additions, produced, as Callahan admits, "by human hands" and which "impart a Spanish Gothic motif to the painting."[41] Suggestions that these were made as late as the seventeenth century are belied by the fact that a copy—dating from probably fewer than forty years after the original appeared—is actually "identical with the original" (except for some "more skillfully done" elements).[42] In fact, there is no convincing proof that the tell-tale artistic motifs were absent from the original. The overlapping of paint that is observed may merely be indicative of stages in the painting process, not of later "additions."

By excluding the obvious artistic elements, pro-authenticity writers such as Callahan have suggested the "original" portions are therefore "inexplicable" and even "miraculous," as Callahan terms the "original figure, including the rose robe, blue mantle, hands and face."[43] Yet while those areas are less thickly painted, evidence that they *are* painted is abundant. For example, infrared photographs show that the hands have been modified (outlined, and some fingers shortened). Also, close-up photography shows that pigment has been applied to the highlight areas of the face sufficiently heavily so as to obscure the texture of the cloth. Moreover, there is obvious cracking and flaking of the Guadalupan Image all along a vertical seam that passes through the "original" areas of mantle, neck, and robe (as well as the nonmiraculous background areas). (See Figure 4.) There are also anomalous lines that infrared photographs reveal in the robe's fold shadows that appear to be sketch lines, suggesting that an artist roughed out the figure in the usual way before painting it.

Additional evidence of artistry in the "original," supposedly miraculous, areas was observed by Glenn Taylor, a professional artist with many years' experience in an impressive variety of portraiture techniques. Studying detailed photographs, Taylor pointed out that the part in the Virgin's hair is off-center; that her eyes, including the irises, have outlines, as they often do in paintings, but not in nature, and that these outlines appear to have been done with a brush; and that the Virgin's traditional likeness, *contrapposto* stance, and other elements are indicative of European paintings of the Renaissance era. To him, "The detailing of the features exhibits the characteristic fluidity of painting." Taylor describes the work as obviously "mannered" (in the artistic sense) and suggests it was probably copied by an inexpert copyist from an expertly done original.[44]

In fact, evidence that the image is indeed merely a painting dates from as early as 1556, when a formal investigation of the cloth was held. Father Alonzo de Santiago testified that the image was "painted yesteryear by an Indian," and another Franciscan priest, Juan de Maseques, supplied more specific information, testifying that the image "was a painting that the Indian painter Marcos had done." Indeed, there was an Aztec painter known as Marcos Cipac active in Mexico at the time the Image of Guadalupe appeared.[45]

In any event, the artist was obviously familiar with one or more Spanish paintings of the Virgin Mary, a fact that suggests that he may have been commissioned to produce the pious fraud. It is certainly well known that "the propagation of Christianity was one of the main purposes of Spanish imperialism, and church and state were closely connected."[46] No doubt as expected, the "miracle" played a "major role" in hastening the conversion of the conquered Indians. Countless thousands came to view the image and, "In just seven years, from 1532 to 1538, eight million Indians were converted to Christianity."[47]

In recent years, one of the silliest examples of "scientific research" conducted on the Guadalupan Image—by "several ophthalmologists" and "a computer expert"—has taken the *acheiropoietos* tradition from the macroscopic to the microscopic level. It concerns "what seems to be the reflected image of a man's head in the right eye of the Virgin" (as Smith describes it), what was once thought to be Juan Diego's own portrait in magical miniature, until someone realized that Aztecs of the time were clean-shaven; thereupon, it was reinterpreted as "a bearded Spaniard." Now with the aid of photo-enhancement techniques (akin to those applied to the Turin "shroud" in hopes of identifying wished-for "Roman coins" over the eyes), still more tiny figures are being "discovered" and assigned to various sixteenth-century Mexican personages, such as Bishop Zumarraga. Meanwhile, the specific methodology is being questioned.[48] And at one point in his own discussion of the endeavor, Smith does wonder whether the proliferating wee people represent anything more "substantial than the human shapes as we see in the clouds, the result of what Father Harold J. Rahn once termed a 'pious imagination.' "[49] As we shall see presently, such imaginings are widespread.

Other Miraculous Pictures

Of the images of the "pious imagination" that Father Rahn described, a common form is the religious picture that is perceived in random shapes. The tendency to see such pictures is ancient. According to D. Scott Rogo:

"Ever since the third century A.D., stories have been recorded of miraculous images of Christ, the Virgin Mary, or other religious figures or emblems, that have suddenly appeared on church walls, windows, or altar cloths."[50]

One such image appeared in 1897 on a wall of Llandaff Cathedral in Wales. Two weeks after the death of the dean, John Vaughan, a "damp spot" appeared on the stone west wall of the cathedral and gradually formed into a facial image. Parishioners thought they recognized this as a portrait of the late dean and also made out, as an integral part of the picture, the letters *D.V.*, which were interpreted as standing for Dean Vaughan. The stain—which, it is now thought, may have been "caused by minute fungi"—eventually dried, and church officials covered the spot with a notice board.[51]

More recently, in 1982, religious spectators at Holden, West Virginia, saw a profile of Jesus in the foliage of a vine-covered tree. The "vision" was reportedly first experienced by one of three youths who were drinking beer. According to a *Charleston Gazette* columnist, "They said it shook him up so that he quit drinking and joined the church." For balance, the paper also quoted a sensible (if ungrammatical) sheriff's lieutenant: "I wouldn't know about any signs, but in my opinion Jesus ain't going to come in no tree."[52]

Yet another tree was the source for a televised news report that began: "Some people think they're seeing a religious sign in Los Angeles." There, in a splotch on a tree in a neighborhood back yard, some religious enthusiasts perceived a portrait of the Virgin Mary. They seemed undaunted when a tree expert explained that the effect was simply due to a fungus.[53]

For a while in December of 1990, a Progresso, Texas, auto parts store claimed the attention of more than a thousand people a day who came to see a reputed image of the Virgin Mary. Making their way past the spark plugs and fan belts, the pilgrims were treated to a foot-wide gray spot in the concrete floor of the shower stall, adjacent to a toilet. "I asked her, 'Why on the floor? Why the bathroom?'" said owner Reynaldo Trevina, a 45-year-old Roman Catholic. He explained that his heart told him to spread the message that the Virgin's appearance on the floor symbolized how many neglect their Christian faith. "So I started telling every customer who came in," said Trevino. "Before I sold them a part, I took them back." But he asked that no one leave money or other offerings. "I don't want this to be commercialized or anything," he said.

Officials of the local archdiocese declined to comment on the image, leaving it to individuals to interpret for themselves. The interpretations varied: One middle-aged woman said that viewing the image caused her pain. "We are in a very troubled world right now," she stated. A fourteen-year-old girl exclaimed, with tears streaming down her face, "She's so beautiful, so beautiful." Yet all an Associated Press reporter could say was that "what could be interpreted as facial features are vaguely discernible in the markings." Mr. Trevino discouraged reporters and others from taking photos, saying, "I want them to take the image home with them in their hearts."[54]

Observers in Fostoria, Ohio, in August 1986 were divided over an image that appeared on a 40-foot-high soybean oil tank. According to *USA Today*, "Whether it represents Christ, or nothing, or as some tourists have claimed, Elvis, depends on the viewer." However, there was no doubt in the mind of the woman who first witnessed the image. "It just jumps out at me," said Rita Ratchen, a 54-year-old drapery maker and self-described good Catholic. She claimed to have witnessed an illuminated figure of Jesus, dressed in a white robe, with his hand on the shoulder of a young boy. Among the nonbelievers was Carl Hunnell, managing editor of Fostoria's *The Review Times*, who termed the resulting pilgrimage to the site "a combination church revival and block party." He added: "I can't take it seriously. You've got some people thumping Bibles and some people swilling beer."

As city officials became concerned about traffic jams, resulting from the hundreds of motorists who lined up to witness the phenomenon, a spokesman for the tank's owner, the Archer Daniel Midland Company, explained the image as "a combination of lighting, rust spots, fog, and people's imaginations." Undeterred, the pilgrims continued their often bumper-to-bumper caravan for a month, until a drunken man, tired of the traffic, obliterated the rust stain with paint-filled balloons.[55]

Among the least likely places for a sacred image would seem to be a forkful of spaghetti illustrated on a billboard. Yet that is what countless motorists reported in May 1991 in Stone Mountain, Georgia. Shrouded in the spaghetti and sauce was the face of Jesus, complete with deep-set eyes, beard, and other features. It was dubbed "the Pasta Jesus" by one skeptical commentator, who gave the following description:

> In the middle of the forkful of spaghetti, is a face. The space between the strands forms hollow eyes. The sauce, noodles and oregano form a blood-drenched mane of hair with a thorny crown, depending on from how far back one views it. Similar to an impressionist painting, the further

back one views it, the more one sees. Like optical illusion art, once you see the face, you cannot *not* see it.[56]

More skepticism came from *Rocky Mountain News* columnist Lewis Grizzard: "In the first place who knows what Jesus really looks like? Until he shows up on 'Donahue' or 'Oprah,' we won't have a clue to his actual appearance." Grizzard added: "I saw the spaghetti billboard on television. I looked at it, but I didn't see Jesus, unless Jesus looks a lot like Bjorn Borg. In the second place," he continued, "if Jesus decided to come back for a little visit, I just can't see God dispatching him to appear on a picture of spaghetti. Can you?"[57]

One who had already answered, in the affirmative, was a woman who had been debating whether to continue singing in her church choir. As she was leaving a gas station she felt compelled to look up, and there was the billboard, one of about twenty such Pizza Hut signs in the area. "And I saw Christ's face," the woman said, adding that she decided to stay in the choir.[58]

Rivaling the pasta picture for foolishness is an image reported in 1978 that is becoming a classic of the genre. While Mrs. Maria Rubio of Lake Arthur, New Mexico, was making burritos, she noticed the pattern of skillet burns on one tortilla. "It is Jesus Christ!" exclaimed the pious woman, and other family members agreed. Mrs. Rubio persuaded a reluctant priest to bless the tortilla, whereupon she built a shrine in her home for the supposedly sacred object. Although a writer for the *Albuquerque Journal* stated cynically, "It looks more like Leon Spinks to me," the story was carried by newspapers nationwide, and thousands flocked from all parts of the United States to witness the miracle, frequently to pray for divine assistance in curing ailments. (Mrs. Rubio's tortilla reminds me of the potato chip collection of Myrtle Young, an inspector at a potato chip plant who has found the crispy slices fashioned in an impressive array of secular shapes: camel, swan, butterfly—even a portrait of Bob Hope.)[59]

Simple illusions can prompt the devout to see religious images almost anywhere. In 1987 Italian police scientists were asked to investigate the supposedly miraculous appearance of Christ on a window pane in the village of Supino, south of Rome. Crowds of pilgrims flocked there in April of that year. Subsequently a forensic report explained that the phenomenon was simply an optical illusion caused by a grimy window. One newspaper said the local Catholic leaders were pleased with the tests, yet believers continued to visit the village even after the dirty pane had been taken away for examination.[60]

Another example of an optical illusion was provided at Santa Fe Springs, California, and reported in the *Los Angeles Times* for January 17, 1981. Homeowners Graziela and Rafael Tascon had concluded that a shadow seen on their garage door in the evenings resembled Jesus Christ—a distinct silhouette of a man crowned with thorns surmounting a cross about three feet tall. As it turned out, the cross was the shadow of a real estate sign stuck in the Tascons' front lawn; the shadow of the head and thorns resulted from a nearby bush; and the light source that cast the shadowy combination was a pair of street lamps opposite the house.[61]

Another widely reported illusion was an "apparition" that appeared nightly on the wall of a suburban Wilkes Barre, Pennsylvania, house in mid-1987. An Associated Press photo showed what looked like a luminous figure wearing a long robe and surrounded by a halo-like glow. Hundreds turned out to see what many insisted was an image of the Virgin Mary. A sensible patrolman, however, realized that the image was simply a reflection of a street light bouncing off a nearby curved-glass window, and demonstrated the fact by obstructing the beam with his hand. "You try to show them, but they won't believe it," he said. "They just believe it's a miracle or something." Finally, the image ceremoniously disappeared when, at the police chief's request, the offending window was opened.[62]

Similarly, images in the shape of crosses appeared on the glass of a bathroom window in a Los Angeles area home, but police and Roman Catholic priests insisted the phenomenon was simply the result of light refracted through the textured glass. Undeterred by the explanation, the faithful lined up by the hundreds to file through the small home. "I think it is something from God. A warning," stated a three-time visitor who had brought her children.[63]

Many additional examples of such wishful thinking are in my files: in Glendale, California, another cross sighting (also a refraction of light through frosted glass);[64] the face of Christ that appeared after dusk on an Estill Springs, Tennessee, freezer (and went away after a neighbor's porch light was relocated);[65] images of Jesus and Mary in the stained glass of an African-American church in Newark, New Jersey (traced to a reflection of street lamps and floodlights that cast shadows from the branches of trees in an adjacent parking lot);[66] a shimmering, multicolored apparition of the Virgin that appeared on the wall of a Catholic church in Colfax, California (attributed to light from a stained-glass window bouncing off a newly repaired light fixture);[67] and so on.

Not surprisingly, similar phenomena are occasionally deliberately faked. That was apparently the case with some mysterious faces that appeared on the floor of a peasant woman's house in the town of Belmez de la Moraleda in Spain. Faces appeared and disappeared, occasionally to reappear or to change expressions. By Easter 1972, hundreds of pilgrims had come to see the phantom portraits. Insofar as one is able to judge from a single photograph—depicting the first visage materializing—the face is indistinguishable from the work of a very amateurish artist. In fact, Scott Rogo says that photographs

> dispel any idea that the faces were merely chance configurations or etchings artificially produced on the floor and walls of the house. While a few are only vague sketches formed out of patterns in the concrete floor, many are genuinely artistic in a rather surrealistic or caricaturistic manner.

(Rogo nevertheless felt these were due to some type of paranormnal phenomena!)[68]

In any event, local newspapers soon charged that the peasant woman was perpetrating a hoax for personal gain. And before long the secular and ecclesiastical authorities had forbidden any tourist trade at the site.[69]

A photograph depicting what was described as "a robed figure, arms outstretched, floating among sinister dark clouds," was circulated in Gastonia, North Carolina, in the spring of 1990. Naturally, it is possible to see, and photograph, "pictures" in clouds—a product of their random shapes that everyone is familiar with. But this picture was different. One photographer observed that the clouds did not look natural. "That's a hoot," he exclaimed. When the photograph was subjected to a computerized analysis that measured its density, the image was shown to lack the three-dimensional properties of genuine photographic images. The person who took the photo was not immediately known.[70]

Whether such "sacred" images are "real" or faked, they obviously depend on the eye—and the emotions—of the beholder. Roman Catholic officials state that reports of miraculous visions and apparitions seem to be increasing worldwide. According to Bishop Francis Quinn of the Sacramento Catholic Diocese:

There is such a hunger and yearning for people to hold onto something . . . to see there is hope and that God is somehow present in the
world. There is a sort of desperation in society. It's become so complex,
and maybe some are overwhelmed. They feel they're losing control.[71]

So powerful is the attraction to experience the divine, that philosopher
Paul Kurtz calls it "the transcendental temptation": "There is the temptation
to believe," Kurtz says, "so everyone believes."[72] Barry Karr, Executive Director of the Committee for the Scientific Investigation of Claims of the Paranormal (CSICOP), agrees: "Once a story gets out, hits the news, it's really
not surprising these things pop up. It creates a bit of a snowball effect."[73]

Although not a single apparition or vision reported in the United States
has ever been authenticated by the Catholic Church[74]—and many have
been exposed as outright hoaxes—the "transcendental temptation" continues
to attract. It is only a matter of time until another vague pattern in yet
another unlikely place moves first one and then thousands of the devout
into a perception of the next "miraculous" image. A cynical hoaxer or
perpetrator of a pious fraud may even help to foster the temptation.

Select Bibliography

Callahan, Philip Serna. *The Tilma under Infra-red Radiation*. Washington, D.C.:
    Center for Applied Research in the Apostolate, 1981. A collection of infrared
    photographs of the Guadalupan Image and a discussion of how they supposedly
    support the claim the image was not painted.
MacDougall, Curtis D. *Superstition and the Press*. Buffalo, N.Y.: Prometheus
    Books, 1983. A critical look at how the press presents supernatural claims—
    such as those of miraculous images—without questioning their validity.
Nickell, Joe. *Inquest on the Shroud of Turin*. Updated ed. Buffalo, N.Y.: Pro-
    metheus Books, 1987. Written with a panel of experts, a skeptical analysis
    of claims that the "shroud" is the burial cloth of Jesus and that its image
    might have been produced miraculously.
Nickell, Joe, with John F. Fischer. "Celestial Painting: Miraculous Image of
    Guadalupe." Chapter 8 of *Secrets of the Supernatural*. Buffalo, N.Y.: Pro-
    metheus Books, 1988. The folkloristic and iconographic investigation debunks
    claims that the image was not wrought by human hands.
Smith, Jody Brant. *The Image of Guadalupe*. Garden City, N.Y.: Doubleday,
    1983. A popular book-length treatment, exaggerating aspects of the claim
    for a miraculous origin of the image.

Wilson, Ian. *The Shroud of Turin.* Rev. ed. Garden City, N.Y.: Image Books, 1979. An apologetic for the notorious "shroud" which attempts to give it a provenance prior to the fourteenth century by equating it with the Image of Edessa.

Notes

1. Thomas Humber, *The Sacred Shroud* (New York: Pocket Books, 1978), p. 84; *The Doctrine of Addai,* quoted in trans. in Ian Wilson, *The Shroud of Turin,* rev. ed. (Garden City, N.Y.: Image Books, 1979). (The manuscript is preserved in Leningrad.)

2. This "official history" is given in translation in Wilson, *The Shroud of Turin,* pp. 272–90.

3. Ibid.

4. Ibid.

5. Ibid.

6. Sir Steven Runciman, in an article on the Edessan Image in the *Cambridge Historical Journal,* quoted in David Sox, *File on the Shroud* (London: Coronet Books, 1978), p. 52.

7. Wilson, *The Shroud of Turin,* p. 130.

8. Ibid., pp. 106ff.

9. *Encyclopaedia Britannica,* 1960 ed., 23:90A, s.v. "Veronica, Saint." For other versions, see *New Catholic Encyclopedia,* 1967, 14: 625.

10. Ibid.

11. From Juliana of Norwich's *Revelations,* quoted in Wilson, *The Shroud of Turin,* p. 108.

12. Humber, *The Sacred Shroud,* p. 85.

13. Ibid., 92.

14. Sox, *File on the Shroud,* p. 51; Wilson, *The Shroud of Turin,* p. 100. The fresco is in the ancient Syrian town of Dura-Europos on the Euphrates River.

15. St. Augustine, *De Trinitate* 8: 4, 5, quoted in Wilson, *The Shroud of Turin,* p. 101.

16. Joe Nickell, "in collaboration with a panel of scientific and technical experts," *Inquest on the Shroud of Turin,* updated ed. (Buffalo, N.Y.: Prometheus Books, 1987), pp. 11–13. Except as noted, information on the Shroud of Turin is taken from this source.

17. Wilson, *The Shroud of Turin,* p. 216.

18. Nickell, *Inquest,* pp. 77–84.

19. Ibid., pp. 85–88.

20. Ibid., pp. 91–94.

21. Ibid., pp. 11–21.

22. Ibid., pp. 41–48, 142–43.

23. For a fuller discussion, see chapter 6, "Post-mortem at Calvary," in Nickell, *Inquest,* pp. 57–75. For a discussion—and defense—of Frei's claims, see Daniel C. Scavone, *The Shroud of Turin,* Great Mysteries series (San Diego, Calif.: Greenhaven Press, 1989), pp. 30–33, 44–46.

24. See also John F. Fischer, "A Summary Critique of Analyses of the 'Blood' on the Turin 'Shroud,' " in Nickell, *Inquest,* pp. 157–60.

25. John Heller, *Report on the Shroud of Turin* (New York: Houghton Mifflin, 1983), p. 168.

26. Nickell, *Inquest,* pp. 95–106. STURP has claimed the "3-D" reconstruction of my images is unsuccessful, but has failed to explain how their "test"—which depends on subtleties of tone—is fair, given that it involved comparing an age-softened shroud image with a contrastingly new one. For a discussion, see Nickell, *Inquest,* pp. 88–91, 104–105. See also Joe Nickell, "Unshrouding a Mystery: Science, Pseudoscience, and the Cloth of Turin," *The Skeptical Inquirer* 13 (Spring 1989): 297–98.

27. Nickell, "Unshrouding a Mystery," p. 296.

28. Scavone, *The Shroud of Turin,* pp. 104–105.

29. Joe Nickell, "Les preuves scientifiques que le Linceul de Turin date du moyen age," *Science et Vie* (France), July 1991, pp. 6–17.

30. Wilson, *The Shroud of Turin,* p. 136; Kenneth E. Stevenson and Gary R. Habermas, *Verdict on the Shroud* (Ann Arbor, Mich.: Servant Books, 1981), p. 104; Heller, *Report on the Shroud of Turin,* p. 212.

31. Jody Brant Smith, *The Image of Guadalupe* (Garden City, N.Y.: Doubleday, 1983), p. 4.

32. Donald Demarest and Coley Taylor, eds., *The Dark Virgin* (N. p.: Academy Guild Press, 1956), p. 2.

33. Joe Nickell and John F. Fischer, "The Image of Guadalupe: A Folkloristic and Iconographic Investigation," *The Skeptical Inquirer* 8.4 (Spring 1985): 243–55; reprinted in Joe Nickell with John F. Fischer, *Secrets of the Supernatural* (Buffalo, N.Y.: Prometheus Books, 1988), pp. 103–117. Except as noted, information for this section is taken from the latter source, and indeed is an abridgement of it.

34. Cleofas Callero, trans., *Nican Mopohua,* in Smith, *The Image of Guadalupe,* pp. 121–25.

35. Marcello Craveri, *The Life of Jesus,* trans. Charles Lam Markmann (New York: Grove Press, 1967), pp. 27–28.

36. Ibid.

37. Anna Brownell Jameson, *Legends of the Madonna as Represented in the Fine Arts* (London: Longman's, Green, 1902), p. xxxiv.

38. Smith, *The Image of Guadalupe,* p. 61.

39. Ibid., p. 20.

40. Philip Serna Callahan, *The Tilma under Infra-red Radiation* (Washington, D.C.: Center for Applied Research in the Apostolate, 1981), p. 10.

41. Ibid., p. 18.

42. Smith, *The Image of Guadalupe,* pp. 12, 68–69.

43. Callahan, *The Tilma under Infra-red Radiation,* pp. 18, 20.

44. Glenn Taylor, personal communication, Lexington, Kentucky, October 4, 1983. For a fuller discussion of the evidence for artistry, see the original report in Nickell with Fischer, *Secrets of the Supernatural,* pp. 108–115.

45. Smith, *The Image of Guadalupe,* pp. 20–21.

46. "Mexico," *Encyclopaedia Britannica,* 1973 ed.

47. Smith, *The Image of Guadalupe,* pp. 10–11.

48. Patrick Tierney, "The Arts," *Omni,* September 1983, pp. 174, 190.

49. Smith, *The Image of Guadalupe,* pp. 79–83, 111ff.

50. D. Scott Rogo, *Miracles: A Parascientific Inquiry into Wondrous Phenomena* (New York: Dial Press, 1982), p. 113.

51. Ibid., p. 125.

52. Curtis D. MacDougall, *Superstition and the Press* (Buffalo, N.Y.: Prometheus Books, 1983), p. 512, citing a report of *Christian Gazette* columnist Don Marsh, September 10, 1982. The previous day, the *Charleston Mail* "Streamer-headlined the AP story" (according to MacDougall), and accompanied it with a photograph.

53. Late evening news, WTVQ-TV, Lexington, Ky., March 27, 1992.

54. "Report of Virgin's Image at Store Draws Crowds," (Progresso) *Courier-News,* December 19, 1990.

55. Ken Meyers, "Faithful Flock to Fostoria," *USA Today,* August 27, 1986; "Image of Christ on Oil Tank Causes Traffic Jams," *The Cedar Rapids Gazette,* August 22, 1986; "Man Pleads Guilty to Defacing 'Christ Image' on Soy Oil Tank," *Courier-Journal* (Louisville, Ky.), October 10, 1986.

56. Lawrence Viele, "The Pasta Jesus," *The Georgia Skeptic* (newsletter of the Georgia Skeptics) 5.2 (March/April 1992): 1, 5.

57. Lewis Grizzard, "A Man of Vision," *Rocky Mountain News,* June 8, 1991.

58. "Christ on a Billboard?" *Courier-News,* May 22, 1991.

59. MacDougall, *Superstition and the Press,* p. 512: Cullen Murphy, "Shreds of Evidence," *Harper's,* November 1991, p. 44. (Cf. "Potato Chip Collector Finds Spud-tacular Fame," *Courier-Journal,* November 5, 1987.)

60. "Image of Jesus in Window Called Optical Illusion," *The Detroit News,* September 9, 1987.

61. MacDougall, *Superstition and the Press,* pp. 511–12.

62. "Reflected Glory," *The Courier-News,* June 4, 1987.

63. Tracy Wilkinson, "Despite Skepticism, Faithful Line Up to View Cross Images in Window," *Los Angeles Times,* August 17, 1990.

64. Terry Spencer, "Glendale Crowd Views Image of Cross," *Daily News* (Glendale, Calif.), August 23, 1990.

65. Unidentified clipping, "Images of Jesus May Vanish with Shift in Lights," Religious News Service, n.d.

66. Michael A. Watkis, "Faithful Report Seeing Sacred Image in Stained Glass of Newark Church, *Newark Star-Ledger,* May 29, 1991.

67. Maria Goodavage, "Apparition Helps Many 'Keep the Faith,' " *USA Today,* December 10, 1990.

68. Rogo, *Miracles,* p. 129.

69. Ibid., p. 128.

70. "Experts Call 'Hugo Christ' Photo Fake," *The Evening Post* (Charleston, D.C.), April 12, 1990.

71. Quoted in Marjie Lundstrom, "Catholic Church Wrestles with Jump in 'Miracles,' " *The Sacramento Bee,* April 7, 1991.

72. Ben Winton, "Controversy over Apparition Sightings Continues," *The Phoenix Gazette,* November 10, 1990. See also Paul Kurtz, *The Transcendental Temptation* (Buffalo, N.Y.: Prometheus Books, 1991).

73. Quoted in Winton.

74. Lundstrom, "Catholic Church Wrestles with Jump in 'Miracles.' "

3

Magical Icons

In addition to those pictures whose very existence is said to represent a miracle, other incredible icons are those that seem to be *animated* (that is, to exhibit behavior as if imbued with life). The concept is ancient.

An example is an Egyptian statue that stands across the Nile from Karnak. Called the statue of Memnon by the Greeks (in whose mythology Memnon was the son of the goddess of the dawn), it is actually one of two 50-foot-tall colossi of Amenhotep III (Pharaoh of Egypt circa 1141–1375 B.C.). The statue became famous for emitting a strange cry or a sound like a mournful voice, supposed to be that of Memnon in response to the greeting of his mother, Eos. The sound was reported occasionally (first by Strabo in 20 B.C., later by Pliny and Juvenal) but always in the morning, perhaps as often as several times a year. Even after the upper part was toppled, the cry continued (until the statue was restored in A.D. 170). Today, authorities attribute the curious phenomenon to a simple fact of physics: Since the statue is hollow, air heated in the interior by the early morning sun escapes through one or more fissures in the granite, thus producing the noise. (Such a phenomenon, although a freak occurrence, is by no means the only example: Napoleon's expedition heard similar sounds at sunrise—once at a quarry and once in a temple at Karnak.)[1]

Of course, miraculous effects could be deliberately contrived. At Alexandria, for instance,

> The great statue of Serapis, which had been made under the Ptolemies, having perhaps marble feet, but for the rest built of wood, clothed with drapery and glittering with gold and silver, stood in one of the covered chambers, which had a small window so contrived as to let the sun's rays kiss the lips of the statue on the appointed occasions. This was one of the tricks employed in the sacred mysteries, to dazzle the worshipper by the sudden blaze of light which on the proper occasions was let into the dark room.[2]

Hero of Alexandria, who lived in the first century A.D., describes an ingenious idol supposedly used by the ancient Egyptians. It is featured in his treatise *The Pneumatics* (which describes various mechanical contrivances) as "Libations on an Altar Produced by Fire." The altar was a heavy pedestal upon which stood the idol, the statue of a goddess holding a vase. When a fire was built upon the altar, presently the figure would—seemingly miraculously—pour out the customary libations. Hero explained that under the fire bowl was an airtight chamber, the air of which expanded as it was heated. This forced the wine from a hidden reservoir up a tube inside the figure and out the vase; as the wine extinguished the fire, the flow stopped.[3]

Hero also described various remarkable automata, for example, "an Automaton which will drink any quantity that may be presented to it." Yet the secret behind the Babylonian idol of Bel (or Baal)—which not only drank huge quantities of wine but also devoured vast amounts of food as well—was a simple one. The story is told in the fourteenth chapter of Daniel (found in Catholic but not Protestant Bibles), "Bel and the Dragon":

> Now the Babylonians had an idol called Bel, and every day they spent on it twelve bushels of fine flour and forty sheep and fifty gallons of wine. (Dan. 14:3)[4]

By this seeming miracle the priests won over King Cyrus to the worship of the idol. Now Daniel, who was very wise and who advised Cyrus in many matters, refused to worship the deity. When the king demanded an explanation, Daniel replied that he believed in a *living* God. Responded

Cyrus: "Do you not think that Bel is a living God? Do you not see how much he eats and drinks every day?" But Daniel laughed and said: "Do not be deceived, O King; for this is but clay inside and brass outside, and it never ate or drank anything." Angry, Cyrus summoned the priests of Bel and proposed a test between Daniel and the group of seventy priests, with punishment of death to the loser. Cyrus arranged to have the food and wine set forth as usual, but to seal the door to the temple so that no one could enter without revealing the fact.

The following morning, the seals were unbroken, yet the food and wine were gone. However, Daniel had set a trap that revealed the priests' trickery. He had instructed his servants to cover the temple floor carefully with sifted ashes. The footsteps of men, women, and children were thus revealed.

> Then the king was enraged, and he seized the priests and their wives and children; and they showed him the secret doors through which they were accustomed to enter and devour what was on the table. (Dan. 14:21)

All were put to death, and Daniel was allowed to destroy the idol and its temple.

Whether or not this story is true (it is most likely only a parable intended to motivate Jews to resist idolatry), it does illustrate the important distinction between *veneration* (paying reverence through an image, which is itself void of value or power, for that which it represents) and *idolatry* (or image worship, in which the image is regarded as the "tenement or vehicle of the god and fraught with divine influence").[5]

Idolatry is thus the result of *animism* (derived from *anima,* "breath"), the belief that objects have life or indwelling souls.

> An image fashioned like a god and having this advantage over a mere stock or stone, that it declares itself and reveals at a glance to what god it is sacred, is believed to attract and influence the god to choose it as his home and tenement. Religious ceremonial is much more hopeful and efficacious for a worshipper who thus has means of approaching the god he worships in visible and tangible form, and even of coercing it.[6]

In its modern expression, animism is often seen in the form of belief in certain miraculous phenomena attributed to religious images—especially pictures and statues of Jesus and the Virgin Mary that weep, bleed, exhibit movement, or the like.

Weeping Icons

With the spread of Christianity have come reports of animated icons. (Broadly speaking, an icon is an image or portrait figure, although the term specially applies to flat or bas-relief representations of sacred personages rendered in the accepted Byzantine fashion.) According to D. Scott Rogo:

> Cases of religious statues, paintings, icons, and other effigies that suddenly begin to bleed or weep have been documented throughout history. Before Rome was sacked in 1527, for instance, a statue of Christ housed in a local monastery wept for several days. When the city of Syracuse in Sicily lay under Spanish siege in 1719, a marble statue of St. Lucy in the city cried continually.[7]

Similar manifestations have been increasingly reported in modern times. Indeed, an entire epidemic swept Roman Catholic Italy in 1953. It began in the home of a young couple, Angelo and Antoinetta Janusso, who lived in a poor district of Syracuse in the island region of Sicily. The couple had received a plaster statue of the Virgin Mary as a wedding gift when they married in March. Then, on August 29, the eighteen-inch statue began to weep in the presence of Mrs. Janusso. This was the culmination of several weeks of upheaval in the Janussos' household.

Antoinetta Janusso was pregnant, and for several weeks she had been suffering "seizures," fainting spells, and attacks of blindness. Local doctors were unable to diagnose her condition, but she seems to have been suffering from hysteria—or, alternatively, to have been feigning the same, although such a protracted bout of malingering would itself be indicative of mental distress.

It is well to keep this in mind in light of the fact that church authorities assessed the weeping phenomenon as genuine and that tests of the liqiud reportedly showed it to be consistent with tears.[8] There was a climate of belief in weeping statues in the city stemming from the previously mentioned case of the weeping statue of St. Lucy, and in any event questions as to the scientific competency and impartiality of the investigators present themselves. Also, if the analyses of the putative tears were like those conducted on samples from the Shroud of Turin—in which, for example, red ocher tempera paint was "identified" as blood—then the situation would be quite different than claimed by proponents.

Scott Rogo stated the obvious when he pointed out that "Antoinetta Janusso's role in the miracle was certainly much more important than any of the original investigators cared to admit." And he may have been closer to the mark than first appears when he suggested the woman's mental state triggered what "may in fact have been a limited form of poltergeist attack"—if we understand poltergeist phenomena correctly. A brief discussion should prove helpful.

The term *poltergeist*—German for "noisy spirit"—applies to a class of allegedly paranormal phenomena characterized by physical disturbances: furniture is moved, smaller objects are sent sailing through the air, and similar disturbances take place, including outbreaks of tapping sounds or of water streaming unaccountably from fully intact walls.[9]

Both believers and skeptics agree that such cases typically revolve around a disturbed individual—usually an adolescent who is thought to be an "agent" of the destructive force. There the agreement ends, however, because proponents of the paranormal suggest the person may merely be exercising unconscious psychokinetic (mind-over-matter) activity, while skeptics suspect that deliberate, if surreptitious, behavior is responsible. The latter theory has numerous solved cases in its favor.

For example, the mystery behind several "poltergeist" fires that plagued an Alabama house was solved by the confession of the family's nine-year-old son. He had had a simple motive, wishing his family to return to the city from which they had recently moved. In another case in a Louisville, Kentucky, home, bottle caps, boxes, and other objects were hurled about. Eventually an eleven-year-old girl admitted she was responsible for the trouble; since her mother was in the hospital, the girl wanted people to pay more attention to her.[10]

Yet another series of disturbances plagued the C. A. Wilkinson family of Tulsa. Mr. Wilkinson suspected "wild electricity" of being the causative agent, but as magician Milbourne Christopher states:

Even objects that were not operated by electricity took on sudden motion. Chairs and tables seemed to vibrate. Pots leaped into the air. One night the commotion was so great that Wilkinson, his wife, and his twelve-year-old adopted daughter bedded down outside in the family automobile.

As usual the disruptions drew curiosity seekers, reporters, and investigators. A trap was laid for a possible human culprit. A light coating of powder was dusted over potential flying objects. The Tulsa *Tribune* duly noted that after the disturbance that followed telltale marks were found on the girl's hands. She confessed that she was the cause of hitherto mysterious turmoil.[11]

In March 1984, the Columbus, Ohio, home of John and Joan Resch was reportedly attacked by a poltergeist. Furniture was overturned, picture frames smashed, glass objects broken, and a telephone handset thrown from its cradle. The family's fourteen-year-old adopted daughter, Tina, described as "hyperactive and emotionally disturbed," was suspected of the shenanigans, which typically occurred when witnesses were looking away from the girl. Although family members, some reporters, and two parapsychologists were apparently duped—at least for a time—some photographs and television news tapes caught the girl red-handed—toppling a lamp, for example—and a TV technician saw her secretly move a table with her foot. As to motive, the noted magician and paranormal investigator James Randi states: "She was admittedly under stress and had good reason to want to attract media exposure: she wanted to trace her true parents, against the wishes of the Resches. And her 'best friend' . . . had a fight with her and broke off their relationship two days before the phenomena began."[12]

Proponents of the poltergeist hypothesis seem undaunted by such evidence of trickery. After all, there will always be cases in which no trickery was discovered because not all cases are adequately investigated by competent experts. Also, there is the tendency of believers to rationalize any contrary evidence. For example, as one says of a case investigated by Hans Bender:

> The incidents centered around Brigitte, a thirteen-year-old daughter. As in other poltergeist cases which seemed to include genuine effects, when these began to wane, the focal person, Brigitte, was discovered to cheat. Bender found the girl's fingerprints on a dish which she claimed the poltergeist had thrown out the window.[13]

Note the unwillingness to draw the obvious conclusion from the evidence. Such rationalizing is simple: whenever cheating is clearly proved, one can fall back on earlier instances in which no trickery was detected. This approach contrasts with that of skeptical investigators who consider one instance of deceit enough to discredit an entire case.

To return to the Sicilian weeping-statue case, it was Mrs. Janusso who was the sole person present when the phenomenon allegedly began (she claimed it was upon suddenly recovering from one of her bouts of "blindness"). It was also she who was invariably present whenever the phenomenon occurred[14] and who claimed to be cured as a result of it. (If she had sought a way out of the predicament she had gotten herself into, the "miracle" would have served to effect a "cure" while diverting attention elsewhere.) Then, as suddenly as it had begun only three days earlier, the phenomenon ceased—immediately after samples had been collected for testing.

As mentioned earlier, though, an epidemic of imitative miracles swept Italy. A housewife in Calabria reported on December 15 that some postcard-size pictures of the Madonna wept bloody tears; the following April 3 a woman in Mezzalombardo claimed that an illustration of Mary clipped from a magazine had begun to weep; and additional reports soon followed, in May 1954 and March 1955. Finally, in March 1957, a family in Ricca Corneta reported that a papier-mâché statue of the Virgin shed tears for several days. All of these occurrences involved weeping madonnas; none had to do with a weeping or bleeding image of Jesus. One must agree with Rogo that they were "no doubt spawned by wide press coverage of the Syracuse miracle."[15]

A pair of New York cases is also instructive. The first began on March 16, 1960, when a framed lithograph of the Blessed Virgin that had begun to "weep" in an Island Park woman's home attracted four thousand visitors within a week, after which a priest at a nearby Greek Orthodox church blessed the house and the tears ceased. (The Greek Orthodox Church is one of a family of Eastern Orthodox churches that split from Rome in 1054, but which still share many customs including the veneration of icons.)

The second case was reported in Ocean Park as soon as the first came to light—by the aunt of the Island Park woman! She informed the priest and also invited representatives of the press, allowing the latter to take samples of the tears. Alas, tests showed they were not genuine tears; however, this did not stop the icon from being publicly displayed and eventually making its way to Los Angeles in 1964. At that time, a local investigator was permitted to take scrapings of the congealed "tears" to find that they were "composed of a solidified sugar solution."[16] This proved that the second case had been a clever hoax, although some of the credulous continued to believe in the genuineness of the first—apparently because no tests had been conducted in that case.

In 1981 in Thornton, California, a ceramic figurine of the Virgin Mary, lodged in the Mater Ecclesiae Mission Church, purportedly began to weep as well as to move and exhibit other phenomena (to be discussed later in this chapter). Soon the church had to be kept open seven days a week to accommodate the hordes of pilgrims who flocked to the site. According to one magazine article, "money poured in, enabling the parish to buy a new roof, air conditioning and such frills as a wrought-iron fence to protect the statue." In addition to money, however, the incredible phenomena also attracted an investigation by the Stockton Diocese.

> The four clerics commissioned to look into the phenomena advanced cautiously and their investigation was shrouded in secrecy—although one priest on the team, Father Robert Pereira, admitted that a "highly specialized scientific laboratory in the Bay Area" was helping to analyze the purported "miracles." Pereira himself was skeptical. He pointed out that many of the events at Thornton do not properly conform to historical cases of weeping statues, cases that definitely proved to be miraculous. Like many Catholic priests and theologians, Father Pereira also worried that the events at Thornton might divert the attention of the masses from the basic teachings of the church.[17]

As a consequence of their investigation, the diocese labeled the phenomena a deception. The commission found that human agency was responsible for the statue's seeming to come to life—i.e., that it was a hoax.[18]

Similarly, in Chicago in May 1984, a 39-inch wooden statue of the Blessed Virgin Mary, enshrined in the Roman Catholic St. John of God Church, supposedly began weeping only two weeks after it arrived at the church. On Tuesday, May 29, the priest, the Rev. Raymond J. Jasinski, together with some parishioners, claimed to witness the phenomenon. By Thursday thousands were hastening to the site—some as mere curiosity seekers, others looking for cures or solace. Soon street vendors had seized the opportunity to hawk photos of the Madonna. Events later took a surprising, violent turn when, on July 25, a man entered the church, pulled out a pistol, and fired three shots at the statue, one hitting its target and lodging in the figure's shin. The unidentified gunman then fled the scene, leaving behind several shocked women who had been kneeling before the Madonna. (He turned out to be a 24-year-old vagrant, who was later tried and found not guilty by reason of insanity.)[19]

Finally, after a year-long investigation, an archdiocesan committee reported its findings. On Tuesday, September 17, 1985, the committee announced that no miracle was involved in the reported weeping, although it left unanswered whether the phenomenon was a deliberate hoax.[20]

Just over a year later, on December 6, 1986, the feast of St. Nicholas, another Chicago effigy reportedly succumbed to the contagious weeping. At St. Nicholas Albanian Orthodox Church, a three-by-five-foot canvas-on-wood icon, depicting Mary with the infant Jesus in hues of gold and scarlet, began to produce moisture. Tears streamed from the Virgin's eyes and moisture also reportedly oozed from her hands. To accommodate the crowds of thousands attacted to the small church, volunteers worked in twelve-hour shifts.

The suspicions of skeptics were further aroused when Bishop Isaiah, chancellor of the Greek Orthodox Diocese who had arrived and officially recognized the phenomenon, said that no scientific testing of the fluid would be conducted nor would any other investigation be made. "In the Orthodox Church, we don't investigate these matters," he said, making emphatic the stonewalling that came from an "Official Statement" released by his office.[21] It stated in part:

Icons have always occupied a prominent place in the life of the Orthodox Christian Church. It can be said that the first one, which was not made by human hands, was the Holy Mandilion which covered the face of Christ at His burial and which had imprinted on it the Holy Countenance. . . .

The weeping icon of the Lord's mother, the Blessed Virgin Mary, which is situated on the iconostasion of the Church of St. Nicholas in Chicago, is not a rare occurrence. The phenomenon is rationally unexplainable. It needs no explanation, whether scientific or natural. The believers do not ask the how, but the why. The why is clear to all. The Lord's mother beckons to the believers and to the unbelievers to awaken from the sleep of materialism and to nourish themselves spiritually. In other words she is inviting to a spiritual reawakening and to penitence all who thirst for Christ and His compassion and mercy.

> The weeping icon of the Holy Theotokos [Mother of God] is a vivid testimony that even in our highly developed age of science, technology, and rampant knowledge, there still remains spirituality and devotion. There still is that awe or mystery about creation especially at this time of the year when all Christians anticipate the coming of God into the world.[22]

Skeptics were quick to point out that the phenomenon was scarcely "rationally unexplainable"; it only remained *unexplained* because no investigation was to be allowed.[23] The archbishop "did not even respond to our request to discuss the possibility of scientific tests," said Michael Crowley, president of the Midwest Committee for Rational Inquiry, a Chicago-based organization that investigates paranormal claims. The refusal, Crowley suggests, could be interpreted as an indication that church officials themselves have doubts concerning the authenticity of the icon.[24]

Another Greek Orthodox icon seems to have caught the weeping condition while on loan to the Chicago Greek Orthodox Church of St. Athanasios and John the Baptist. This began on October 17, 1990, when the icon of St. Irene Chrisovalantou, patron saint of the sick and of peace, supposedly began to cry immediately after a service for peace in the Persian Gulf. Returned to its home (the church of a breakaway Orthodox faction) in Astoria, Queens, New York, on October 23, the icon attracted additional thousands of pilgrims over the following days as it was reputed to continue weeping.[25] However, the tears dried up after the Gulf war ended. (See Figure 5.)

Although an investigation was refused at the time, on May 11, 1991, I was able to examine the icon, under rather limited conditions, in company with members of the New York Area Skeptics (NYASk). A previous NYASk ultraviolet-light examination had revealed only some streaks and markings that were clearly not the result of weeping. Our examination included stereomicroscopic viewing which also failed to show traces of any tearstains.[26] Subsequently, forensic analyst John F. Fischer and I obtained a videotape of the earlier, October 1990, phenomenon. At first we regarded the evidence as too ambiguous to assess, but further study indicated that there were wet-looking streaks that seemed to have been on the painted panel rather than the clear plexiglas cover. It appeared to us that the two "rivulets" flowed down the face just to the outside of the eyes and that the scale of the "tears" was greatly disproportionate to the diminutive size of St. Irene's face. These observations suggested to us a rather crude hoax.[27]

A curious sequel to the story of the St. Irene icon came just before Christmas 1991. On December 23, three armed men and a woman burst into the church, forced two priests and four others to lie on the front altar, pried the icon from its case, and fled. Whether they sought the icon for its alleged powers, or for the estimated $800,000 value of its gold frame encrusted with jewels,[28] could only be speculated upon. Said Bishop Vikentios:

> Only we need the icon back, we don't care for the gold or the jewels.
> It is a holy icon, it is a miracle icon. She is the patron saint of peace.
> We don't know why the Lord allowed this to happen.[29]

Within a few days, however, the icon was returned—although missing the frame and most of its jewels—anonymously through the mail.

A final (?) episode in the icon saga came when representatives of the mainstream church—the traditional Greek Orthodox Archdiocese of North and South America (mentioned earlier in the stonewalling of the 1986 Chicago weeping-icon case)—suggested that the breakaway faction that owns the icon might have staged the theft as a hoax. "We have doubts about the tears and so on," added the archdiocese's press officer. To what appeared as a case of the pot calling the kettle black, members of the breakaway Greek Orthodox Christians of North and South America, responded that the other church was simply envious of the icon.[30]

I will mention only one other case—or rather several cases that centered around a single priest—that captured national press attention in 1992 when statues at his St. Elizabeth Ann Seton Church in Lake Ridge, Virginia, and elsewhere, began to weep copiously. The priest is the Rev. James Bruse who, before being ordained, was enrolled in the *Guinness Book of World Records* in 1978 for riding a roller coaster for five straight days. According to *USA Today*, tears from a three-foot fiberglas statue of the Virgin "seem to fall only in the presence of Bruse" and "even statues at other churches have cried in Bruse's presence." Bruse has also claimed to have the stigmata—in this case, welts on his wrists and bleeding feet—wounds that ostensibly imitate those of the crucified Christ. (Stigmata will be discussed in a later chapter.)[31] According to the *Washington City Paper*, ". . . with the exception of the one in the sanctuary, all of the statues at St. Elizabeth's that have purportedly wept . . . are located in Bruse's private office." The paper added, "But most suspicious is Bruse's silence and his refusal to allow the statue to be examined."[32]

I followed the story closely—being aided by reporters from *USA Today, The Washington Post,* and other newspapers, who phoned me to discuss the matter at length. Upon learning the facts, I challenged Bruse, in the pages of the *Washington City Paper,* to permit the statue of the Virgin to be examined under controlled conditions. I later sent him a certified letter along with a copy of the newspaper article in whch I made the challenge.[33] To date, I have received no reply.

How are statues made to weep? One possibility is *condensation—* moisture collecting on a cool surface. For example, when the glass-eyed "Pilgrim Statue of Fatima" purportedly wept while on a ten-day display in New Orleans in July 1972, a skeptical archdiocesan spokesman stated: "There are all sorts of possible causes. This is a very humid climate here."[34] If one could go back through the centuries to the very first "weeping" statue, it might well have been due simply to the effect of condensation.

However, few statues are like that at Fatima (carved of wood with separate glass eyes) which might favor condensation in the proper region to produce "weeping." The usual effect of condensation, on a porcelain figurine, for instance, would be an overall fogging of the surface, not localized streaming of "tears."

A second possibility is *deliberate hoaxing.* Although elsewhere I have considered such elaborate hypothetical scenarios as hollow statues with tubes attached to pinhole-sized "tear ducts" and the use of chemical preparations (such as calcium chloride, a crystalline powder that draws moisture from the air and eventually liquefies),[35] I expect that such contrivances are used rarely if at all. It is a simple matter to use an eyedropper filled with water (or better still a briny solution, or even real tears!), applying it when no one is around. Or a small, concealed sponge could work wonders when one pretends to wipe nonexistent tears from an icon and then returns the damp handkerchief to its awestruck owner. A novelty squirt ring is another possibility,[36] although early in this century a French abbé merely sprinkled on a picture water from a nearby vase when he thought no one was looking.[37] Other possibilities will occur to the inventive.

James Randi describes how Mazola oil was the secret ingredient for a fake "weeping" stained glass window at a New Orleans church in 1989. Placed on the window early in the morning, the oil suspends on the glass, blending with its hues. As the sun rises during Mass, the oil begins to glimmer, as if the glass had begun to weep. Then, as the glass becomes warm, the oil starts to trickle down the window. Explained a reporter, "windows are also safer to rig than statues or icons, because often they are set out of arm's reach and can't be admired closely."[38]

A third explanation for weeping icons is *imagination*. As one little girl said, after confessing to some "poltergeist" disturbances, "I didn't throw all those things. People just imagined some of them."[39] The same can be true of weeping effigies. Explains Barry Karr, Executive Director of CSICOP:

> There are a lot of people who really want miracles because they want to be part of something miraculous, and people will claim to see things and experience things, not necessarily fraudulently, but based on a high level of expectation. They got there expecting to see something, and anything can turn into a miracle.[40]

Something of the sort may have taken place at churches visited by the catalytic Father Bruse, where statues and a stained-glass window supposedly wept. Stated a reporter: "Maybe they did cry. Or maybe people first saw Bruse and then thought they saw the objects weep."[41] (We shall see more of the role imagination plays in animating statues later in this chapter).

Finally, related to the previous possibility, imagination, there is the effect of *illusion*. For instance a "weeping" portrait of Mary at the Greek Orthodox Shrine of St. Michael in Tarpon Springs, Florida, in 1989, proved to be completely dry. Dr. Gary Posner, founder of Tampa Bay Skeptics, discovered that the "icon" was nothing more than a *photograph* of the notorious "Guiding Mother of God Weeping Icon" from the St. Nicholas Albanian Orthodox Church in Chicago (discussed earlier).[42]

I witnessed a different illusion when I examined the St. Irene icon in Queens, New York. The glistening varnish and certain surface irregularities created a play of light that produced the appearance of weeping. A religious supplicant predisposed to see tears (the legend of St. Irene held that "tears were always to be found in her eyes"[43]) could, especially if carrying a candle, see in the resultant glimmering in the tiny eyes, aided by vertical cracks and other streaks, the effect of tears.[44] Aided in part by the sad expression of St. Irene, we easily experienced the illusion of seeing tears welling up in the saint's eyes, although a low-power stereo microscope showed us the true state of affairs.[45]

Bleeding Effigies

An astonishing series of apparently miraculous events occurred in 1985 on December 8—the Feast of the Immaculate Conception. A two-foot statue of the Virgin Mary in the home of a Montreal, Quebec, railroad worker named Jean-Guy Beauregard began weeping. When the phenomenon attracted the predictable assortment of the pious and the curious, Beauregard's landlord asked him to move the statue. He took it to a lakeside town on Montreal's northwestern outskirts, Sainte-Marthe-sur-le-Lac, to the home of friends, Maurice and Claudette Girouard.

Soon, the Blessed Virgin's tears began to turn bloody, and the "contagion" we noted earlier infected nearby icons, statues, and crucifixes which also started weeping and bleeding. Thousands of pilgrims waited in the brutal winter cold to view "the Miracle of Sainte-Marthe," as many as 12,000 in one week. Still, church authorities were cautious, even skeptical. The local bishop, the Rev. Charles Valois of St. Jerome Diocese, sensibly labeled the affair "an exaggeration of the marvelous," adding:

> God seldom speaks by extraordinary means but rather through the Bible and the teachings of the church. It is not through such means as these [weeping statues] that we are going to find out what the Lord wants to say to us.[46]

And then, as soon as it had begun, the Associated Press reported that the "bubble burst"; the "miracle" was "all a hoax—not even a very clever hoax." Newsmen from the Canadian Broadcasting Corporation had been permitted to borrow a "miraculous" icon and had taken it directly to a scientific laboratory. There, examination showed that blood had been mixed with a coating of pork and beef fat so that—when the room warmed slightly—the substance would liquefy and run like tears. A Montreal newspaper reported that the owner of the effigies confessed he had used his own blood to produce the effects.[47]

The Miracle of Sainte-Marthe is only one example of an alleged phenomenon that has occurred since antiquity. One documented case from the last century featured Rose Tamisier, a French stigmatic who claimed to receive visits from The Virgin Mary and who caused a picture of Christ to emit actual blood. According to Brewer's *A Dictionary of Miracles,* Tamisier was educated at a convent "where she made herself notorious," claiming to be visited constantly by the Virgin Mary. Leaving the convent, she returned to her native village where she became known as a miracle worker. She allegedly grew a miraculous cabbage sufficient to feed the entire village for weeks, while she herself ate nothing—except consecrated wafers brought to her by angels. As Tamisier's fame spread, her body became marked with unusual stigmata, and she "now entered on her great achievement," causing a picture of Christ "to emit real blood"—her first exhibition taking place on November 10, 1850. Although the "miracle" was examined and pronounced genuine, the following year Tamisier was tried at Nimes on a charge of imposture, and—"after a long and patient investigation"—was found guilty and sentenced to six months' imprisonment, in addition to being fined 500 francs and costs.[48]

Another French case began in 1913 when rumors circulated about remarkable phenomena occurring at the home of the Abbé Vachère at Mirebeau-en-Poitou. Supposedly, a picture of Christ bled, wafers consecrated by the abbé dripped blood, and a statue of Christ in a nearby grotto produced a bloody sweat. The reports intrigued psychical investigator Everard Feilding, a devout Catholic, who traveled to Mirebeau in the company of the great Irish poet William Butler Yeats.

The abbé, a charming sixty-year-old gentleman, explained how he had acquired two oleographs of Christ in 1906. (An oleograph is a type of color print imitative of an oil painting.) He claimed that one morning, five years later, while saying Mass in the private chapel of his home, he observed dark stains on the forehead of one of the images that hung over the altar. Later that day, the stains had condensed into a liquid resembling blood, and two days after that stains had formed themselves into a "crown of thorns" configuration. Soon, the picture bled daily and, by the following month, began to weep as well. The abbé also began to hear voices bemoaning the decline in religion. The following year, 1912, brought added miracles, including wafers unaccountably breaking open and issuing blood.

But by 1914 the abbé's superiors ordered him to turn over the bleeding picture, whereupon his second oleograph, which had been kept at a cottage he owned, also began to weep and bleed! At this point Feilding arrived and was permitted to take samples of the bloodlike substance. Back in England, Feilding had these analyzed by London's Lister Institute which determined that the substance was not human blood—although the exact composition of the substance could not be determined. It did, however, contain a microorganism typically found in stagnant water.

When Feilding returned to Mirebeau on Easter 1915, Vachère explained that—as a result of increasing skepticism about the miracles on the part of the bishop—Rome had excommunicated him. During the three days he spent at Mirebeau, Feilding paid several visits to the abbé's home—always finding the oleograph wet but never seeing the bleeding actually begin. Finally, the investigator proposed a test: He would dry the picture, then seal it in the chapel to see if it produced blood when no one had access to it. After initial resistance the abbé acquiesced, but allowed Feilding only to lock rather than seal the chapel door. However, the investigator secretly placed a piece of paper in the hinge in such a way as to fall if the door were opened.

Upon returning to the chapel some hours later, Feilding discovered that the picture was wet but that the slip of paper had been dislodged. Informed of the fact, Vachère became enraged, then suggested that his sacristan might have given the door a shake upon finding it locked and thus dislodged the paper. Feilding thought this tenable. Nine years later, Feilding and his wife paid a last visit to the now elderly abbé upon learning of still new miracles: a statue of the infant Jesus, for example, had begun to bleed. Just before Feilding was to take new samples of the blood from the oleograph, his wife believed she saw Vachère surreptitiously sprinkle water on the picture from a nearby vase. (This probably would have been to remoisten the blood that presumably had earlier been placed on the picture.) This time, tests of the liquid showed it was indeed human blood.

Feilding was reluctant to believe that the kindly old man could be guilty of such deceit, and he had trouble making up his mind about the affair. Scott Rogo, however, has postulated that the abbé's "unstable mental disposition, his devotion, and his fascination with the stigmata" (he had corresponded with a German stigmatist) resulted in "a poltergeist attack that mimicked the appearance of a religious miracle."[49] Failing to appreciate virtually every clue that points to the obvious answer—pious hoaxing—Rogo asserts: "This theory is further supported by the fact that sometimes religious figures would bleed in homes that the abbé merely visited!"[50] (Exclamation point, indeed!)

Turning from France to northern England, on March 17, 1920, a middle-class housewife claimed that a crucifix in her home had begun to drip blood. But there are ample reasons to doubt the authenticity of the phenomenon, not the least of which is that the woman, a Catholic convert, had earlier laid claim to a miraculous healing, divine visions, spirit sightings, psychic abilities, and the stigmata, as well as burn marks on her arm which she claimed resulted from being touched by a soul from purgatory! And the bleeding crucifix? This was reported the very day after the local newspaper carried an account of Abbé Vachère and the "miracles" at Mirebeau![51] The poor woman seemed determined to mimic every such phenomenon she read about.

An interesting variant on the bleeding-icon phenomenon occurred in France in 1954, at the time the weeping-statue rage was sweeping neighboring Italy. An effigy responded to injury—in this case, a statue of Saint Anne (the legendary mother of Mary[52]). The statue belonged to a hotel owner in Entrevaux named Jean Salate. Salate claimed that he broke a finger on the statue in a fit of anger and that the statue responded miraculously by emitting thirty drops of blood during the day and again the following morning. While throngs of the pious gathered to witness the miracle, and chemical analysis proved that the blood was genuine, rumor soon spread that Salate had himself faked the phenomenon.[53]

In contrast to the preceding case, no wound or blemish was necessary to cause a plastic-encased portrait of Jesus to exude blood. The affair began on May 24, 1979, when Mrs. Kathy Malott visited her grandmother, Mrs. Willie Mae Seymore, at the latter's Roswell, New Mexico, home. It was reportedly Mr. Malott who first noticed a "tear" of blood just under the right eye of the wallet-sized picture. Soon, a trickle flowed from the spot and pooled at the bottom of the picture, where it was inserted into the frame of a larger picture. "The blood was running from the picture just as if I had cut my finger," said Mrs. Seymore.[54]

The family phoned a priest who seems to have been skeptical of the phenomenon. He not only declined an offer to visit the residence to view the picture, but he labeled the matter "ticklish" and said that any participation by the Roman Catholic Church would have to be approved by the archbishop. But rather than pursue that avenue, the family then telephoned the local newspaper, which in turn arranged to have a medical technician from a local hospital test the red substance. He reported that it was "bona fide blood" but did not confirm whether it was human or not. According to one (unverified) source, "An even more bizarre note was added when the blood was discovered to be still uncongealed after 24 hours."[55] Actually, the newspaper that "broke the story"[56] described the blood as *coagulating at the base of the frame*" and again as a *"dried substance*" (emphasis added).

A 1971 Italian case supposedly indicates that blood can not only flow spontaneously from holy images but also be supernaturally manipulated into pictorial images. A lawyer living in Maropati said he awoke on the morning of January 3 to find blood (subsequently confirmed as such) dripping from a painting of the Madonna that hung over his bed. The phenomenon was repeated on subsequent occasions, but soon the flows began to disobey gravity and run *horizontally* in rivulets so as to produce bloody crosses on the white wall immediately beneath the painting! Or rather we are asked to *believe* that they did. The "facts" in the case—colorfully related by Rogo[57]—come from the supermarket tabloid, the *National Enquirer*.[58] An accompanying photograph shows that while the blood on the painting did have the appearance of rivulets, the crosses were composed of thicker markings; the crossbars, especially, resembled swabbed *strokes* more than actual flows. And while the *Enquirer* article was titled "Vatican Investigates Claim that Painting Weeps Human Blood," Rogo makes no mention of the alleged investigation's conclusions—which must have fallen somewhere between the "dubious" and "fake" ranges.

More remarkable than simple crosses was the bloody portrait of Jesus that formed on a bedroom wall in Cosenza, Calabria (Italy), sometime between 1955 and 1961. Sister Elena Aiello, who reputedly suffered bleeding stigmata on her hands, claimed that one day the blood splashed onto the wall next to her bed, and the blood formed an image of Jesus' face. It is difficult to imagine, however, how anyone who glanced at the picture—an image resembling a child's drawing[59]—could keep from laughing aloud at the sight. But just when we think we are at the limits of human credulity, we sadly witness a further extreme.

Other Animated Figures

Not only do sacred images weep and bleed but they also close their eyes and exhibit other movement—even, in one case, the ability to stroll about the church in the middle of the night. Believe it, or not!

Earlier in the chapter we discussed fake idols and automata employed by the ancients. Such devices may also have been used in churches even as late as the Renaissance. According to a question posed to the religious magazine *This Rock:*

I heard that during the Reformation there were many miraculous statues exposed as frauds. These statues were said to be able to speak, but after they were torn down it was shown that they were actually mechanical dummies.

Responded the magazine:

Every age is confronted with the problem of bad taste in liturgical art. (Our own is no exception.) During the late Middle Ages and into the Renaissance artists strove for naturalism in the production of the visual arts of painting and sculpture. At the same time the study of engineering and mechanics was progressing.

These two began to come together. Mechanical clocks were invented, and aside from their use as timekeepers, they became items of visual delight and entertainment. Today in Germany, Switzerland, and other Northern European countries you still can see examples of mechanical clocks combined with moving figures; the clocks not only keep time, but perform little mechanical plays. The cuckoo clock is a descendant of this art form.

Churches and shrines undoubtedly sported statues articulated with mechanical lips. With their movements they would be considered entertaining but not miraculous. Anyone could see such devices at work outside the church on the towers of town halls and guild halls. In erecting such statues the churchmen of those days might justly have been accused of bad taste, but not of fraud.[60]

Be that as it may, in 1866, at a small house owned by two "devoutly religious" sisters in Bari, Italy, a figure of the infant Jesus began to exhibit remarkable powers. First, the foot-high waxen image began to sweat blood, which the sisters collected in phials. They turned one room of their home into a shrine for the figure, which they exhibited in a glass case. Not only did the figure continue to exude blood for two years, but it also began to exhibit movement. Allegedly, its eyes shifted angle; on occasion, it would be discovered seated in an upright position instead of reclining; and its arms would even be found outstretched![61]

The affair was reportedly investigated with favorable results, but it does not appear that the "blood" was ever analyzed (it suspiciously gave off "an odd cinnamon odor"[62]), or that the phenomena occurred under controlled conditions, or that anyone ever actually witnessed the movements as they occurred. In fact, it is not even clear that there were witnesses to the changed poses of the figure, i.e., that they were supported by anything more credible than the allegations of the sisters. But one notes that the figure was of wax—which is easily softened and manipulated—instead of a material like porcelain.

A more modern case involving the alleged movement of a statue has interesting features. In 1985, a figure of the Virgin Mary in a grotto at Ballinspittle, County Cork, Ireland, reportedly began to sway gently, the alleged phenomenon first having been reported by a teenage girl. "The statue was swaying back and forth and then forward," said the girl's mother. "At one point we thought the top would crack off." Subsequently, thousands of visitors flocked to the village of 200 to view the statue, which is adorned with a halo of blue lights. Dozens of people, including several news reporters, also claimed to have witnessed the Virgin's movements.

Nevertheless, although it was reported that church officials did not "want to dampen piety," they were unhappy about the affair. One parish priest attempted to dissuade his congregation from reporting the phenomenon, and the bishop of Cork, Michael Murphy, prohibited the holding of a Mass for the Feast of the Assumption at the grotto. It remained for a group of scientists from University College, Cork, to discover the truth about the statue. They too, saw the figure sway, yet a motion-picture camera revealed no such movement had occurred![63] They soon determined that the effect was an illusion. According to the science magazine *Discover:*

> It is induced when people rock gently back and forth while looking at the statue. At dusk, when the sky is grey and landmarks are obscured, the eye has no point of reference except the halo of blue lights. Therefore, say the scientists, the eye is unable to detect the fact that one's head and body are unconsciously moving. The viewer who sways is likely to get the impression that not he but the statue is moving.

The scientists added: "None of us is out to belittle anybody's beliefs. It's simply that we believe there's a physical explanation."[64]

Later, some religious observers who were undeterred by the rational explanation began to claim that they had also seen the statue's hands and feet move. Needless to say, no proof was offered of this, and the effects were doubtless due to the power of suggestion combined with the illusory effect of prolonged staring. In any case reports of the phenomenon ceased abruptly on October 31. As three Roman Catholic nuns and thirty worshipers watched—horror-stricken—three men smashed the statue. Interestingly, their motives do not appear to have been impious ones. The Associated Press reported: "Police had to restrain a crowd gathered outside the courthouse as the three accused men walked inside holding Bibles."[65]

Less than two years later, similar phenomena were being reported in Sri Lanka. In July 1987, a sixteen-year-old schoolboy claimed he saw a plaster statue of the Virgin make a slight sideways motion of her clasped hands. The following night, a 70-year-old retired merchant said he witnessed the statue's left eye move. Soon hundreds were gathering nightly before the white-and-blue statue that stood in a grotto outside St. James Church. The parish priest encouraged the reports, saying: "I think it is some sort of sign to us that Our Lady is heeding to our prayers, that she is ready to help us at any moment." He promised a scientific analysis of the phenomenon as soon as the crowds diminished, but apparently no proof of the "miracle" was forthcoming and the matter soon passed into obscurity.[66]

Clearer results were reported in Pennsylvania in 1989. The case began on Good Friday at the Holy Trinity Church in Ambridge, a quiet Ohio River mill town fifteen miles northwest of Pittsburgh. During the service a luminous, life-sized crucifixion figure of Christ reportedly closed its eyes. At first, no one claimed to have seen the eyelids actually moving, only that the eyes had been about one-third open when the statue was relocated in January, and that during the special three-hour prayer meeting the eyes were observed to be shut. However, the pastor of the church, Rev. Vincent Cvitkovic, was soon reporting additional claims: "At times the eyes seem to be opening and a little later seem to close again." In addition, he said that the statue changed color—from vivid tones on Good Friday to dull ones after—and gave off "a glistening sheen, like perspiration."[67] Other worshipers claimed that, miracle or no miracle, they felt better—"cleansed" and "calmer"—after gazing at the crucifix.[68]

The affair drew contrasting reactions, however. A pastoral counselor at Catholic University in Washington, D.C., Rev. Richard Delillio, did not feel the events were very positive. "People have a basic need for meaning and happiness in their lives," he said, explaining that many cannot resist the attraction of sensational claims. "When something like this comes along, it's the way of easy surrender."[69] And Dr. William Dinges, who teaches religion at Catholic University, took a "cautious, guarded" view, stating, "The human capacity for self-deception is incredible."[70]

"The crucifix—which depicted a still-living Christ with partially open eyes and mouth—originally hung at eye level in a corner of the church. In January, after undergoing restoration, the crucifix was raised fifteen feet above the altar, to a position in front of a stained glass window. An artist who helped with the restoration, and who "touched up" the eyes with acrylic paint, said that the eyes were open at the time the crucifix was hung. Rev. Cvitkovic reportedly had videotape showing the eyes both open and closed.

An investigation was soon launched by the Roman Catholic Diocese of Pittsburgh. Bishop Donald W. Wuerl appointed a commission to examine the evidence and report on the astonishing phenomena. Alas, after careful study of the before-and-after videotapes, the commission found "no convincing evidence" that the statue closed its eyes during the Good Friday service. When close-up views of the face from each videotape showed the eyes in a similar, partially open position, the commission rejected claims that a miracle had occurred. Commission members stated that they felt the witnesses were sincere but could have been deceived by the church's lighting and by the angles of viewing.[71] These elements, coupled with pious imagination, were apparently also responsible for the other reported phenomena: the perspiration-like sheen and the brightening and dulling of the colors.

In the wake of the commission's report, Rev. Cvitkovic was barred from celebrating Mass, and he responded by resigning. Having once said to disbelievers in the alleged miracle, "I'm not that smart to even think of a hoax,"[72] the priest was never apparently suspected of deliberate deception. A clue to the actions of diocesan officials may be that the church had been a center from which Catholic pilgrims departed for the shrine at Medjugorje, Yugoslavia—a "miraculous" shrine drawing official church disapproval.[73] Also, as the priest's brother explained: "I think there were complaints about people not going to church where they belong because they were coming and enjoying Mass at Holy Trinity."[74]

Undeterred by such skepticism, the Rev. Frank O'Grady and several parishioners of Our Lady of Pompeii Roman Catholic Church in Paterson, New Jersey, claimed to have witnessed a color-changing statue in 1992. The 30-inch figure of Mary—a replica of the life-size International Pilgrim Statue of Our Lady of Fatima (one of several Fatima statues said to exhibit miraculous phenomena such as weeping[75])—stands to the left of the altar. One witness saw the base of the statue turn a "dark,

dark pink," while another said the figure once "turned the brightest blue"; other colors were also reported. In fact, the statue is actually "white with blue and pink tones," and the color-changing effect appears to correlate with the motive force of the viewers. For example, according to a signed testimonial, "One woman present began to cry and we all began to sing to the Virgin Mary and the colors became bolder and more vivid as we sang."[76] Not surprisingly, therefore, many people were unable to witness the alleged color change and went away disappointed.[77]

Perhaps the most incredible of the animated statues was the one we discussed earlier that allegedly wept in a Thornton, California, church in 1981. The four-foot, sixty-pound statue of Our Lady of Fatima was a factory-made product shipped from the Fatima, Portugal, manufacturer to the San Francisco Bay area in 1968. A Portuguese-American grain farmer purchased the statue from a church supply store, donating it to the Mater Ecclesiae Mission Church in memory of a son-in-law who had died in an accident. For some thirteen years, the statue was immobile.

Then, on March 13, 1981, according to the statue's unofficial care-taker, a retired asparagus grower named Albert Amaro: "We found her [the statue] in front of the altar with her rosary wrapped around the crucifix about 25 feet from where she had been standing the night before." The statue was replaced, but ten days later was back at the altar. "On the morning of April 13 we found her at the altar again," said Amaro. "She was moving every 13th of each month and once or twice in between."[78] Even bolting the statue in place did not deter its nighttime strolls, which did not cease until it was relocated near the altar.

Although the wandering ceased, new manifestations began to be reported: The Virgin's eyes changed angle from time to time; she tilted her chin; and her hands, pressed together in prayer, moved from a po-sition near her heart to one at her chin. These changed positions were documented in photographs, and some photo backgrounds revealed images of Jesus that had appeared mysteriously. There were also the tears—allegedly beginning to flow the first time the statue was moved.

But there were problems as well: No one actually witnessed any of the phenomena as they occurred, and one who touched the statue's tears found the liquid "oily and sticky"—indicating that the tears were not genuine. Bishop Roger Maloney of the Stockton Diocese began an investigation of the affair, appointing four clerics as a commission to examine the evi-dence. The result was that the statue's "weeping" and nighttime visits to the altar were branded a probable hoax. The movements of the Madonna's eyes, chin, and hands as supposedly shown in photographs were apparently nothing more than the result of variations in photographic angles. Two photos which showed the image of Christ in the background were examined by a forensic scientist and revealed as the handiwork of a hoaxer.[79]

For their efforts, the investigating clerics were denounced as "a bunch of devils" by some who refused to accept their findings. One stated, "The Bishop and his cronies won't recognize [the miracles] because they're afraid of the tens of thousands of people who will come here."[80]

The reactions were similar to those in Quebec when the bleeding-statue hoax was exposed. According to *The Wall Street Journal,* many worshipers sent the local bishop hate mail, complaining that—never mind the evidence—he still should have pronounced the event miraculous![81] This end-justifies-the-means attitude of the defenders of such "miracles" mirrors that of the hoaxers who obviously believe that a good motive—bringing revenues to the parish, renewing the faith of believers, or attempting to confound the skeptics—is justification for perpetrating a hoax in the guise of a miracle.

The consequences can, however, be a mixed blessing. The St. Nicholas Albanian Orthodox Church's crying icon drew as many as 5,000 visitors a day, and the revenues from such throngs can be impressive—as the Thornton, California, parish learned. But there is often a down side to the occurrences. Police have had to respond to unruly gawkers and even acts of violence. And as one priest states: "I think it is a shame that so many people need this kind of thing . . . to lead them to prayer and to be closer to God."[82] Indeed, the belief in animated statues recalls the ancient idolatry of those who came under the influence of the priest of Bel.

These matters aside, there is still the question of whether any miraculous icons and effigies exist—after the cases of hysteria and hoaxes have been subtracted. The answer is that there simply is no credible evidence that there are. A near-laboratory test for icons and statues has long been at hand: museums and galleries. Those attract throngs of people—including the religious faithful—yet the animated-statue phenomena are never reported. That is because the images are in a controlled environment where hoaxing would be more difficult—and less remunerative.

Select Bibliography

Hebert, Albert J. *Mary, Why Do You Cry? Photos of Her Images in Tears.* Paulina, La.: Privately printed, 1985. An astonishingly credulous, mostly pictorial presentation of the weeping-Madonna phenomenon, together with that of bleeding statues.

Kosova, Weston. "Why Is This Woman Crying?" *Washington City Paper,* April 24, 1992. A thorough, critical analysis of the weeping/bleeding-effigy phenomenon in general and the Lake Ridge, Virginia, weeping-statues case in particular.

Rogo, D. Scott. "Bleeding Statues and Weeping Madonnas." Chapter 7 of *Miracles: A Parascientific Inquiry into Wondrous Phenomena.* New York: Dial Press, 1982. A credulous look at the animated-effigy phenomenon, less from the point of view of a religious defense than as a parnormal—e.g., "poltergeist"—manifestation.

Notes

1. Rupert T. Gould, *Enigmas* (New York: Paperback Library, 1969), pp. 32–46; Walter B. Gibson, *Secrets of Magic Ancient and Modern* (New York: Grosset & Dunlap, 1967), pp. 14–15; "Memnon," *Encyclopaedia Britannica,* 1960 ed.

2. S. Rapoport, *History of Egypt,* vol. XI (New York: Grolier Society, 1904), pp. 231–32.

3. Gibson, *Secrets of Magic Ancient and Modern,* pp. 21–22; see also Hero of Alexandria, *The Pneumatics of Hero of Alexandria,* a facsimile of the 1851 Woodcraft edition, introduced by Marie Boas Hall (New York: American Elsevier, 1971).

4. The text is from *The Revised Standard Version Common Bible* (New York: William Collins, 1973).

5. "Idolatry," *Encyclopaedia Britannica,* 1960 ed.

6. Ibid.

7. D. Scott Rogo, *Miracles: A Parascientific Inquiry into Wondrous Phenomena* (New York: Dial Press, 1982), p. 161.

8. Ibid., pp. 173–78.

9. D. Scott Rogo, *The Poltergeist Experience* (New York: Penguin, 1979).

10. Milborune Christopher, *ESP, Seers & Psychics* (New York: Thomas Y. Crowell, 1970), pp. 149–63.

11. Ibid., p. 146.

12. James Randi, "The Columbus Poltergeist Case," *The Skeptical Inquirer* 9.3 (Spring 1985): 221–35.

13. Rogo (*Miracles,* p. 175) states that the statue "continued to weep even

while being transported to police headquarters, where it was inspected before being returned to Angelo later that night." But this could mean simply that water, surreptitiously placed on the icon before it was taken away, had not dried when a policeman thought to look at the statue en route. Rogo makes no mention of the statue producing a fresh flow of tears at the police station.

14. W. G. Roll, "Poltergeist," in Richard Cavendish, ed., *Encyclopedia of the Unexplained* (London: Routledge & Kegan Paul, 1974), p. 198. Roll was one of the two parapsychologists mentioned in the Resch case.

15. Rogo, *Miracles,* p. 178.

16. Ibid., pp. 178–79.

17. Stephen Magagnini, "When the Madonna Wept," *Fate,* March 1984, pp. 42–46.

18. Marjie Lundstrom, "Catholic Church Wrestles with Jump in Miracles," *The Sacramento Bee,* April 7, 1991; Curtis D. MacDougall, *Superstition and the Press* (Buffalo, N.Y.: Prometheus Books, 1983), p. 521.

19. Jerome Clark, "Chicago's Virgin Weeps," *Fate,* December 1984, pp. 84–86; Jonathan Dahl, "Icons Shedding Tears Are a Mixed Blessing to Congregations," *Wall Street Journal,* January 30, 1987.

20. "Church Says 'Weeping' of Statue Not a Miracle," *The Courier-Journal* (Louisville, Ky.), September 19, 1985.

21. "Virgin Mary Painting 'Weeps' in Illinois Church," *USA Today,* December 12, 1986; Tasia Kavvadias, "Icon's 'Miraculous Sign' Draws Multitude," *Chicago Tribune,* December 15, 1986.

22. "Official Statement on the weeping Icon of the ever Virgin Mary at the St. Nicholas Albanian Orthodox Church in Chicago, IL," issued by the Office of the Chancellor of the Greek Orthodox Archdiocese of North and South America, December 12, 1986, and reproduced in *M.C.R.I. News* (the newsletter of the Midwest Committee for Rational Inquiry), February 1987, p. 3.

23. Ibid.

24. "Shawn and Madonna," *Free Inquiry* 8.1 (Winter 1987/88): 19.

25. Mireya Navarro, "Saint's Weeping Portrait Draws Curious and the Faithful," *New York Times,* November 5, 1990.

26. See Joe Nickell, "Weeping Icon Revisited—Still Dry-Eyed," *The New York Skeptic* (Newsletter of the New York Area Skeptics), Summer 1991, pp. 6–7.

27. Examination of St. Irene videotape, conducted at Gotha, Florida, by Joe Nickell and John F. Fischer, August 6, 1991.

28. "Congregation Prays for Return of Stolen Icon," *Newark Star-Ledger,* December 25, 1991.

29. "Gunmen Steal 'Weeping Icon' from a Church in Queens," *New York Times,* December 24, 1991.

30. "Greek Factions Duel over Theft of the Icon," *Newark Star-Ledger,* January 2, 1992.

31. Carol J. Castaneda, "Statue Attracts the Faithful," *USA Today,* March 23, 1992. See also Weston Kosova, "Why Is This Woman Crying?" *Washington City Paper,* April 24, 1992, pp. 24–33.

32. Kosova, "Why Is This Woman Crying?" p. 26.

33. Nickell in Kosova, "Why Is This Woman Crying?" p. 28; Joe Nickell, certified letter to Rev. James Bruse, May 29, 1991.

34. "Priest Says He Photographed Statue of Madonna Weeping," *The Toronto Star,* July 21, 1972. For a series of photographs of the weeping, see Albert J. Hebert, *Mary, Why Do You Cry?* (Pauline, La.: Privately printed, 1985), pp. 4–12.

35. Kosova, "Why Is This Woman Crying?" p. 28. See also "The Scientist Who Makes Icons Weep," *Newsweek,* October 26, 1987, p. 79 (describing physicist Shawn Carlson's use of salt crystals to cause a copy of the "Mona Lisa" to "weep").

36. A "Squirt cigarette lighter" is also advertised in the catalog *Things You Never Knew Existed,* 1990, Johnson Smith Company, Bradenton, Florida.

37. Rogo, *Miracles,* p. 168 (footnote).

38. Kosova, "Why Is This Woman Crying?" p. 28.

39. Christopher, *ESP, Seers & Psychics,* p. 149.

40. Kosova, "Why Is This Woman Crying?" p. 28.

41. Ibid., p. 30.

42. Gary P. Posner, "Tampa Bay's Weeping Icon Fiasco," *Skeptical Inquirer* 14 (Summer 1990): 349–50.

43. Nickell, "Weeping Icon Revisited," p. 7.

44. Ibid.

45. Ibid.

46. "Bleeding, Crying Statue of Virgin Mary a Hoax," *The Tampa Tribune,* January 18, 1986.

47. Ibid.

48. E. Cobham Brewer, *A Dictionary of Miracles* (Philadelphia: Lippincott, 1884), pp. 184–85.

49. Rogo, *Miracles,* pp. 164–71.

50. Ibid., p. 170.

51. Ibid., pp. 172–73.

52. She is known only from apocryphal writings. See John Coulson, ed., *The Saints* (New York: Hawthorne Books, 1958), p. 32.

53. "Blood and Tears," in *The Unexplained: Mysteries of Mind, Space and Time,* vol. 6 (New York: Marshall Cavendish, 1984), p. 824.

54. Rogo, *Miracles,* pp. 184–85.

55. "Blood and Tears," p. 824.

56. The Santa Monica, California, *Evening Outlook,* May 29, 1979, quoted in Rogo, *Miracles,* 184–85.

57. Rogo, *Miracles,* pp. 158–60; photo following p. 64.

58. Lloyd Mallan, "Vatican Investigates Claim that Painting Weeps Human Blood," *National Enquirer,* September 5, 1971. Rogo cites no other source.

59. Janet and Colin Bord, *Unexplained Mysteries of the 20th Century* (Chicago: Contemporary Books, 1989), p. 265.

60. "Quick Questions: Did the Churches Use Talking Statues?" *This Rock,* January 1992.

61. Rogo, *Miracles,* p. 183.

62. Ibid.

63. "Those Who Sway Together Pray Together," *Discover,* October 1985, p. 19; "Is Anybody There?" a program on paranormal phenomena aired on the Discovery Channel, May 13, 1991, at 1:00 A.M.

64. Quoted in "Those Who Sway Together," p. 19.

65. "3 Accused of Smashing Statue of Virgin Mary," *The Herald-Leader* (Lexington, Ky.), November 2, 1985.

66. "Church Crowds Strain to See if Statue Moves," unattributed clipping (apparently from the *New York Times,* August 1987); Janet and Colin Bord, *Unexplained Mysteries,* p. 353.

67. Carol Memmott, " 'Miracles' Many, but Proof Hard to Come By," *USA Today,* April 12, 1989.

68. "Devout Flocking to Crucifix," *Courier-News,* April 2, 1989.

69. Quoted in Memmott, " 'Miracles' Many."

70. Ibid.

71. "No Proof of a Miracle Found at Pittsburgh Church," *Washington Post,* July 8, 1989. The photographs were shown side by side on an episode of the "Unsolved Mysteries" TV program, September 27, 1989, and again on January 10, 1990.

72. Quoted in Memmott, " 'Miracles' Many."

73. "Diocesan Investigators Dismiss 'Miracle,' " *Free Inquiry* 5.2 (December 1989):2.

74. "Priest Resigns over Crucifix Mystery," *The Express,* August 15, 1989.

75. Hebert, *Mary, Why Do You Cry?* pp. 1–9.

76. A January 17, 1992, testimonial signed by eight persons, quoted in Ivette Mendez, "Religious Phenomenon: Parishioners Stunned by Fatima Statue's Color Changes," *The Newark Star-Ledger,* May 20, 1992.

77. Mendez, "Religious Phenomenon."

78. Memmott, " 'Miracles' Many."

79. Magagnini, "When the Madonna Wept," pp. 44–46.

80. Ibid., p. 46.

81. Dahl, "Icons Shedding Tears Are a Mixed Blessing to Congregations," p. 11.

82. Quoted in Magagnini, " 'Miracles' Many," p. 45.

4

Mystical Relics

The veneration of relics—objects associated with a saint or martyr—has taken place since the first century A.D. It is based on a concept of "beneficent contagion":

> Its basis is the idea that a man's virtue, or holiness, or protective healing powers, do not die with him; they continue to reside in his body and can be tapped by any believer who in some way makes contact with his corporeal shrine. Mere proximity is enough: the medieval pilgrim was satisfied if he could but gaze on the tomb of his cult-object.

Moreover:

> If the body is dismembered, so the belief goes on, the power within it is not diminished; on the contrary, each part will be as full of potency as the whole. The same thing applies to anything that the cult-object touched while alive or, indeed, to anything that touches him after he is dead. All these inanimate containers of a supposedly animate force— whole bodies, bones, hair and teeth, clothes, books, furniture, instruments of martyrdom, winding-sheets, coffins and (if the body is cremated) the ashes that are left—are dignified by the name of "relics" and credited with the grace that once resided in their owners.[1]

Even something that has *touched* the relic can be imbued with some of its power, as is reputedly the case with the Shroud of Turin discussed in Chapter 2. As another example, when Constantina, the empress of Byzantium, wrote to Pope Gregory and asked for the head of St. Paul, the latter softened the effect of his refusal by sending a cloth that reputedly had touched the saint's head. When the cloth was cut, blood supposedly flowed from it.[2]

The response to such alleged miraculous powers of relics, including the powers of healing and of protection, was profound:

> Before long, every Christian priest aimed to have a relic of some sort under his church's altar, and with good reason. Whether he liked it or not, a belief in relics and in their alleged power to work miracles formed the core of religion as experienced by the majority of his congregation—many of whom still carried memories of pagan temples and sacred groves in their blood. Holy bones and the like were venerated in every town and village and, unsurprisingly, a wholesale business in fakes arose to meet this explosion of demand.[3]

So prevalent had relic veneration become in St. Augustine's time (about A.D. 400) that he deplored "hypocrites in the garb of monks" for hawking the bones of martyrs, adding with due skepticism, "if indeed of martyrs."[4] By the Middle Ages,

> The living bodies of likely future saints were covetously watched by relic mongers; when Thomas Aquinas fell ill and died at a French monastery [in 1274], his body was decapitated and his flesh boiled away by monks greedy for his bones. It is said that Saint Romuald of Ravenna heard during a visit to France that he was in mortal peril because of the value of his bones—he fled homeward, pretending to be mad.[5]

About 403, Vigilantius of Talouse condemned the veneration of relics as being nothing more than a form of idolatry, but St. Jerome defended the cult of relics—on the basis of the miracles that God reputedly worked through them.[6] According to a recent writer:

> So widespread and insistent was the demand for relics that in the ninth century a specialized corporation was formed in Rome to discover, sell and transport holy relics to all parts of Europe. . . . Roman catacombs were ransacked for old bones, which were duly identified with suitable

saints. Some became hydra-headed—a number of churches claimed to have the head of John the Baptist.[7]

Sometimes "proofs" were offered that the relics were authentic. For instance, those of St. Briocus of Great Britain—an arm, two ribs, and a vertebra—were placed in a church at Angers, whereupon "they jumped for joy at the honor conferred upon them." Of course, whether this re-action is merely the stuff of pious legend or is evidence of a staged miracle cannot now be determined.[8] And then there was the hand of St. William of Oulx, a one-armed peasant, which was said to have repeatedly refused burial by pushing itself through the coffin; so the hand was severed and retained as a relic known as the "Angelic Hand."[9]

Here and there were such relics as the fingers of St. Paul, St. Andrew, John the Baptist, the doubting Thomas—even one of the Holy Ghost! Teeth attributed to St. Apollonia (reputedly effective in curing toothaches) were beyond counting; a tooth of St. Peter was supposedly discovered—resting on his tomb—600 years after his death; and then there was the gargantuan tooth of St. Paul, although some believed it came from "one of the monsters of the deep." For St. Peter there were also parings from his own toenails, his chains, "filings" from the chains, and vials of his tears. There was even a vial of sweat from St. Michael from the time he had contended with Satan. The Vatican still preserves relics of St. Andrew, along with an ornate reliquary for St. Matthew's arm. No fewer than three churches preserved the corpse of Mary Magdalene; another, alas, possessed only her foot.

An entire cemetery was despoiled to provide one monastery with the relics of St. Ursula and her legendary 11,000 virgin martyrs. (The legend depended on a scant, fifth-century reference to a tomb of virgin martyrs. Due to ignorance of Latin epigraphy, the Roman numeral for 11 (XI) was mistaken for 11,000. As the cemetery surrounding the church of the Virgins was excavated for relics, the name Ursula was appropriated from the tombstone of an eight-year-old girl. Names for numerous other female martyrs were provided by "revelations"—despite the fact that many of the bones recovered were those of men. That fact, however, "did not affect their curative value."[10]

Astonishingly prolific were "relics" associated with Jesus, whose fore-skin was preserved in no fewer than six churches. Miraculously preserved as well were Jesus' swaddling clothes, hay from the manger, some of his baby hair, his pap-spoon and dish, his milk teeth, gifts from the Wise

Men, and the cloak with which Joseph covered the infant at Bethlehem. Later relics included a preserved tear that Jesus shed at Lazarus's tomb, his "seamless coat," one of the vessels in which he had changed water to wine, the tail of the ass upon which he had ridden into Jerusalem, and so on.

The crucifixion was especially well-represented. The Sainte Chapelle in Paris possessed the entire crown of thorns—although this was not the only one, and individual thorns turned up at other churches. Several nails that had been used to affix Jesus to the cross also turned up. Fragments of the True Cross were so prolific, critics say, that there were enough to build a ship. One piece of the cross was kept in a compartment of a crucifix by St. Colette—supposedly a gift from St. John the Evangelist, who sent it from Heaven. He also sent St. Colette a gold ring as proof that Christ had selected her as his virgin bride.

There remained a few relics of Joseph, such as his staff and hammer, in addition to various plows fashioned in his carpentry shop that were worked on by the young Jesus. Relics of Mary were more numerous, however: some of her hair was preserved, together with her shirt and vials of her breast milk. So were chips of rock on which a few drops of Mary's milk had fallen, turning the rock white and imbuing it with curativie powers. At Loretto, in Italy, pilgrims visited the Holy House in which Mary lived at the time of the Annunciation; it had supposedly been miraculously transported there from Palestine.[11]

And, of course, the burial of Christ was also well represented. There were bits of the angel's candle which lit his tomb, the marble slab on which his body was laid, the "napkin" (*sudarium*) that covered his face, and other burial clothes—some still fragrant with myrrh—including the forty "true" shrouds mentioned in Chapter 2. In the seventh century, a French bishop named Arculph reported seeing a shroud of Christ on the island of Iona (off the coast of Scotland). Arculph related a tale of how this shroud had been stolen by a converted Jew, later passed into the hands of infidel Jews, and claimed by Christians—with an Arab ruler judging the dispute. The ruler placed the shroud in a fire from which it rose in the air, unscathed, and fell at the feet of the Christians, who deposited it in a church.[12]

Among the macabre relics that are still preserved today and that remain the subject of considerable controversy are the "blood" of St. Januarius, a vial of a congealed substance that mysteriously reddens and liquefies on certain occasions; the Pozzuoli stone, which exudes Januarius's blood;

the "incorruptible" bodies of numerous saints, which resist the natural tendency to decay; and some curious "relics" imprinted with the scorched handprints of souls from purgatory. Let us look at each in turn.

The Blood of St. Januarius

According to legend, San Gennaro—St. Januarius—was born at Naples near the close of the third century A.D. and was bishop of Benevento when he was martyred during the persecution of Christians by Diocletian. The story goes that after lions refused to harm Januarius and his companions, they were cast into a fiery furnace but remained uninjured. Finally, they were beheaded at Pozzuoli, and two vials of Januarius's blood were (according to later legend) taken with his remains to the Neapolitan catacombs. Januarius's reputed relics were disinterred in the fifth century, housed in various locales over the next several centuries, and permanently enshrined in a Naples cathedral in the latter thirteenth century.[13]

According to the testimony of eyewitnesses dating back to at least the fourteenth century, what is represented as the martyred saint's congealed blood periodically liquefies, reddens, and froths—in apparent contravention of natural laws. Religious zealots call this a miracle, yet a writer for *New Scientist* notes it is a flawed miracle, and *The Oxford Dictionary of Saints* terms it an "alleged" one.[14] A spokesman for the Catholic Church states, "It may not be a miracle, but whatever it is, it somehow functions outside the realm of ordinary laws."[15]

The "blood" half fills a pear-shaped ampule, but a narrow, adjacent vial is now essentially empty (its contents supposedly dispensed to wealthy families in the eighteenth century). The vials are mounted in a cylindrical silver case which has clear glass faces for viewing, as well as a handle by which it can be held or fitted into an ornate monstrance. (See Figure 6.)

The Januarian ritual takes place several times annually: on the Saturday preceding the first Sunday in May (commemorating the relics' entry into Naples) and the following eight days, as well as the octave beginning on the saint's feast day (September 19, the anniversary of his legendary death)—a total of seventeen days. The "miracle" has also been invoked "at the time of the visits of distinguished persons, or when other relics are exhibited to fend off calamities."[16] During the ritual, a priest exposes the congealed blood before another reliquary supposed to contain the martyr's skull (but which apparently contains only small bone fragments).

"Give us our miracle!" beseech members of the congregation. "St. Januarius, delight us!" After a time, the liquefaction usually occurs, greeted by an enthusiastic response, and the reliquary may be taken on a procession through the cathedral or even beyond. If the phenomenon fails to occur, tradition holds that disaster is imminent. (After one such failure the archbishop of Naples, when pressed to identify the threat, named "neopaganism," which his flock interpreted to mean the "rise of Italian communism."[17])

One modern eyewitness report was given by a Naples physician, Dr. Giorgio Giorgi, in a 1970 Italian parapsychology journal. He described how the case was held up and slowly rotated; then, Giorgi states:

> After about four minutes, certainly no longer, I was disconcerted to see just in front of my nose, at a distance of little over three feet, that the clot of blood had suddenly changed from the solid state into that of a liquid. The transformation from solid into liquid happened suddenly and unexpectedly. The liquid itself had become much brighter, more shining; so many gaseous bubbles appeared inside the liquid (shall we call it blood?) that it seemed to be in a state of ebullition.[18]

What Giorgi qualifies as *seemingly* ebullient, however, others characterize by saying that the blood "melts, bubbles up, and flows down the sides of the vials" or even that it "bubbles and boils." Still others, however, using less emotionally charged wording, merely say that the substance is seen to "froth."

Additional features of the Januarian phenomenon are reported. In answer to skeptics who have suggested the liquefaction results from increased temperature (attributed to nearby candles and electric lights, or to body heat from those in the chapel, even to warmth from the priest's hands), proponents of paranormal hypotheses counter that the phenomenon acts independently of temperature and sometimes occurs more readily in September than in May.

Actually, blood would be accelerated in its coagulation if heat were applied, and tests supposedly show the substance is blood. In 1902 and again more recently, researchers were permitted to tilt the reliquary so as to pass a beam of light through the film that remained on the inner wall of the vial. They claimed their resulting spectroscopic analysis proved the presence of genuine blood.

It is also maintained that, after its liquefaction, the substance exhibits variations in volume and weight. The normal level in the vial can either rise or fall; sometimes the weight decreases as the volume *increases,* and vice versa. Such data are reputed to be beyond all physical laws—indeed, to be a miracle, one incapable of even being duplicated by a hoaxer. One Catholic writer held that the various aspects of the phenomenon proved the existence of God, the existence of the human soul and its survival at death, the legitimacy of "the cult of saints," and ultimately the "divine mission" of the Catholic Church.[19] (The Church itself, however, makes no such claims.)

To assess the Januarian phenomenon, forensic analyst John F. Fischer and I initiated an investigation that spanned several years and consisted of three major phases: (1) researching the provenance of the vials, including their legendary source; (2) studying the observed phenomena; and (3) conducting relevant laboratory experiments. As we shall see, the "miracle" does not fare well under such scrutiny.

The blood relics' provenance, for example, falls in the undocumented-to-suspicious range. First of all, the Church has never been able to verify the existence of San Gennaro as an actual historic personage: No contemporary reference to him has been discovered, nor does his name appear in any of the early Roman martyrologies. Moreover, there is absolutely no historical record for the saint's blood relics prior to 1389 (when an unknown traveler reported his astonishment at witnessing the liquefaction). And the legend of their acquisition—that Januarius's nurse was present at his beheading and obtained some of his blood in two vials that were then placed in his funeral urn—is as improbable as it is modern. The legend dates from the sixteenth century, some two hundred years after the vials appeared in Naples.

The suspicions that naturally follow from this dubious provenance increase when another fact is considered: There are additional saints' bloods that liquefy—some twenty in all—and virtually every one of them is found in the Naples area. Such proliferation, which a skeptical Father Herbert Thurston termed "a rather useless manifestation of the divine omnipotence"[20]—seems less suggestive of the miraculous than indicative of some regional secret.

Turning to the phenomenon that has garnered such attention, about which more reports have supposedly been written than on any other miracle of Catholicism,[21] it is important to note that no sustained scientific scrutiny of the blood relics has ever been permitted. Also, descriptions of the liquefaction vary, and it is not always easy to separate what may be permutations in the phenomenon's occurrence from differences attributable to individual perceptions. (Whether inconsistency is compatible with the miraculous is a question perhaps best left to theologians.)

Assertions that the substance in the vials is genuine blood are based solely on spectroscopic analyses that employed antiquated equipment and that were done under such poor conditions as to cast grave doubts on the results. Moreover, even if the assertions were accepted at face value, the possibility of other substances being present would have to be acknowledged, and the researchers themselves admitted that certain dyes could even be mistaken for hemoglobin. Indeed, the liquefied "blood" is altogether more viscous than genuine blood, which would, of course, remain dark and coagulated. To call that which is inconsistent with blood "miraculous blood" is at best to employ faulty logic.

There are also serious problems with the weighings of the vial that are supposed to prove that the substance therein changes weight. The reported measurements were at best somewhat crude, and a recent authority reports, "Tests performed during the last five years by using electric balances failed to confirm any weight variation."[22]

As to the alleged changes in volume, it should be noted that those variations, too, "seem to be no longer reported."[23] In any event, there is a ready hypothesis to explain the alleged occurrence, based on the observation that the substance in the vial can apparently recongeal as quickly as it frequently seems to liquefy. Indeed, "the blood often solidifies during the procession, despite the jarring of the vial."[24] If the reliquary was being swirled about when the material began to congeal, it could—in a thickened and thus opaque film—coat the upper portion of the vial to any height; it could even give the appearance that the vial was full. According to one authority, "there is no means of telling whether the mass is solid throughout, or whether empty space is enclosed within a solid crust thus accounting for the apparent variation in volume.[25]

Other claims associated with the "miracle" also fail to withstand scrutiny. One is the claim that the substance supposedly "boils." According to one authority, the expression is "inexact." In fact, "There is no actual boiling, simply a formation of foam"[26]—as may appear on the surface of almost any liquid. And as to the substance changing color "from dark red to bright red,"[27] that appears to correlate exactly with the liquefaction. Therefore, it may simply be due to the fact that when the substance is congealed no light passes through it and it is viewed only in reflected light; however, when it has liquefied, and a flashlight (formerly a candle) is held behind the case, light is transmitted through the vial. Thus the "blood" can indeed seem (as described earlier) "much brighter, more shining."

Finally, there is the liquefaction itself, the essential Januarian manifestation that has been the subject of literally centuries of debate. Skeptics have long suspected that—whatever the substance in the vials is—it is susceptible to melting whenever the reliquary is sufficiently warmed. Although this is denied by the miraculists—who point out that the phenomenon sometimes occurs in December but not in May, when the temperature is warmer—it is also true that it does take place more often in May and September. In addition, as a skeptical Father Thurston pointed out concerning the other liquefying blood relics in the Naples area, the feast days of all the saints involved fall in the warm season.[28]

Actually, the subject of temperature is much more complex than is implied by a discussion of the time of year involved. Of more obvious significance than the outdoor temperature is the indoor one. While it is true that the miraculists publish tables presumably demonstrating lack of constant relationship between church temperature and the time it takes for liquefaction to occur, they completely ignore a multiplicity of additionally relevant factors. For example, what was the temperature of the reliquary in its niche (or, in recent years, its vault), and how long had it been at that temperature before being brought to the proximity of electric lights, candles, people, and other thermally radiating sources?

Other factors to be considered are the humidity, the thermal conductivity of the surface the reliquary rests on in its vault, the heat of the hands holding the reliquary (a source of heat apparently not applied to the thermometer used by Neapolitan researchers), and many other factors. Suffice it to say that despite the scientific appearance fostered by publishing multi-column tables, scientific rigor has scarcely made its acquaintance with the Januarian phenomenon.

What can be said, by way of approximation, is that the liquefaction seems to occur at about the room temperature of the chapel, about 19–27° C (or about 66.2–80.6° F), and after the lapse of varying times depending on certain physical factors. Rationalist scholar Pierre Saintyves insisted the liquefaction never takes place when the temperature is below 17° C. Indeed, the ritual was formerly also performed on December 16, but the liquefaction occurred relatively rarely on those occasions—apparently due to the colder temperature—and those observances have been discontinued.

Saintyves theorized that the substance was blood, to which—to prevent decomposition—some preservative such as "essence of balsam or aromatic resin" had been added. A mixture of blood and wax has also been suggested, as have additional concoctions: blood and chalk; an aqueous suspension of chocolate powder, casein, and other ingredients; a mixture of tallow, ether, and carmine; and so on.

Not surprisingly, there were problems—of homogeneity (the tallow mixture stratified into three layers), of effect (for example, one experimental vial has to be heated in a candle flame), of history (neither chocolate nor ether nor carmine was available in Italy in the fourteenth century), and of the probable effects of age (resins, for example, might harden over time).[29]

John Fischer and I have offered our own "generic" solution to the problem. As a "thought experiment" consider a vial half-filled with a non-drying oil (e.g., olive oil) that will remain liquid at even cool temperatures. To it is added a substance (e.g., melted beeswax) that forms a mixture which is normally congealed at room temperature. Only a small amount of this is added, sufficient that, when the whole is cool, the mixture is solid, but when slightly warmed, the trace of congealing substance melts and—slowly or even quite suddenly—the mixture liquefies. A pigment must be added—say dragon's blood, known from classical times and popular in the Middle Ages. (Leaving aside such an oil-and-wax mixture, there are substances that already have the sharp temperature gradient necessary to reproduce the Januarian phenomenon—coconut oil, for example.)

Along such lines, we have produced our own vials of "blood" (dubbed "St. Februarius") which perform with sufficient success to permit us to say this: however accurately we may have guessed the secret, we will wager we are much closer to the formula than anything proposed by the paranormalists. As one authority states: "A very important fact is that liquefaction has occurred during repair of the casket, a circumstance in which it seems highly unlikely that God would work a miracle."[30]

In 1991, before we could publish our research, a team of Italian scientists made international headlines with their own solution to the Januarian mystery. Writing in the journal *Nature,* Prof. Luigi Garlaschelli (Department of Organic Chemistry, University of Pavia) and two colleagues from Milan, Franco Ramaccini and Sergio Della Sala, proposed "that thixotropy may furnish an explanation." A thixatropic gel is one capable of liquefying when agitated and of resolidifying when allowed to stand. The Italian scientists, creating such a gel by mixing chalk and hydrated iron chloride with a small amount of salt water, reported a convincing replication of the Januarian phenomenon.[31] (See Figures 7 and 8.)

In response, Bernard J. Leikind—a physicist who had been kind enough to review our work—commented that he found the Italians' idea "plausible, as is the one that you considered." While noting that the precise answer "cannot be decided until tests on the material are made," Leikind concluded: "The real point is that since there are at least two plausible naturalistic explanations for the liquefaction, both well within the range of normal behavior of materials, there is no reason to require divine intervention."[32]

Januarius and the Pozzuoli Stone

Associated with the legendary St. Januarius is another "miracle" involving his "blood"—not that contained in the vials in Naples but rather one involving a quite different relic and thereby warranting a separate discussion.

Housed in the monastery church at Pozzuoli, a town about nine miles from Naples, this relic is purportedly the stone upon which Januarius' execution was carried out. Of course, as skeptics have explained, *stones* are never used for beheadings because they will damage the blade of the axe or sword. Therefore, the pious may choose an alternate legend. This holds that the stone—a block of marble featuring an oblong cavity—was the basin in which Januarius' nurse (or serving woman), Eusebia, washed her hands after filling vials with the martyr's blood.

The stone stands in a niche where lighting and viewing conditions are not the best. Nevertheless, at least "under electric light," the stone's cavity "seems" to be "reddish brown, with unevenly distributed spots." Supposedly, the cavity reddens when Januarius' blood liquefies in Naples, although skeptics attribute this perception of reddening to pious imagination and focused lighting. Nevertheless, "people say" that the stone also sometimes exudes blood, as it reportedly did in 1860 when a Neapolitan church dedicated to St. Januarius caught fire. The stones also allegedly bled on September 19 (the martyr's feast day) in 1894. Bits of cotton were supposedly used to sponge off the blood on these occasions. According to one writer who has researched the Pozzuoli phenomenon at some length:

> On May 31, 1926, one of these pieces of cotton was submitted by Father Padulano to the laboratory of legal medicine at Naples. The analysis revealed that it contained human blood. Of course the narration of this case necessitates the use of the conditional tense, because nothing can prove that it is not a product of fraud, even though it may be unintentional.[33]

There has been considerable speculation over what causes the exudations:

> It has been supposed that heat or humidity used to cause them, but this hypothesis seems false. On September 19, 1902, Prof. Sperindeo, after having extinguished the candle in the chapel, took the temperature of the room every five minutes while the phenomenon was going on. This temperature remained constant, at 1° C, and even had the tendency to decrease at the end of the observation. In September 1927, Monsignor Rocco used a hygrometer to measure the humidity in the niche. The machine registered 62 when the spots became a vivid red, and 100 when they returned to dark red. This measurement remained constant during three consecutive days. We cannot therefore blame the intervention of humidity.[34]

Nevertheless, skeptics remain unconvinced. In fact, there are numerous reasons to doubt the Pozzuoli "miracle," one reason being that the tales related about the stone's reputedly preternatural properties exhibit *motifs* (or narrative elements) common to folktales: "revenant [i.e., ghost] as blood" and "ineradicable bloodstain after bloody tragedy."[35] There are many such tales in which each of these motifs appears.

For example, in classical mythology, when Tripas' son, Erysichthon, cut down a sacred oak—in which lived a Dryad (i.e., a wood nymph)— blood flowed from the cuts of the axe.[36] Again, on an occasion when the Trojan hero Aeneas and his men gathered myrtle, they saw the wood was bleeding and heard the voice of their dead comrade Polydorus call out from his unmarked grave.[37]

Other tales dramatize the supposedly "ineradicable" quality of a bloodstain. For example, there is the story of Castle Lockenhaus in Austria, whose sixteenth-century owner, a Countess Bathori, was rumored to have murdered young girls and to have drunk their blood. Under the castle arch is a faint, brownish patch of earth that turns blood-red whenever rain falls on it. "Efforts have been made to remove the stain, but with no avail. Some mysterious power has given it a permanence that defies explanation and the power of modern science to get rid of it."[38] Or so the castle's caretaker tells credulous tourists. Apparently the "blood" has never been analyzed and confirmed as such. As to the stain's reddening in the rain, there is nothing unusual about that since moisture typically brightens a dull color.

Another indelible-stain story was one that John F. Fischer and I investigated in 1978. It involved an eastern Kentucky farmhouse with mysterious sounds and a door that "bleeds"—all attributed to a century-old tragedy. Investigation, however, turned up mundane sources for the sounds, and analysis of the blackish stain on the door revealed that it was not blood. We traced the streaks to water-borne substances—decaying leaves, dirt, etc.—that had washed down from the roof.[39]

In the case of the Pozzuoli stone "miracle," one authority has observed: "It is regrettable that no analysis of the phenomenon has yet been made with sufficient control." In any case, authorities indicate that "the exudations would tend to be less evident nowadays,"[40] although this fact has not kept the matter from being hyped by popular writers and miraculists.

More recently, additional proofs against the authenticity of both the legend and the miracle have been discovered. As it turns out, the stone actually comes from a sixth-century marble altar.[41] And as for the reddish traces, they are now known to be residues of old paint![42] Like the Januarian phenomenon in which the "blood" of the saint periodically liquefies, the Pozzuoli "miracle" appears to be simply a pious hoax launched in earlier times—in both cases the "relics" being no more than fabrications intended to deceive the credulous. It seems that, over the centuries, they have been eminently successful.

The Incorruptibles

Among the most incredible of relics are the entire corpses of saints and other holy persons that have remained incorrupt—i.e., that have not succumbed to decay even though their bodies were supposedly neither embalmed nor otherwise preserved by artificial means. Their study broaches such subjects as death and burial, disinterment, and preservation of bodies—topics that the writer of a credulous book on the subject admits "would at first appear of morbid and macabre interest, but which eventually proved to be stimulating and fraught with mystery."[43]

The earliest-known saint whose body was supposedly incorruptible was St. Cecilia, the patroness of music. Martyred about A.D. 177, she became the subject of a legend that in actuality is "a fabrication devoid of historical truth," according to an authoritative dictionary of saints. In fact, the story of St Cecilia's virginal marriage (she was forced to wed against her will but retained her virginity by converting her husband to Christianity) was plagiarized from a popular history.[44]

In any case, in the year 822, when Pope Paschal I desired to relocate her remains in a place of honor but was unable to find her grave, says a further legend, St. Cecilia appeared to him in a dream and revealed the location. More than seven centuries later, in 1599, during restoration of the saint's basilica, two marble sarcophagi were discovered, one of which contained her reportedly incorrupt body. I say *reportedly* because the clerics scarcely looked at the body, let alone examined it:

> Peering through the ancient veil which covered the body, they noted that Cecilia was of small stature and that her head was turned downward, but due to a "holy reverence," no further examination was made.[45]

Since the face was apparently not in view and the body was fully clothed and observed only through a veil, how could one know the condition of the remains, much less be certain that the body had not been embalmed? Cecilia came from a noble family who would have been expected to provide her with full funerary treatment. If the body had been eviscerated and treated inside and out with resin, which was used in antiquity for embalming, and if other conditions were favorable, the body might well have been preserved. Given this possibility, the "mysterious and delightful flower-like odor" which reportedly emanated from Cecilia's coffin[46] might be considered evidence of the use of an aromatic resin like balsam (an oleoresin containing the preservative benzoic acid and commonly used for embalming).[47]

A similar explanation may account for the "suave fragrance" given off by the body of St. Sperandia (1216–1276) which was found intact two years after her death and may well have been embalmed in some fashion. (The body is now "dry . . . with only a slight tendency to darken.") Then there is the body of Blessed Mattia Nazzarei of Matelica (1252–1319). (The term *blessed* is applied to one who has been beatified but not yet canonized a saint.) The corpse emitted "a sweet fragrance" and exuded a "blood-fluid." (In recent years, in light of "a slight deterioriation of the body," it has been "enclosed in plastic.") The funeral rites for St. Antoninus (1389–1459) were delayed for eight days (a situation that would certainly seem to invite embalming), but during that time the body remained "intensely fragrant." Similarly, the body of St. Maria Maddalena de' Pazzi (1566–1607), which was entombed beneath the high altar of a monastery church and disinterred a year later (to be moved into the cloister), was found well preserved and soon began to exude ". . . a liquor as oil, more odiferous [odoriferous: fragrant] than balm."[48]

In more than one instance of an "incorruptible" corpse, investigation has shown that the body had, in fact, been embalmed. For example an examination of the corpse of St. Charles Borromeo (1538–1584) revealed that, in actuality, "the body of the Saint had been embalmed in the usual manner shortly after death." (A credulous writer states that "this was not held directly responsible for the preservation of the body almost three hundred years after the Saint's death," yet one should keep in mind several additional facts: that the body was never buried in the ground but in a tomb; that its condition was monitored on several occasions, with new vestments and coffins being provided; that, when it was found in a humid environment, it was removed until the condition was rectified; and that it has been kept during the past three centuries in a presumably airtight reliquary under excellent environmental conditions.)[49]

Another example is that of St. Philip Neri (1515–1595). Four years after he was interred, above the first arch of the nave in a small chapel, his body was found "covered with cobwebs and dust" yet so well preserved—medical men attested—as to be "undoubtedly miraculous." This case merely indicates the state of credulity, even among physicians, at the time (or else the peer pressure they felt to attest to the miraculous). In fact—as has always been known—Philip's "viscera were removed and the body embalmed in a simple fashion after the Saint's autopsy in 1595." Also a recent reference to the body's "last embalmment" suggests that the corpse had been repeatedly maintained.[50]

The condition of many saints' corpses that have been pronounced incorruptible is frankly unknown—or at least has gone unreported in the standard text on the subject, Joan Carroll Cruz's *The Incorruptibles* (1977). Among them is St. Alphege of Canterbury (954–1012), whose body was reportedly free of corruption in 1022 although its present state is unmentioned. Also, "no trace or relic remains" of St. Waltheof (d. 1159) to say whether the remains have been preserved or not.[51]

Moreover, numerous supposedly incorruptible bodies have been destroyed —some during the Reformation (when relic veneration was attacked by Protestants), others during the French Revolution and at other times. For example, during the religious wars of 1561, Protestants burned the corpse of Blessed Bertrand of Garrigua (d. 1230), and French revolutionaries in 1791 buried the corpse of St. Jeanne de Lestonnac (1556–1640) in a pit with a horse's carcass where the body was reduced to a skeleton. What the state of such incorruptible bodies would have been had they had not been destroyed is a question best answered in light of those corpses that have remained.

In many additional cases, details of burial, exhumation, etc., are completely unreported so that there is no real basis on which to honestly base a claim of incorruptibility. Take the body of St. Margaret of Cortona (1247–1297) for instance. There is no mention of her body *not* being embalmed in some way, or of the conditions prevailing during her original interment. (The corpse is now described as "dry.") Another example is that of Blessed Margaret of Lorraine (1463–1521)—puzzlingly listed as an incorruptible, even though her body was apparently not exhumed for 250 years, whereupon the remains were found in the form of a "thin, skeletal body." (Only a few bones now exist.)[52]

Still other relics must be classified as, at best, *formerly* incorruptible. For instance, although St. Coleman (d. 1012) was hanged and his body reportedly remained on the tree "for such a lengthy period that the preservation was acknowledged as miraculous," nevertheless it was his "bones" that were found when his grave was subsequently opened. (In this case we must wonder at the accuracy of the original account, which may be no more trustworthy than other medieval legends.) Similarly, the body of St. Edward the Confessor (1004–1066) was exhumed thirty-six years after his death and found "perfectly incorrupt"; yet when the coffin was opened in 1685, the remains "had been reduced to a skeleton." The body of St. Albert the Great (1206–1280) is another case of former incorruptibility: the remains now "consist only of bones." Then there is the case of St. Agnes of Montepulciano (1268–1317). When her body was placed inside the walls of a church's main altar, "unfortunately the tomb retained an excessive amount of humidity and this provoked the decomposition of most of the body."

A similar fate struck the once incorruptible body of St. Francis of Rome (1384–1440) which was discovered preserved several months after her death when it was transferred to a tomb. However, when the tomb was opened two centuries later, "only the bones were found at this time." Likewise, "only the skeleton remains" of the Blessed Eustochia of Padua (1444–1469), which was reportedly still preserved as late as 1633. Other incorruptibles who eventually turned to skeletons included St. Cuthbert (d. 687), St. Anthony Maria Zaccaria (1502–1539), St. John of God (1495–1550), St. Stanislaus Kostka (1550–1568), Blessed Alphonsus de Orozco (1500–1591), St. Camillus de Lellis (1505–1614), and Blessed Rose Philippine Duchesne (1769–1852). Although St. Francis de Sales (1567–1622) is cited among the saints whose bodies have supposedly remained incorruptible, the fact is that his body was embalmed; even so, eventually "only dust and bones were found." Another embalmed relic was that of St. Jeanne Françoise de Chantal (1572–1641) which nevertheless became skeletalized; today, "A composite figure of St. Jeanne, clad in the habit of her order, contains the bones of the Saint which are connected with silver cords." Similarly the bones of the once incorruptible St. Vincent de Paul (1580–1660) are now "encased in a wax figure," as are those of many others, including St. Pacifico of San Severino (1653–1721), St. Veronica Giuliani (1660–1727), Blessed Anna Maria Taigi (1769–1837), and St. Pierre Julien Eymard (1811–1868).[53]

Still other "incorruptible" bodies are more accurately described as mummified; that is, the body is desiccated—a condition that can occur naturally under certain conditions (such as being kept in a dry tomb or catacombs)[54] or be induced by embalming. For instance, the body of St. Urbald of Gubbio (c. 1100–1160) was officially examined in 1960 and found to have "become quite mummified, having brown, dry skin with the texture of leather"—scarcely a description suggestive of miraculous incorruptibility. Similarly, there is the dismembered body of St. Agatha (d. 251), which is preserved in different reliquaries, with only the arms, legs, and breasts being exhibited in a glass case. Although described as "incorrupt" they are acknowledged to be "rather dried and dark."

Similarly the body of St. Zita (1218–1278), viewed through her glass-walled reliquary, "appears somewhat dark and dry." Again there is the corpse of Blessed Andrew Franchi (1335–1401), reportedly labeled incorrupt on being viewed in 1911; but when it was last examined in 1966, a medical report "described it as being completely mummified." Also, "The head is without hair and is detached from the body, while the upper lip, the point of the nose, all the toes, and parts of the fingers are missing." The body of Blessed Osanna of Mantua (1449–1505) has likewise become "hazel brown" and "is tried and darkened and wrinkled with age," and that of St. Rose of Lima (1586–1617) was supposedly discovered incorrupt although a few years later it was "found somewhat wasted and desiccated." A similar description attends the remains of St. Vincent Pallotti (1795–1850): In 1949 they were found "dry, partially mummified," yet the hands and face required covering—the latter with "a silver mask made from the impression of the original death mask." The same treatment was given the relic of St. Madeleine Sophie Barat (1779–1865). Likewise, forty-five years after the death of St. Jean-Marie-Baptiste Vianney (1786–1859), his remains were found "dried and darkened," but the viscera were removed as a conservation measure and the face was "covered with a wax mask which reproduces the features of the servant of God."[55]

What was described as "a slight mummification" affected the corpse of St. Catherine Laboure (1806–1876). It must have seemed threatened because "to insure the preservation of the body" there was injected into it "a solution of formaldehyde, glycerine and carbolic acid" (i.e., an embalming fluid). (One does wonder why—if the body was as intact as described—the "incorrupt hands" were amputated and kept in a separate reliquary, having been replaced *in situ* by wax hands.[56])

In some cases artificial means have been used to help preserve a corpse or to conceal its poor condition—even though miraculists continue to cite these saints' relics as evidence of incorruptibility. Take, for instance, St. Edmund Rich of Canterbury (1180–1240), whose body was pronounced incorrupt "several years after his death" but which is "now brown in color with skin resembling parchment"; we learn that "in later years it appears that artificial methods were employed to conserve it." Again there is the corpse of St. Clare of Montefalco (1268–1308)—described as "dry but perfectly flexible"—yet whose body is almost totally concealed in robes, the head covered with a crown, and the face shielded with a veil. A more remarkable case involves the corpse of St. Bernardine of Siena (1380–1444). His body was reported as incorruptible twenty-six years after death.[57] However,

> The body has been examined several times during the years, the last examination occurring in August 1968. The body at that time was found wrapped in tobacco leaves, and it was determined that preservatives had been used during a previous exhumation. Parts of the body are held together by various means, and chemicals were applied to the relic to maintain its condition.[58]

Less serious is the state of preservation of St. Rita of Cascia (1381–1457). Despite reports to the contrary, her garments are not original but have been replaced many times over the ages. About 1650 the body, which appears to be mummified,[59] began to show signs of deterioration. One eyebrow and a cheekbone became dislodged and were "repaired with wax and string as the two medical examinations of 1743 and 1892 indicate."

The corpse of St. Catherine of Bologna (1413–1463), which became "darkened" over the centuries, is supposedly still "incorrupt" although during World War II the hands and feet required "a light coat of wax for protection," and in 1953 these relics received a "protective covering" in the form of a glass urn. Sometimes the maintenance of an "incorruptible" corpse can take a bad turn, as was the case with that of Blessed Archangela Girlani (1460–1495): when it was examined in 1932, "unfortunately this skin of the face was injured at this time by the faulty application of a chemical, which stripped away part of the flesh." (Had this not occurred, one wonders, would any mention have been made of the "chemical"?) Better results were undoubtedly obtained with another relic, the body of St. Angela Merci (1474–1540) which is kept in a glass case in the Casa St. Angela in Brescia, Italy, and has the appearance of an ornately dressed and crowned mummy. In 1930 a priest made "a chemical treatment of the relic with natural resin to preserve it." Likewise, the relic of St. Benedict the Moor (1526–1589) having became "a little dry and hard" and rather unsightly, "the face of the Saint was covered some time ago with a thin wax mask."[60]

In still other cases the reputed incorruptibility appears to be some-what uneven. Consider, for example, the body of the Blessed James of Bevagna (1220–1301). Although the left foot was purloined as a relic, the remainder is supposedly "perfectly entire"; however, the face, hands, and right foot are said to be "the best parts." In another case, that of St. Peregrine Laziosi (1265–1345), we are told, "Although some of the bones are exposed, the lower legs and feet, the arms, skull, neck and chest are well covered with flesh, which is of a predominately black color." St. Josaphat (1580–1623) is held to be in "an amazing state of preservation," although "the face has predominately skeletal features." A similar state attends the corpse of St. Lucy Filippini (1672–1732), whose "venerable face . . . is the only part of the relic which has suffered a little, and this is covered with a silver net, contoured to resemble her features."[61]

Still other cases seem to exhibit many of the features we have con-sidered thus far. For example the remains of St. Nicholas of Tolentino (1245–1305) were supposed to be incorrupt and placed on exhibit, whereupon someone amputated his arms. Subsequently, the body "com-pletely decomposed" except for the arms, which became "mummified"; yet the remains have been "arranged in a simulated figure that is cov-ered by an Augustinian habit" and the skull "covered with silver."[62]

In at least two instances, the body of a saint remained relatively incorrupt (eventually seeming to mummify), even though means had been taken to hasten the decomposition. The first was that of St. Francis Xavier (1506–1552) and was done so that the saint's bones might more easily be sent home from an island in the Far East. Nevertheless, after ten weeks "the coffin was raised and the body found to be perfectly preserved under the lime." Eventually it became "dry and shrunken in size" and the interior had to be braced with wires, although the mystery of its original resistance to the "destructive agent" of the lime is still cited. In reality there is no mystery: Contrary to popular belief, the chemical does not hasten the destruction but actually has a *preservative* effect on a corpse! "The lime combines with body fat to produce a hard soap that resists invasion by insects and bacteria, and retards putrefaction."[63]

A second instance, the relic of St. Paschal Baylon (1540–1592), also involved the application of "quicklime"—used "so that the flesh would be quickly consumed, producing glossy white bones," which were felt "would look impressive in a shrine." After eight months in "this caustic agent" the body was discovered to be "miraculously preserved in the flesh." Knowing the true effects of lime, we can understand—if not share in—the wonderment of the priest who stated at the time: "Human language is inadequate to portray such a spectacle."[64]

To summarize this litany of examples, it should be clear that while there are indeed some notable instances of preservation of saints' corpses, there are also many accompanying reasons to account for them: embalming (sometimes unknown to the viewer or deliberately concealed), natural mummification (fostered by tomb or catacomb—rather than earthen—burial), periodic examination and conservation of the relics, and so on. But, as we have also seen, many of the instances of alleged incorruptibility cannot be verified or—more importantly—are clearly disproved by the facts: numerous instances in which the bodies were eventually reduced to bones or have had to be subjected to extensive restoration in order to be placed on view.

Such facts can serve as an antidote to exaggerated claims for incorruption—claims like those captioning the cover photo of a credulous book, *The Incorruptibles*. The caption reads: "The incorrupt body of Saint Bernadette Soubirous of Lourdes, France (1844–1879), preserved intact for 100 years without embalming or other artificial means." Now it would take an autopsy by independent authorities to determine whether (like the corpse of St. Catharine Laboure) St. Bernadette had been given injections of embalming fluid. But in any event, the book does note that when the body was first exhumed, thirty years after St. Bernadette's death, it was found "emaciated," and ten years later the face had to be covered with a wax mask.[65] This explains the lifelike appearance of the saints who appear in close-up photos.

It is also well to keep in mind that this phenomenon is likewise claimed by other religious traditions, including Buddhists,[66] and there are parallel examples of the incorruptibility of bodies even of ordinary people. For example, a young man who had fallen into the lead cellar of the Bremen Cathedral in the eighteenth century was discovered "in an excellent state of preservation." Soon afterward,"members of the German aristocracy requested burial there and their mummified bodies can now be viewed in their open caskets."[67]

Small wonder that the author of *The Incorruptibles* concedes:

> The presence or absence of faith will undoubtedly determine the viewpoint with which one would accept this phenomenon of incorruption. For those who habitually search for a natural socioeconomic explanation for everything, there are no arguments which will suffice to satisfy their doubts.[68]

Burning Handprints

A curious phenomenon that hitherto seems to have received little attention outside of religious sources is the "Mystery of the Burning Handprints" (according to an article of that title).[69] The handprints—scorched into the pages of books or onto consecrated cloths or the like—are usually alleged to be from the unrequited spirits of the dead.

According to the story behind one such "relic":

> At the end of the 17th century there was a profound friendship between the hermit of the chapel of St. Romedius in the castle of Thaur and the priest and dean of Thaur, Georg Meringer. It is said that both had agreed that the one who died first would give the other a sign from the next world. Father Meringer died first.
>
> In October 1659, toward 11 o'clock at night, the hermit heard someone knocking at his door. He was in the process of decorating the altar of the chapel with paper flowers stored in a wooden box. He subsequently heard the voice of the dead priest bemoaning his fate. During his lifetime the priest had forgotten to celebrate two masses that had been paid for, and it was for this reason that he was still suffering in purgatory.
>
> The hermit asked for a sign to confirm the supernatural nature of this message. Lo and behold, suddenly he saw the imprint of a burning hand appear on the bottom of the little box of flowers.
>
> Thereafter the hermit saw to it that the two masses in question were celebrated. Finally, in a dream, Father Meringer appeared to him and told of his deliverance.[70]

Afterward, Emperor Franz II of Austria closed the church, prompting the resident priest to write in his journal (dated 1784): "By supreme order, our House of God, being considered superfluous and unimportant for the pastorate, had to be closed. In our 'enlightened' epoch, the contemplation of the relic, even in another church, is not allowed." The priest transferred the box to his own room, but today it is exhibited for veneration behind a protective grille in the little church of St. Romedius.

What is the rationale behind such *burning* handprints? According to the German mystic, Margarete Schaeffner—who claimed to have received burning handprints on cloth on at least five occasions—the imprints were from spirits in purgatory. (In Catholic teachings, purgatory is a place, or condition, of temporary punishment wherein those who died in God's grace must expiate their sins. Theologians have held that in purgatory souls are actually "tormented by material fire."[71]) Thus Georg Siegmund has suggested that the imprints "may have been symbolic allusions to the 'sweeping fire' which cleanses the soul." But by "symbolic allusions" Siegmund does not mean to imply that the imprints are not genuine. Indeed, he states, "In my opinion these apparitions were materializations—souls of the dead who physically materialized for a short time in order to manifest themselves in the world of our senses."[72]

Siegmund is aware of the apparent contradiction in supposing that nonmaterial entities, as spirits are imagined to be, can actually burn or even leave traces on physical objects. "However," he says, "it does not follow that therefore we should reject cases such as those outlined here." He adds: "Even if we are not in a position to explain the actual process by which such materializations form, the evidence of this phenomenon is so strong that we can hardly doubt its reality." Then, as if supporting his assertion rather than undermining it seriously, Siegmund asserts, in his very next sentence, "It is noteworthy, I think, that the size and the form of the burned handprints do not always correspond to the normal anatomical size and structure of the human hand."[73] By this convoluted reasoning, that which is *prima facie* evidence of fakery is actually taken as support for the miraculous!

In this light, consider the example provided by a little eighteenth-century prayer book, only about 6 × 10 centimeters, that is the respository for another manifestation of burned handprints. The imprint of the fingers, palm, and wrist has penetrated from the eighteenth page of the opened book, through ten previous leaves, to the front cover. Supposedly this occurred when a member of the Hackenberg family in Czechoslovakia was returning from a pilgrimage which he had undertaken in order to fulfill a pledge made to his deceased father. During his morning prayers he suddenly fell asleep, whereupon his father appeared and spoke to him, saying: "I am delivered [from purgatory]. As a sign of my deliverance, I leave you a burned handprint in your prayer book." Then the pilgrim awoke to find the imprint at the very location of the morning prayer.[74]

Improbable on the face of it, this story becomes even less credible when we consider that—as Siegmund concedes—"the burned imprint of the hand was no larger than that of a child, whereas the deceased was an adult."[75] Siegmund seems unable or unwilling to draw the obvious conclusion, speaking lamely about "the possibility that the story has been altered over the years" and adding defensively, "But the relic speaks for itself." Indeed it does, and it bespeaks fakery. The scaling of the size of the hand to fit the page is a detail that points to an amateurish forger; so is the crudeness of the anatomy (as shown in a photo), since both the thumb and little finger appear proportionally too long. Also (as one observer noted), "The fingers give the impression of being composed only of bones"[76]—a fact that makes little sense in terms of the pilgrim's story but would be consistent with a hot cast-metal "hand" which, unlike a real human hand, failed to flatten slightly when pressed, instead remaining rigid so that a lesser surface area imprinted.

A German cloth said to bear "the imprint of six charred fingers"[77]— a sign supposedly left by a soul in purgatory—is another "relic" that perhaps best speaks for itself. Yet another is a thumbprint burned into a sixteenth-century book of sermons that today reposes in the library of the dean of Hall in the Tyrol. The burn penetrates the leather cover and sixty-four of the volume's antique pages, leaving a burn that is "notable for its sharpness and depth,"[78] if not for its credibility.

Another scorched book is a missal kept in a church in the Saar (now in Germany). During celebration of a Mass for a deceased priest, scorches supposedly appeared in the book to mark selected passages. A "clairvoyant" in the congregation claimed she saw the shadow of an apparition twice approach the book and touch it with his finger, smoke arising from the book each time. The priest, however, saw and smelled nothing, leaving open the possibility that the burns had been produced earlier. Indeed, this possibility gains credibility from the fact that (as Siegmund notes), "curiously enough, the margins or the blank pages of the book were never touched."[79] Apparently the hands that opened the book and turned the pages were as cool as those of any hoaxer!

There is at least one case that departs from the souls-in-purgatory genre, although it is no less instructive—in more ways than one. It involves a burned handprint on a great oak table in a Polish museum, supposedly once the tribunal table in the Hall of Justice. According to a legend, during a lawsuit in 1637 a wealthy nobleman claimed a widow's property as his own and bribed the judges. When they decided in his favor, the distressed widow gestured toward a crucifix on the wall and cried: "If Satan himself were the judge, he'd give a fairer judgment." In consequence, around midnight gathered judges wearing black wigs which concealed tiny horns. The judges forced the horrified court clerk to witness their "satanic tribunal." The attorney for Satan presented the widow's case and the occult tribunal found for the widow. On the crucifix, the legend continues, Christ looked away in shame. The following day the clerk discovered the black handprint on the table—the "seal" given to the case.

One who has studied such relics described the imprint on the table as "rather large," adding: "What attracts our attention is that its digits do not resemble the imprints of different fingers; the impression given is more diagrammatic than realistic." A photograph confirms this assessment.[80]

Other examples could be given, but these should be sufficient to characterize this peculiar form of "relic" and its attendant legends. Evidence in these cases reveals them to be, at best, unsubstantiated and incredible, and, at worst, probably spurious. Certainly, such burned imprints are easy to produce, as my example in Figure 9 demonstrates.[81] Yet Siegmund disparages skepticism regarding the phenomenon, adding: "This same obsolete 'rationalism' survives today and underlies the crusade against the legitimacy of evidence for the paranormal." Just why we should take the phenomenon seriously, he neglects to say.

Select Bibliography

Brewer, E. Cobham. *A Dictionary of Miracles*. Philadelphia: J. B. Lippincott, 1884. A reference work that includes many examples of incredible relics and their legendary powers.

Cruz, Joan Carroll. *The Incorruptibles*. Rockford, Ill.: Tan Books and Publishers, 1977. A credulous account of more than a hundred cases of the phenomenon of the incorruption of saints' bodies.

Nickell, Joe, with John F. Fischer. "Miraculous Blood." Chapter 9 of *Mysterious Realms*. Buffalo, N.Y.: Prometheus Books, 1992. An investigative look at the liquefying "blood" of St. Januarius and the related "miracle" of the Pozzuoli stone.

Rogo, D. Scott. "The Miracle of St. Januarius." Chapter 8 of *Miracles: A Parascientific Inquiry.* New York: Dial Press, 1982. A credulous account of the phenomenon of St. Januarius' liquefying "blood" with speculation as to its supposedly paranormal nature.

Siegmund, Georg. "Mystery of the Burning Handprints." *Fate,* June 1981: 42–51. Abridged from the author's presentation to a Catholic parapsychological conference, an uncritical account of the phenomenon of burned handprints: supposedly the marks of spirits in purgatory.

Notes

1. Christopher Pick, ed., *Mysteries of the World* (Secaucus, N.J.: Chartwell Books, 1929), p. 101.

2. Ibid., p. 102.

3. Ibid.

4. St. Augustine, quoted in "Relics," *Encyclopaedia Britannica,* 1973 ed.

5. Karl E. Meyer, "Were You There When They Photographed My Lord?" *Esquire,* August 1971, p. 73.

6. "Relics," *New Catholic Encyclopedia,* 1967.

7. Meyer, "Were You There When They Photographed My Lord?" p. 73.

8. E. Cobham Brewer, *A Dictionary of Miracles* (Philadelphia: J. B. Lippincott, 1884), pp. 262–63.

9. Except as noted, information on such relics comes from Joe Nickell, *Inquest on the Shroud of Turin* (Buffalo, N.Y.: Prometheus Books, 1983; rev. ed. 1987), wherein additional documentation is given.

10. Howard W. Haggard, *Devils, Drugs, and Doctors* (New York: Harper & Row, 1929), p. 301; John Coulson, ed., *The Saints* (New York: Hawthorn Books, 1958), p. 439.

11. See n. 8.

12. Nickell, *Inquest,* p. 53.

13. Except as noted, information on St. Januarius is adapted from Joe Nickell with John F. Fischer, *Mysterious Realms* (Buffalo, N.Y.: Prometheus Books, 1992).

14. James Hansen, "Can Science Allow Miracles?" *New Scientist,* April 8, 1982, pp. 73–76; David Hugh Farmer, *The Oxford Dictionary of Saints* (Oxford: Clarendon, 1978), p. 208.

15. Kathrine Jason, "Bubbling Blood," *Omni,* July 1982, p. 92.

16. From an English translation of David Guerdon, "Le sang de Saint Janvier

se liquefie et se cogule depuis des siècles," *Psi International Bimestrial* 5 (1978): 9–29.

17. "Starting Out on a Journey of No Return," *Time,* May 17, 1976, p. 25.

18. Giorgio Giorgi, quoted in translation in D. Scott Rogo, *Miracles* (New York: Dial Press, 1982), p. 193.

19. Leon Cavène, *Le célèbre miracle de Saint Janvier à Napels et à Pouzzoles* (Paris: Gabriel Beauchesne, 1909), p. 346.

20. Quoted in Guerdon, "Le sang du Saint Janvier."

21. Rogo, *Miracles,* p. 189.

22. Ennio Moscarella, *Il sangue di S. Gennaro vescovo e martire* (1989), cited by Prof. Luigi Gerlaschelli et al., letter to Joe Nickell, November 5, 1991.

23. Moscarella, *Il sangue di S. Gennaro,* p. 401.

24. Guerdon, "Le sang de Saint Janvier."

25. John Coulson, ed., *The Saints: A Concise Biographical Dictionary* (New York: Hawthorn, 1958), p. 239.

26. Hubert Larcher, *Le sang: peut-il vaincre la mort?* ([Paris]: Librairie Gallimard, 1957), p. 277.

27. Ibid., p. 278.

28. Guerdon, "Le sang du Saint Janvier."

29. See n. 13.

30. Coulson, *The Saints,* p. 239.

31. Luigi Garlaschelli et al., letter to *Nature* 353 (October 10, 1991): 507; "Scientists Say 'Miracle' No Mystery," *Chicago Tribune,* October 10, 1991; "Shakeup over Sacred Blood," *Science News,* October 12, 1991, p. 229.

32. Bernard J. Leikind, letter to Joe Nickell, November 4, 1991.

33. Guerdon, "Le sang de Saint Janvier"; Rogo, *Miracles,* pp. 195–96.

34. Guerdon, "Le sang de Saint Janvier."

35. Stith Thompson, *Motif-Index of Folk Literature,* rev. ed., vol. 2 (Bloomington: Indiana University Press, 1955), p. 466.

36. Robert E. Bell, *Dictionary of Classical Mythology* (Santa Barbara, Calif.: ABC/CLIO, 1982), p. 29.

37. Ibid., p. 30.

38. Perrott Phillips, ed., *Out of This World: The Illustrated Library of the Bizarre and Extraordinary,* vol. 12 (N.P.: Phoebus/BPC, 1978), p. 58.

39. Joe Nickell with John F. Fischer, "Bleeding Door: Enigma on Deadening Branch," chapter 9 of *Secrets of the Supernatural* (Buffalo, N.Y.: Prometheus Books, 1988), pp. 119–28.

40. Guerdon, "Le sang de Saint Janvier."

41. Moscarella, cited by Garlaschelli (see n. 22).

42. Ibid.

43. Joan Carroll Cruz, *The Incorruptibles* (Rockford, Ill.: Tan Books and Publishers, 1977), p. 21.

44. Coulson, *The Saints,* p. 107.

45. Cruz, *The Incorruptibles,* p. 44.

46. Ibid., p. 45.

47. Resins were used in mummifying and embalming the dead from very early antiquity to comparatively modern times. (See "Mummy," *Encyclopaedia Britannica,* 1960 ed.). *The Oxford English Dictionary* (compact edition, 1971) cites a use of the adjective *balsamate,* meaning "embalmed," from 1470.

48. Cruz, *The Incorruptibles,* p. 48.

49. Ibid., pp. 190–93.

50. Ibid., pp. 210–12.

51. Ibid., pp. 64, 69–70.

52. Ibid., pp. 83, 94, 162, 237–38.

53. Ibid., *passim.*

54. Ibid., pp. 31–33; *The Sun,* February 18, 1992 (citing natural mummies of monks in the Capucin catacombs of Palermo, Italy).

55. Cruz, *The Incorruptibles, passim.*

56. Ibid., pp. 281–85.

57. Ibid., pp. 83–84, 103–105.

58. Ibid., pp. 127–28.

59. Ibid., illus., p. 134.

60. Ibid., *passim.*

61. Ibid., pp. 95, 115–16, 232–34, 254–55.

62. Ibid., pp. 96–98.

63. See Phil McArdle and Karen McArdle, *Fatal Fascination* (Boston: Houghton Mifflin, 1988), p. 119.

64. Cruz, *The Incorruptibles,* pp. 204–209.

65. Ibid., front cover; pp. 288–89.

66. Janet and Colin Bord, *Unexplained Mysteries of the 20th Century* (Chicago: Contemporary Books, 1989), p. 270.

67. Ibid.; Cruz, *The Incorruptibles,* p. 33.

68. Cruz, *The Incorruptibles,* p. 42.

69. Georg Siegmund, "Mystery of the Burning Handprints," *Fate,* June 1981, pp. 42–51.

70. From an old account, quoted in Siegmund, "Mystery of the Burning Handprints," pp. 42–43.

71. "Purgatory," *Encyclopaedia Britannica,* 1960 ed.

72. Siegmund, "Mystery of the Burning Handprints," p. 48.

73. Ibid., pp. 47–48.

74. An old account supposedly preserved by the Hackenberg family, cited in Siegmund, "Mystery of the Burning Handprints," pp. 48–49.

75. Ibid., p. 49.

76. A Dr. Stampfl, director of the seminary at Weidenau, in a report of November 1, 1922, cited in Siegmund, "Mystery of the Burning Handprints," p. 48. See also the photographs in ibid., p. 45.

77. Ibid., pp. 42–43, 51.

78. Ibid., p. 50.

79. Ibid., pp. 49–50.

80. Ibid., p. 51; see also the photograph in ibid., p. 49.

81. I made the imprint by tracing a child's hand on a sheet of brass, cutting it out, and heating it on the eye of a stove.

5

Pentecostal Powers

Some Christian fundamentalists (those who believe in the literal truth of the scriptures) place special emphasis on what are called "charismatic gifts of the spirit." These miraculous (i.e., divinely bestowed) gifts can come to those who undergo "baptism in the Holy Spirit"—an experience the resurrected Jesus promised to his disciples at the first Pentecost.[1] As one authority explains the difference between water baptism and Spirit baptism:

> I believe we can see this distinction as two operations of the one Holy Spirit. In the first, the Holy Spirit comes to give new life and the new birth. Water baptism is the outward and visible sign of that new birth. While in the other the Spirit anoints or empowers Christians for their witness and ministry. Jesus said, "you will receive power when the Holy Spirit comes on you, and you will be my witness" (Acts 1:8).[2]

Among the "supernatural gifts" of the Spirit are speaking in tongues, prophesying, healing by the laying on of hands, and experiencing other miracles.[3] Due to a passage in the Gospel of Mark, some adherents also include taking up serpents and drinking poisons—to demonstrate their imperviousness to noxious substances.

Because of the association with the Pentecost (the Jewish feast that marked the end of the grain harvest), Christians who emphasize such "gifts"

101

are known as Pentecostals—particularly when they represent a separate denomination within fundamentalism.

Although there have been various Pentecostal movements over the centuries, the modern one began with members who were mostly former Baptists or Methodists. In 1906 at a prayer meeting on Azuza Street in Los Angeles, several revivalist-minded Christian leaders met to pray for an outpouring of the Holy Spirit. This led to an outbreak of "praying in tongues," and as a consequence modern Pentecostalism was born. A few years later, in 1914, the Assemblies of God—the largest Pentecostal group—was organized. In addition, the Church of God and various other independent churches also practice Pentecostalism, and increasingly the movement is making inroads into mainstream religions such as Catholicism. In this case the adherents are usually called charismatics, after the theological term *charism* (from the Greek *charisma,* or "gift").[4]

Many fundamentalists disparage Pentecostalism because they believe the gifts of the Spirit (outlined in 1 Cor. 12:7-11) were intended only for those early disciples who were specifically anointed by Christ. Regarding these, when Paul refers to "that which is perfect" in the thirteenth chapter of 1 Corinthians, he is thought to be foretelling the New Testament:

Charity never faileth: but whether there be prophecies, they shall fail; whether there be tongues, they shall cease; whether there be knowledge, it shall vanish away. For we know in part, and we prophesy in part. But when that which is perfect is come, then that which is in part shall be done away. (1 Cor. 13:8-10)

Pentecostalism is often also derided for what is perceived as its adherents' uncontrollable hysterics, such as dancing with wild gyrations, exhibiting seizure-like bodily motions while "going under the power," and speaking or praying in tongues—all of which has earned the charismatics the sobriquet "holy rollers." To their critics, charismatics may appear as overly emotional people under the spell of semi-charlatans.[5]

Indeed, the examples of several prominent Pentecostal/charismatic preachers have often seemed to justify the latter criticism. Jimmy Swaggart, for example, was defrocked as an Assemblies of God minister in the wake of sexual misconduct and other excesses; and Jim Bakker survived revelations about his lavish lifestyle only to be convicted and imprisoned for defrauding his flock of $158 million.[6] Even Pat Robertson, whose televangelistic success has helped gain recoginition for charismatic Christianity, has been accused of "operating on the edge of ethics." According to critic Jeffrey Hadden, a sociology professor at the University of Virginia, "He used [a business] built by contributions of religious people donating to a religious organization to build a personal fortune."[7]

Nevertheless, Pentecostalism has an undeniable appeal to many—especially the economically disadvantaged (where ignorance and superstition prevail, critics note), some 87 percent of them living in actual poverty.[8] Also it is apparently growing in strength in North America, England, and Latin America. What is its attraction? According to one adherent:

> The most important basis for the growing acceptance of Pentecostal Christianity is a basic hunger in the human psyche for a taste of the miraculous. The truth is that most Christians have a basic dissatisfaction with the quality of their spiritual life and long for something more and something deeper. There is within most of us an insatiable appetite for the supernatural, and mundane Christianity leaves us wanting. We all long for the assurances of God's reality in our lives. Rational theologies do not seem to satisfy us, and we look for the ecstasies that are described by the mystics.[9]

This being the case, therefore, "the Charismatic movement has spokespersons who know how to capitalize on such spiritual hungers."[10]

Unfortunately, as in other instances of capitalizing on someone's needs, there is ample room for abuse. For example, the Rev. Peter Popoff (who will be discussed more fully later) was publicly exposed when his special gift of prophetic discernment turned out to be blatant trickery.[11] Deception—including self-deception—has also been alleged in other charismatic "miracles." This naturally raises the question, Are there "gifts of the Spirit" that can stand scrutiny—that are indeed genuine evidence of the miraculous? Let us take a closer look at some of the more widely touted phenomena: glossolalia (speaking in tongues), divine prophecy, and imperviousness to fire and poisons (including poisonous snakes).

Speaking in Tongues

To charismatics, speaking in tongues—or what is known in psychological circles by the Greek term *glossolalia*—is an essential aspect of Christianity. It first appears in the New Testament as a fulfillment of Christ's promise that his apostles were soon to "be baptized by the Holy Ghost":

And when the day of Pentecost was fully come, they were all with one accord in one place. And suddenly there came a sound from heaven as of a rushing mighty wind, and it filled all the house where they were sitting. And there appeared to them cloven tongues like as of fire, and it sat upon each of them. And they were filled with the Holy Ghost, and began to speak with other tongues, as the Spirit gave them utterance. (Acts 2: 1-4)

It should not be thought from this that the concept was a new one. Incoherent utterances that supposedly result from an altered state of consciousness or religious ecstasy are a practice common to many religions. In the Greek oracles, for example, the priests of Apollo at Delphi, supposedly under the influence of the god, issued such babblings which were then interpreted by the priests.[12]

The "gift of tongues" was also practiced by the old Israelite prophets. Indeed, "to prophesy" usually meant just such ecstatic and incoherent speech as is reported in 1 Samuel 10:10 concerning Saul: ". . . a company of prophets met him; and the Spirit of God came upon him, and he prophesied among them."[13]

Similar trance-like utterances have recurred in Christian revivals through the ages—for example, among thirteenth-century mendicant friars; the Jansenists, or followers of Cornelius Jansen (1585-1638); the early Quakers; the converts of John Wesley (1703-1791), who founded Methodism; the Shakers (i.e., "Shaking Quakers," the frenzied worshipers of the United Society of Believers in Christ's Second Appearing); and many other revivalists.[14]

Several references to different types of "tongues" in the New Testament can cause confusion. For example, the mention of "other tongues" in 1 Corinthians 14:21 has been interpreted as referring "to the disciples preaching in languages they were not familiar with"—i.e., supposedly practicing xenoglossy. As we know from modern cases, there are many glossolalists "who can, on certain occasions, start speaking languages they knew years ago but thought they had forgotten." (Such recollection is an example of what psychologists term *cryptomnesia,* or "hidden memory.") For example, as psychologist Robert A. Baker relates in his *Hidden Memories:*

In one reported case, a woman reported alternating dual personalities in which "A" was the normal, primary personality with "B" the secondary personality believing she was the reincarnation of a Spanish woman of the previous century. At times this patient spoke automatically in a tongue consisting of fragmented Spanish with a few traces of Italian—totally untranslatable into English. Inquiries determined that while the patient was attending convent school she did, periodically, overhear three Mexican girls talking Spanish to each other. Unconsciously, she assimilated their speech. The death of the patient's father came as a severe emotional blow and precipitated the personality split. This situation was aggravated by her infatuation with a man of half-Spanish blood and full Spanish appearance who was the emotional source that precipitated her secondary personality. While she may have learned some Spanish words from her lover, her sample of Spanish contained references suggesting that she heard the three Mexicans orally repeating lessons in Spanish history. There were also a number of words which sounded like Spanish but were not.[15]

Some glossolalists merely jabber in a manner that resembles a known foreign language (in much the same way that comedian Sid Caesar used to produce hilarious renditions of "German" and "French" that might easily pass as such to anyone who was not actually conversant with those languages). However, such utterances are linguistically no more than false languages.[16]

Indeed, it appears that some people may—while half-listening to a glossolalist—superimpose their own inner "voices" into the pseudolanguage so as to make intelligible what is not. This may be the explanation behind such anecdotal cases as the following, related by Harold Hill in *How to Live Like a King's Kid:*

> When another man came and sat in the prayer chair, I laid hands on him and prayed for him in the Spirit, praying in tongues. When the prayer was over, the scoffer was babbling like a baby, crying up a storm, slobbering all over his expensive blue serge suit.
>
> "What ails you?" I asked.
>
> "Well," he said, "I don't know if the man in the chair got anything, but God spoke to me when you prayed for him, because you were praying in High German. I'm a student of High German, and I doubt if even you know it, because it's a rare language."
>
> I said, "I don't know any German, high, low or medium."
>
> "Well," he said, "God spoke to me in perfect High German and said, *Who are you to scoff at any of My gifts?*" And that big blubbering man got saved, and the next day, I heard him praying for someone in a new language. He was really turned on.[17]

In fact, there is no proof of any recognizable language uttered by a glossolalist which cannot be accounted for by one or another psychological explanation.[18]

Passages in 1 Corinthians describing "an *unknown* tongue" (14:2,4) and "the tongues of . . . angels" (13:1) refer to a supernatural language that is comprehended only by God and angels.[19] But, says one charismatic writer:

> Some have argued that the speaking in tongues at Pentecost was different from that described by Paul in 1 Corinthians. In fact they were exactly the same. The only difference lies in the circumstances. At Pentecost the gift was given at the moment when the disciples were baptized in the Spirit, and the audience were unbelievers. The languages were unknown to those who spoke them, but recognized by those who heard them. For the listeners, therefore, the tongues took on the form of prophecy and a sign, thus fulfilling the words of Joel " 'they will prophesy' " (Acts 2:18). On the other hand, in the Church in Corinth the gift, in its normal use in church worship, was in a language unknown both to speakers and listeners, hence the command to have "interpretation."[20]

Be that as it may, Paul's instructions as to interpretation are earnestly given:

> Now, brethren, if I come unto you speaking with tongues, what shall I profit you, except I shall speak to you either by revelation, or by knowledge, or by prophesying, or by doctrine? And even things without life giving sound, whether pipe or harp, except they give a distinction in the sounds, how shall it be known what is piped or harped? For if the trumpet give an uncertain sound, who shall prepare himself to the battle? So likewise ye, except ye utter by the tongue words easy to be understood, how shall it be known what is spoken? for ye shall speak into the air. (1 Cor. 14:6–9)

Therefore, Paul said, "Wherefore let him that speaketh in an unknown tongue pray that he may interpret" (1 Cor. 14:13). Again Paul stated:

> If any man speak in an unknown tongue, let it be by two, or at the most by three, and that by course; and let one interpret. But if there be no interpreter, let him keep silence in the church; and let him speak to himself, and to God. (1 Cor. 14:27–28)

Otherwise, Paul asked, if the unlearned or unbelieving come into the church when there is mass speaking in tongues, "will they not say that ye are mad?" Indeed, the Baptist fundamentalist minister Jerry Falwell once compared speaking in tongues to "the belly rumblings of someone who had eaten too much pizza."[21] Likewise the Vatican sees glossolalia as an "uncouth manifestation of demon possession."[22]

Nevertheless, one adherent insists that while *speaking* in tongues may produce only vain babblings,

> *Praying* in tongues is quite another thing. Sometimes the feelings and yearnings of a Christian are so intense and so profound that the ordinary words of human languages cannot express them. There are occasions when what is happening in the mind is so awesome that there are no words in the common vocabulary that can convey its meaning. According to Pentecostals, it is in such times that the individual can become surrendered to God and let the Holy Spirit prompt in him or her prayers and praise in sounds that make no sense to anyone who may be listening. These sounds are not meant to be interpreted because they are not a message from God. Instead these "words" are "groanings" of the heart of the Christian. They are feelings toward God and they are sounds which only God understands and appreciates.[23]

Some would go further, however, maintaining that glossolalia is actually a miraculous phenomenon, in that it is entirely the Holy Spirit speaking through the person. Writes convert Susy Smith:

> This would undoubtedly seem to be true on certain occasions at least, especially when there is specific prophecy. Frequently in church services of the Pentecostal type or in prayer meetings, an individual stands up and gives a message in tongues. This is often quite disconcerting to the novice who observes it, because the speaker may sound overly dramatic and pretentious. Then someone else gives an interpetation in English. But when the prophecy is accurate and the event comes to pass, it is hard not to be convinced that something supernormal is involved.[24]

Smith does not provide a case study to illustrate her claim but, as we shall see later in this chapter, claims of divinely bestowed prophetic utterances simply cannot be accepted uncritically.

In fact, as should already be clear, glossolalia is simply pseudolanguage that will vary according to the personality of the individual, the circumstances under which the phenomenon is produced, and so on. According to Baker, "some individuals in the throes of religious ecstasy will babble excitedly, emitting screams, yells, moans, and groans that are punctuated at random by streams of meaningless babble."[25] With televangelists such as Swaggart, Bakker, and Robertson,

> Their glossolalia has no discernible grammatical structure and semantically, syntactically, and in every other linguistic way defies the logic of any human language spoken anywhere on earth. Their utterings are merely a flowing cadence of made-up nonsense words, often multisyllabic, that when strung together and punctuated with hand gestures, facial expressions, and variations in tone and volume can convince even the most skeptical that one is, indeed, talking in an obscure esoteric language that bears, at times, faint resemblance to American Indian dialect, Russian, Swahili, or something else strange but at moments vaguely familiar.[26]

Thorough analysis of many expressions of glossolalia has shown that it is indeed "linguistic nonsense." A professor of anthropology and linguistics at the University of Toronto, Dr. William T. Samarin, conducted an exhaustive five-year study of the phenomenon on several continents and concluded:

> Glossolalia consists of strings of meaningless syllables made up of sounds taken from those familiar to the speaker and put together more or less haphazardly. The speaker controls the rhythm, volume, speed and inflection of his speech so that the sounds emerge as pseudolanguage— in the form of words and sentences.
>
> Glossolalia is language-like because the speaker unconsciously wants it to be language-like. Yet in spite of superficial similarities, glossolalia fundamentally is not language.

Samarin also noted that, according to more than half of the glossolalists he studied, it was easier to speak in tongues than in ordinary language. "You don't have to think—just let the words flow. One minister said he could 'go on forever: it's just like drumming.' "[27] Similarly, Martin Gardner reported, "I myself, while researching this article [on glossolalia], began to practice tongue speaking and now can babble it fluently. 'Drawk cabda erfi esnes nonton.' "[28]

In fact, glossolalia was presented as little more than a verbal trick or vocal performance, rather like ventriloquism or yodeling, in the 1972 film *Marjoe*—a documentary exposé of Pentecostalism's excesses. Featuring Marjoe Gortner, the former child evangelist known as "Marjoe the Miracle Child," the film included one scene that showed several older women surrounding a younger one and attempting to teach her to speak in tongues. They repeatedly blurted brief utterances that she was to try to mimic. Marjoe followed with his own rendition of some chanted gibberish and a cynical, shrugging explanation of how easy the phenomeon was to reproduce.

Studies of charismatics indicate they are psychologically no different from other people except for their prevailing belief in the supernatural, their emphasis on speaking in tongues, and a noted lack of emotional inhibition. They are often given to weeping and wailing, to conversing directly with God, and to seeing visions. According to Martin Gardner:

> The autobiographies of [Oral] Roberts, the Bakkers, Swaggart, and Robertson drip with episodes of weeping. Tammy sobs on almost every page of her book, and her husband, someone recently said, cries if the breakfast toast burns. Swaggart constantly works up crocodile tears while he sings, waves the Good Book, begs for money or asks forgiveness for his sins. . . . Oral has described several visions of Jesus and angels and in 1986 revealed that Satan had invaded his bedroom and tried to strangle him. When Robertson bought his first television station his devout mother had a vision of large bank notes floating down from heaven into her son's hands. Tammy's visions are marvelous. In one of them Jesus wore a helmet and brandished a sword.[29]

In the final analysis, then, "the gift" of speaking and praying in tongues is by no means evidence of the miraculous or the supernatural. Instead it is merely "psychobabble," a nonsensical form of utterance that—depending on the motives of the practitioner—falls somewhere between conscious deception and pious self-delusion.

Prophecy

Another charismatic "gift of the Spirit" is prophecy, but since belief in prophetic powers is not limited to Pentecostals, or even to the religious, our discussion of the topic must necessarily be rather far-ranging.

The term *prophet* derives from the Greek word for one who uttered or interpreted an oracle—not his own thoughts but a revelation "from without." Although prophecy now popularly refers to what parapsychologists would term *precognition* ("foreknowledge"), actually the Greek word did not denote "fore-telling" but "forth-telling"[30]—a distinction that remains important, as Pentecostal writer Tony Campolo explains:

> In reality, to exercise the gift of prophecy is to *forth*tell the word of God. In more familiar terms, to prophesy is to preach the truths and judgments of God for this generation. With this *forth*telling there may be some *fore*telling, but that is only a secondary dimension of what is declared. The preacher may predict what will happen to the people if they do not heed the word of God and change their ways. But primary to prophecy is a declaration of what God expects His people to do and how He expects them to change.[31]

Therefore, the Old Testament prophets were not prognosticators in the popular sense. As Owen Rachleff explains in his *The Occult Conceit:*

> Jeremiah, for one, was a religionist whose prophesies about the fall of Jerusalem were no more extrasensory than someone today predicting the onset of a third world war. Ezekiel was a preacher who couched his message in elaborate poetic imagery, which his followers could interpret as they chose. Ezekiel preached the themes of redemption and revival; his was a realistic message of patent probability, not a prophecy as such. The great Hebrew prophets never claimed clairsentient or clairvoyant powers of a supernatural nature; their purpose after all was not future-casting but religious instruction. Though they reportedly experienced visions and flashes of insight, we must remember that their fallacies and wrong guesses were not recorded by their followers who, like many biographers, may have glamorized their subjects so as to make them appear infallible. Besides, many of Ezekiel's visions, like those of St. John the Divine, are submerged in obscurity and as yet remain ostensibly "unfulfilled."[32]

Nevertheless, since the prefix of the Greek word for prophet (i.e., "pro-") could mean "before" in time, and since prophecies typically dealt with future knowledge and events, the concept of prophecy as "prediction" was a logical outcome. To the popular mind prophecy became virtually synonymous with fortune-telling.

Certainly, the ancient world was rife with seers—ranging from degenerate soothsayers to the Greek oracles, the most famous of which was the one at Delphi. Again Rachleff states:

> It is quite obvious that the Oracle was simply intoxicated by some form of narcotic that had been naturally or artificially dissolved in the waters of the spring. The pertinent factor, however, especially as it concerns modern precognition, is the subsequent interpretation given her ravings by the Delphic priests. Most often these interpretations were offerings of good advice on matters of war, marriage, finance, and the like. But when the priests were asked for specific predictions—the bane of all seers—they cloaked their reports in clever ambiguities that, coupled with the ambiguous conditions of human life, served as an effective ploy. Thus the name of a king or prince babbled by the Oracle might mean prosperity or calamity for the kingdom or personal harm (or fortune) for the king. If the king was later involved in a crisis, either good or bad—as kings or rulers are wont to be—the priest could take credit for a significant prophecy; something, they would say, was in the air concerning their king.[33]

Old Testament writings could also be reinterpreted as prophetic. Later Christians mined that richly metaphorical ore to "discover" various passages that are supposedly prophetic of Jesus Christ as the Messiah. Some are held to accurately foretell such key events in Jesus' life as his birth at Bethlehem, his miraculous healings, his arrest and scourging, and his crucifixion. On the other hand,

> These and other such verses are, of course, not universally accepted as prophecies of Christ as the Messiah. In Jewish commentary, for example, the famous Suffering Servant passages of Isaiah (beginning in Chapter 42) are sometimes interperted as referring to Israel itself (on the basis, for instance, of Isaiah 49:3: "And he said to me, 'You are my servant, Israel, in whom I will be glorified.' "); and at least one commentator, Julian Morgenstern, has demonstrated a connection between this theme and pre-Semitic harvest rituals that indicate the very ancient salvationary role of a despised and executed figure.[34]

Others see certain New Testament details as having been deliberately appropriated by the Gospel writers from the Old Testament. For example, Isaac Asimov points to a passage in Matthew—one absent from the other gospels—"which may well have arisen merely out of Matthew's penchant for interpreting and describing everything in accordance with Old Testament prophecy, ritual, and idiom. . . ."[35]

Biblical writers aside, probably the most famous seer of all times was Nostradamus—Michele de Nostredame (1503-1566), the French seer whose prophetic utterances show his attraction to astrological signs and portents. Eventually, although some viewed him as a heretic or warlock, Nostradamus became wealthy and honored, especially at the French court. Henry II's queen, Catherine de Médicis, was a patron of astrologers and sorcerers.[36]

In recent times it has become fashionable to try to demonstrate that Nostradamus correctly prophesied modern events. However, Nostradamus's prophecies were written in quatrains whose vague and symbolic poetry could be subjected to different interpretations at different times.[37] Owen Rachleff characterizes Nostradamus's prophecies as "exquisite examples of ambiguity, aided by a keen sense of history."[38]

In this century astrologer Evangeline Smith Adams (1868-1932) became known as "America's female Nostradamus." Indeed, it is claimed that she predicted her own death, which occurred on November 10, 1932. Even if the story is true, Miss Adams, ill of heart disease, had merely announced that she would die before the year's end. Many seriously ill people know—or guess—that they have only months or even weeks to live. Actually, however, according to a popular book on astrology, there is no proof that she made such a prediction. There is merely a *claim* that that was so, which a friend of hers made *after* her death. The book refers to the claim as providing a "touch of myth."[39]

A similar judgment applies to Adams's contemporary, Edgar Cayce (1877-1945), the so-called sleeping prophet. By entering a "trance" state Cayce supposedly provided thousands of people with accurate medical readings (which will be discussed in the next chapter) as well as numerous clairvoyant prognostications. For example, he predicted that the mythical sunken continent of Atlantis would rise again, about 1968, but the elusive continent failed to appear. Nevertheless, before his death, Cayce told numerous clients that in their previous lives they had been Atlantean citizens.[40]

More recently, Jeane Dixon (b. 1918) seems to have inherited Nostradamus's mantle. She claims her professed ability is God-given: "I think He has given me a number of visions because He knows I'll tell others about them. I'm a little girl who can't keep a secret."[41]

Mrs. Dixon's fame rests largely on the claim that she predicted the assassination of President John F. Kennedy. The May 13, 1956, issue of *Parade* magazine did report: "As to the 1960 election, Mrs. Dixon thinks it will be dominated by labor and won by a Democrat. But he will be assassinated or die in office, though not necessarily in his first term." Later she explained that her prediction was a revelation: "A vision is a revelation; a revelation is a word of God and cannot be changed." However, according to Milbourne Christopher:

> As we know now, the election was not "dominated by labor." She did not name the Democrat she said would win; no date was given for the president-to-be's end; and his announced demise was qualified with Delphic ingenuity "assassinated or die in office, though not necessarily in his first term." Thus if the president served a single term, it would be within four years; if he was re-elected, there was an eight-year span. Such a surmise was not illogical for anyone who has studied recent American history. . . .[42]

Christopher continues:

> In January 1960 Mrs. Dixon changed her mind. Kennedy, then a contender for the Democratic nomination, would not be elected in November, she said in Ruth Montgomery's syndicated column. In June she stated that "the symbol of the presidency is directly over the head of Vice-President Nixon" but "unless the Republican party really gets out and puts forth every effort it will topple." Fire enough shots, riflemen agree, and eventually you'll hit the bull's-eye.[43]

Mrs. Dixon has fared less well with other predictions: Eisenhower did not "appoint five-star General Douglas MacArthur to an exceedingly important post." Neither did "Russia move into Iran in the fall of 1953." Mrs. Dixon was wrong in 1965 when she prophesied that "Russia will be the first nation to put a man on the moon," and wrong again the following year: on May 7, 1966, dramatically holding her crystal ball and peering over the footlights of an auditorium at the University of Southern California, Mrs. Dixon confidently announced that the Vietnam War "will be over in ninety days." Instead, it lasted nine more years. The list of Mrs. Dixon's wildly erroneous predictions and of her notable failure to "see" major events could continue *ad infinitum*.[44]

Not only are dedicated practitioners of clairvoyance like Nostradamus and Dixon able to "see" beyond space and time—according to proponents of ESP—but so are ordinary people. Witness the *Titanic* disaster. What has since been termed "the most astounding instance of prophecy" is found in an 1898 novel, *The Wreck of the Titan,* written by an obscure author named Morgan Robertson. Fourteen years after this disaster novel had slipped into obscurity, the events it described came shockingly true: The *Titanic*—the largest ship in the world—sank on its maiden voyage across the Atlantic.

Not only did the *Titan* and *Titanic* have similar names, but they were of similar size (70,000 and 60,000 tons respectively) with too few lifeboats; both sank in April in the North Atlantic after striking an iceberg; and both resulted in a great loss of life (most of the *Titan*'s 2,300 passengers and 1,503 of the *Titanic*'s 2,206).

Prophecy? Clairvoyance on the part of Morgan Robertson? Apparently not: First of all, despite apocryphal claims to the contrary, Robertson never claimed to be prescient. Moreover, there were glaring differences between the two ships—Robertson's fictional vessel had an auxiliary sail that the *Titanic* lacked. Finally, there is every indication that Robertson had researched his topic and merely made extrapolations from available facts. Ships traveling the North Atlantic route faced no danger so great as that posed by icebergs, and the danger was at its peak in April. As to the similar names, both mean gigantic and either was thus an obvious choice; it is even possible that the novel influenced the naming of the real ship.[45]

Even so, after the sinking of the *Titanic* many survivors and others came forward to claim they had had forebodings or premonitions of the disaster. But as Daniel Cohen points out:

> A hundred or a thouand times in an average person's life he or she may have a dream or some other vague premonition of disaster. When disaster really does strike, we tend to think it was foretold, forgetting all the times the dreams and hunches were wrong. Add to this very human response another one, a selective memory that tends to add or subtract details in order to make them conform to what actually happened, and we have the psychological conditions that create an outpouring of "I knew it was going to happen," every time some unexpected and dramatic tragedy takes place. And the sinking of the great ocean liner was surely laden with both drama and tragedy.[46]

Occasionally, there is quite a different relationship between dramatic events and an apparent premonition or clairvoyant vision. Such was the case in 1981, when Los Angeles "psychic" Tamara Rand allegedly predicted the shooting of President Reagan—foretelling that the attempted assassin would have the initials "J. H." and a surname similar to "Humley" (his name was John Hinkley), that Reagan would be shot in the chest during a "hail of bullets," and that the event would take place in the last week of March or the first week of April (it actually occurred on March 30). The predictions were reputedly given on a talk show taped January 6 in Los Vegas.

Associated Press reporter Paul Simon thought Rand's story was too good to be true and, upon investigating, discovered that it was: the videotape was a fake, filmed the day *after* the attempted assassination, as Rand's co-conspirator, KTNV talk show host Dick Maurice, later confessed. Rand deliberately made her "predictions" less specific than possible to deflect suspicion.[47]

Among the most attention-getting prophecies are those that predict the biblical apocalypse or other doomsday scenarios. For example, consider the prophecy made by the founder of the Church Universal and Triumphant, Elizabeth Clare Prophet (whose surname, incidentally, is genuine: she is the former Mrs. Mark Prophet). She has predicted that the world will end in a nuclear holocaust, and her followers have located themselves on a Montana ranch where they are busy building fallout shelters, stockpiling weapons, and otherwise preparing for Armageddon. Ms. Prophet captured national headlines with her reported prediction that the end of civilization would occur on April 23, 1990. Prophet denies having set the date, but local residents disagree. "She has postponed the date at least four times over the last year," said Richard Meyer, a hardware store owner. "Every time it doesn't happen, she says it is because of church prayers." Ms. Prophet's visionary view was that changes in Eastern Europe and elsewhere were part of a Soviet design to distract and weaken the West so that a massive nuclear strike could be launched.[48] Apparently she was unable to foresee that—quite contrary to her scenario—what would actually happen would be the collapse of the Soviet Union!

Another religious doomsday prophecy was prompted by the Gulf War. The Rev. Charles Taylor, host of a nationally syndicated radio program titled "Today in Bible Prophecy," preached that the war with Iraq was a prelude for an attack upon Israel by Soviet and Arab forces, resulting in "a seven-year period of tribulation that will lead to the final battle of Armageddon." He added, ". . . we know things are very close because God has given us the indication."[49] Alas for the Rev. Taylor's prophetic powers, such events have not materialized and—once again—there was a failure to see the dismantling of the Soviet Union.

Countless such cases—many of them chronicled in Charles Mackay's classic work, *Extraordinary Popular Delusions and the Madness of Crowds* (1841)[50]—have occurred throughout history, not only attesting to the failure of prophecy but also bearing witness to the credulity of countless occultists and religious zealots.

Taking Up Serpents

Certain practices of some fundamentalist Christians are too extreme even for many ardent Pentecostals, yet these practices also claim scriptural authority. In Luke, Jesus said to a group of his followers:

> I behold Satan as lightning fall from heaven. Behold, I give unto you power to tread on serpents and scorpions, and over all the power of the enemy, and nothing shall by any means hurt you. (Luke 19: 18–19)

Also, according to a passage in the gospel of Mark, when Jesus appeared to his disciples after his resurrection, he said:

> He that believeth and is baptized shall be saved; but he that believeth not shall be damned. And these signs shall follow them that believe; In my name shall they cast out devils; they shall speak with new tongues; they shall take up serpents; and if they drink any deadly thing, it shall not hurt them; they shall lay hands on the sick, and they shall recover. (Mark 16: 16–18)

The latter passage may be spurious, however. Unlike the King James Version of the Bible, modern translations separate this final portion of Mark's gospel (vv. 9–20) from the main text. According to Gerald A. Larue, emeritus professor of biblical history and archaeology at the University of Southern California:

> These verses, written in a style different from the rest of the gospel, are not found in the best and most reliable ancient manuscripts. They were compiled out of material from the other gospels during the second century C.E. and appear to represent a reaction against the abrupt ending of the original writing.[51]

There is, in fact, "no indication that drinking poison or handling poisonous reptiles to demonstrate faith became a popular pastime in the early church."[52]

Nevertheless, in a consequence of these passages, certain Christian charismatics believe their faith provides them with immunity to serpents and certain other harmful things, just as they are given the ability to speak in tongues and the power to heal by the laying on of hands.

The practice in modern times seems to have originated in 1909 with one George Went Hensley, an illiterate Church of God preacher. Hensley was preaching about the Mark 16 passage in an outdoor service near Cleveland, Tennessee, when a box of rattlesnakes was overturned next to his pulpit. Hensley picked up the snakes and continued preaching—thus becoming known as "the original prophet of snake handling."[53]

No major Pentecostal denomination now endorses snake handling, and it has been specifically rejected by the Church of God. Even so, some rural congregations continue the practice, including the Free Pentecostal Holiness Church (with churches in Virginia, Kentucky, Tennessee, and North Carolina) and various independent churches scattered throughout Appalachia, such as the Church of the Lord Jesus in Jolo, West Virginia.[54] One source states that West Virginia is "the last state in which ritual snake handling remains legal,"[55] but Georgia's stringent 1940s law was annulled in a 1960s revision of the state code.[56] In any event, legal or not, the practice persists in several states where authorities often turn a blind eye to it on the basis of religious freedom.

The churches are invariably small, rural edifices like one small-town Alabama church described as "a converted store and filling station with a crude fiberboard facade, a miniature steeple and a sign out front that reads, 'The Church of Jesus with Following Signs.' " One observer described the congregation of that church as consisting of "hard, angular women and men with slicked hair and bad teeth."[57] They are typical of the poor (usually white) and relatively uneducated members who comprise the snake-handling sects.[58]

The practice of taking up serpents is actually part of regular worship in the churches that include "hillbilly-type singing," fervent preaching, and "witnessing" (or "testifying": making "an open declaration in public of one's religion"[59]), speaking in tongues, and the like—all punctuated with ecstatic yells and exhortations—until the participants have all been roused to fever pitch.[60] Then, when the Spirit moves them, some members begin to take up serpents: copperheads, rattlesnakes, or cottonmouth moccasins.

At one such service, the preacher—who was on trial for attempting to murder his wife—was described in this way:

> The power of the singing contorts Glen Summerford's face into a reddish mask and seems to wipe away the woes that have made him a pariah everywhere but in this cramped room. His body convulses as he hops from one leg to the other in a feverish jig. He sips from a jelly jar full of water that he says is laced with strychnine.
>
> This is the moment, he says, when the Lord enters the room.
>
> He reaches beneath his pulpit and pulls out the proof of his faith—two copperheads and a rattlesnake.
>
> The copperheads twist around his finger like vines while the thick rattlesnake musses his hair with its tongue. Two dozen worshipers are entranced.[61]

Similar activities characterize other snake-handling services, including one held at the Church of the Lord Jesus Christ in Kingston, Georgia, in 1990—only six days after one member, 48-year-old Arnold Loveless, was fatally bitten by a rattlesnake, and only two days after his funeral was held in the church's wood-paneled sanctuary. According to the *Atlanta Constitution:*

> The Rev. Carl Porter, the pastor, warned the three dozen people in the pews, "We've got some serpents up here. They'll bite you, and they will kill you. If you get one of them out, that's between you and the Lord."
>
> But the first rousing song of the evening was only a few choruses old when Mr. [Byron] Crawford, 28, and Gene Sherbert, another church member, felt led to take up the snakes.
>
> As others in the church stood, clapped and swayed, Mr. Crawford sang a gospel song, sounding like a young Elvis Presley, whom he vaguely resembles.
>
> "He's the God of Alabama. He's the God of Tennessee. He's the God right here in Georgia. He's the God for you and me," he sang, accompanied by electric guitars, cymbals, drums and tambourines.
>
> For about 15 minutes, verse after verse, he held the copperheads, sometimes raising them to face level.
>
> Mr. Sherbert, meanwhile, held a 2½-foot rattlesnake much like the one that killed Mr. Loveless. At one point, he placed it, writhing, on the pulpit.[62]

Mr. Crawford told a reporter that he had been handling snakes for over ten years and had been bitten four times—once each by a cottonmouth moccasin and a copperhead and twice by rattlesnakes. The last time, he said, "it swelled me up a little," but he insisted that he had never sought medical treatment for a snake bite. Gesturing toward a wooden box that contained the copperheads he had brought to the service, Crawford stated: "If I'm going to live by this right here, it's good enough to die by."[63]

Adherents of the practice insist that taking up serpents should only be done when worshipers truly feel the Holy Spirit is upon them. One minister of the sect says he attempted to stop a service at his church several years ago when he believed that a man who had taken up snakes did not have God's blessing. "The man lays in the hills of Georgia today. He got killed by a snake bite. They [the snakes] wouldn't stop. But they [the congregation] stopped the meeting when the boy got bit and died."[64]

The urge to caution in handling snakes, however, may reflect more shrewdness than piety. While poisonous snakes are indeed dangerous and must be handled carefully, the knowledge that the rural snake handlers bring to the practice can be most helpful. For example, unless snakes are hot, hungry, or frightened, they move little and are relatively unaggressive.[65] Also, snakes raised from hatchlings can become accustomed to handling.[66] Large snakes grasped firmly behind the neck will be unable to bite, and, "once they are off the ground they are much less likely to bite and can usually be held safely."[67]

In addition to these general practices, there are some that apply to different species of snakes that handlers can take advantage of. For example, the rattlesnakes that are used in the services are often the eastern timber rattlers, not their more deadly and more combative diamondback cousins of the western United States. It is well known that "the timber rattler is not an aggressive creature."[68] Similarly, the cottonmouth moccasin is distinctive in that, while quite poisonous, "it doesn't attack people often."[69] As to the copperhead, while its bite is painful, "its poison . . . is rarely strong enough to kill."[70]

Moreover, while snake bites should certainly be treated, the fact is that—fortunately—venom is rarely injected directly into a blood vessel, which would provide the most deadly threat.[71] Moreover, snake bites vary in the amount of venom injected: With a *mild* snake bite, the strike is a glancing one and the result is minimal pain; a *moderate* snake bite causes some localized pain and swelling but not a general sick feeling; and a *severe* snake bite causes excruciating pain, discoloration and swelling, and a generalized sick feeling.[72] Multiple bites—as in the case cited earlier by the preacher—are the most deadly, since venom can be injected with each bite,[73] and the attack of several snakes could therefore be life-threatening in the extreme.

Also, the effect of snake bites varies considerably depending on the health and size of the victim, the speed of venom absorption, and the location of the bite, which fortunately is usually in the extremities.[74] Remaining calm—since panic helps spread the venom more quickly[75]—is essential, as snake handlers well know. Consider this report on one victim's response:

> He collapsed during the service but refused to call a doctor. The congregation circled around him and prayed, *and for days he lay on his mother's couch.* Faith, he believes, healed him. (Emphasis added.)[76]

Applying ice packs to the wound can be helpful in slowing the spread of the poison and thereby lessening the shock to the body's system.[77]

Typically, in the case of media reports that mention the lack of medical help a snake bite victim receives, it is well to consider that that does not necessarily mean *all* treatment—such as the at-home administration of constriction bands and lancing and suctioning of the wound—was forsaken. Such treatment would usually greatly minimize the harmful effects of snake bite.[78] At least, keeping a wound clean and allowing it to drain well reduces the attendant risks of infection and gangrene.[79]

The extent to which trickery is resorted to in snake-handling demonstrations may be debated. The wife of one such handler—Glen Summerford of the Church of Jesus Following Signs in Scottsboro, Alabama—made a number of accusations against her husband in the course of his trial for attempting to murder her. (Summerford was convicted of twice forcing his wife, at gunpoint, to place her hand into a cage of snakes until she was bitten, then standing by for two days as she lay near death.) According to Mrs. Darlene Summerford, her husband sometimes employed defanged snakes, adding that if a snake doesn't sense fear, "it ain't going to bite you. Glen knows how to handle them," she stated.[80]

Those who do receive snake bites are told that it was their lack of faith that caused them. Stated Byron Crawford of his most recent of four bites (mentioned earlier): "If I'd kept my mind on the Lord, I wouldn't have got hurt."[81] Yet when a devout member of the sect dies from snake bite, the others resort to rationalization. For instance, when Arnold Lee Loveless died, his pastor, the Rev. Carl Porter, stated his belief that everyone's fate is predestined from the beginning of creation.[82] It seems ironic that that notion could co-exist with a view of individual faith and responsibility, yet perhaps it is no more ironic than the fact that "the original prophet of snake handling," George Went Hensley, died in 1955 of a snake bite sustained during a religious service.[83]

Other Immunities

As already indicated, Mark 17:18, which refers to the taking up of serpents, also promises that "if they drink any deadly thing, it shall not hurt them." Although, as we have seen, this passage is in an apocryphal section of Mark's gospel and there is no evidence the practice was engaged in by early Christians, nevertheless the drinking of strychnine regularly accompanies snake handling in some of the independent "Holy Roller" churches. By authority of Luke 10:19, which tells how Christ promised a group of seventy disciples that "nothing shall by any means hurt you," some worshipers also demonstrate supposed immunity to fire and/or to electrical shocks.

Interestingly enough, strychnine seems to be the poison of choice among the Christian zealots who claim invincibility over its harmful effects. Why strychnine? Probably because of its unique properties.

Strychnine is a poisonous alkaloid discovered in 1817 and found in certain species of *Strychnos* such as St. Ignatius' beans. Although it has been used in rodent poisons, it has also been used medicinally—in cathartic preparations and as "a tonic and stimulant for the central nervous system."[84] In the latter case, the specific effects consist of excitation of the motor areas of the spinal cord. Small doses "increase the sensibility of touch, sight, and hearing," whereas "large doses" cause difficulty in swallowing and "twitching of the muscles"[85] (which would seem to fit in well with the Pentecostal penchant for exhibiting seizure-like convulsions and similar manifestations of going under the power). Overdoses of strychnine can, of course, cause death.

That some snake-handling Pentecostals actually drink strychnine is attested by the deaths in 1973 of Jimmy Ray Williams and Buford Pack. They died after drinking the poison during a worship service in Tennessee, where that practice is illegal. (A year later, Mr. Pack's brother, Liston, attempted to have the U.S. Supreme Court overturn the Tennessee law, but he was unsuccessful.)[86] However, when others drink strychnine and survive—which is supposed to provide evidence of the miraculous power of faith—questions are raised about the concentration of the solution and the amount actually imbibed.

For instance (as mentioned in the discussion on snake handling), Alabama preacher Glen Summerford (convicted of attempting to murder his wife by snake bite) sipped "from a jelly jar full of water that he says is laced with strychnine." Of course whether the water actually contained the poison—and if so, how much—is unknown. That Summerford displayed "a small vial of white powder" to a reporter and offered to allow it to be tested means nothing.[87] We do not even know whether the preacher—accused of the deceptions—did more than pretend to sip the liquid, or whether (before or after) he had ingested a common antidote, such as egg white, for that poison.[88]

In any case, it is interesting that Summerford—like other strychnine-drinking Pentecostals—was ostensibly sipping the poison before handling snakes. It is interesting because the administration of strychnine has been advocated *to treat certain physiological effects resulting from snake bite.*[89] It would appear that a healthy person could sip a small amount of a diluted solution of strychnine without serious harm, and that, in the event of snake bite, the presence of the substance in the body could actually have a beneficial effect.

Immunity from fire is another form of invincibility the Christian faithful allegedly attain. Members of the Free Pentecostal Holiness Church, especially, are prone to light kerosene lamps improvised from bottles and—according to D. Scott Rogo—"perform sometimes remarkable exhibitions of fire immunity" such as holding the lamps to their hands and feet without being harmed.[90] Rogo's source was "scientific investigation" by a New Jersey psychiatrist, Dr. Berthold Schwarz, who reported:

> On three occasions, three different women held the blaze to their chests, so that the flames were in intimate contact with their cotton dresses, exposed necks, faces and hair. This lasted for longer than a few seconds. Twice, at separate times, one of the "most faithful of the saints" slowly moved the palmar and lateral aspects of one hand and the fifth finger in the midpoint tip of an acetylene flame (produced by the reaction of calcium carbide and water in a miner's headlamp). He did this for more than four seconds, and then repeated the procedure, using the

Figure 1: The Shroud of Turin? Actually, a negative photograph of an experimental rubbing image made from a bas-relief by the author. Is this how the reputed Holy Shroud of Christ was created, or was it instead produced by a miraculous burst of radiant energy at the moment of Jesus' resurrection?

Figure 2: The Image of Guadalupe, as copied in an altar painting at the Santuario de Guadalupe in Santa Fe, New Mexico. The original—venerated at a shrine in Mexico City—is said to be a miraculous self-portrait of the Virgin Mary. (Photo by the author.)

Figure 3: Detail of altar painting at the Santuario de Guadalupe, depicting the Virgin's imaginary appearance to a peasant named Juan Diego in 1531. (Photo by the author.)

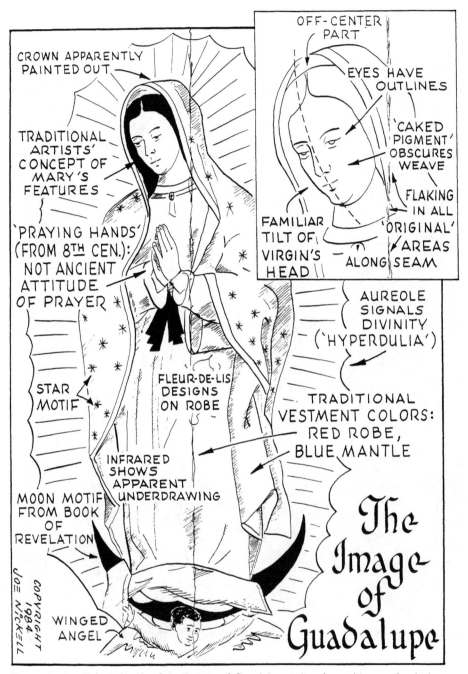

Figure 4: Analytical sketch of the Image of Guadalupe, showing evidence of painting. However, believers in the Image's authenticity maintain that beneath the painted areas, and in certain supposedly unretouched areas, an "original," miraculous portrait exists.

Figure 5: A "weeping" icon at a Greek Orthodox church in Astoria, Queens, New York. Photographed here long after the "tears" had dried, the saint still appears to be crying due to her painted expression and surface irregularities in the image. (Photo by the author.)

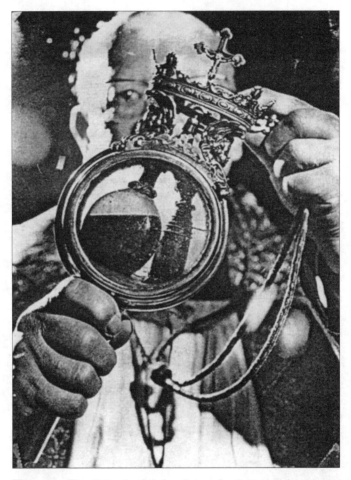

Figure 6: The "blood of Saint Januarius," having just been transformed from its usual congealed form to a liquefied state. (Photograph from Catholic News Service.)

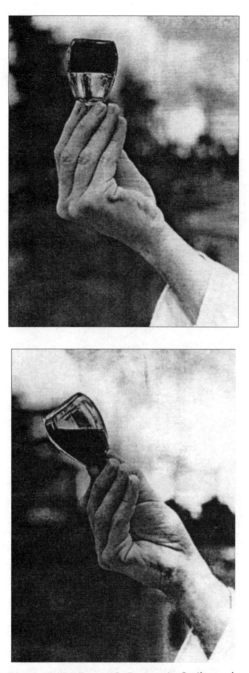

Figure 7 (top) and 8 (bottom): Italian scientists' duplication of the Saint Januarius phenomenon. Congealed "blood" (top) suddenly liquefies (bottom) in a seemingly miraculous fashion. (Photo courtesy of Luigi Garlaschelli, Franco Ramaccini, and Sergio Della Sala.)

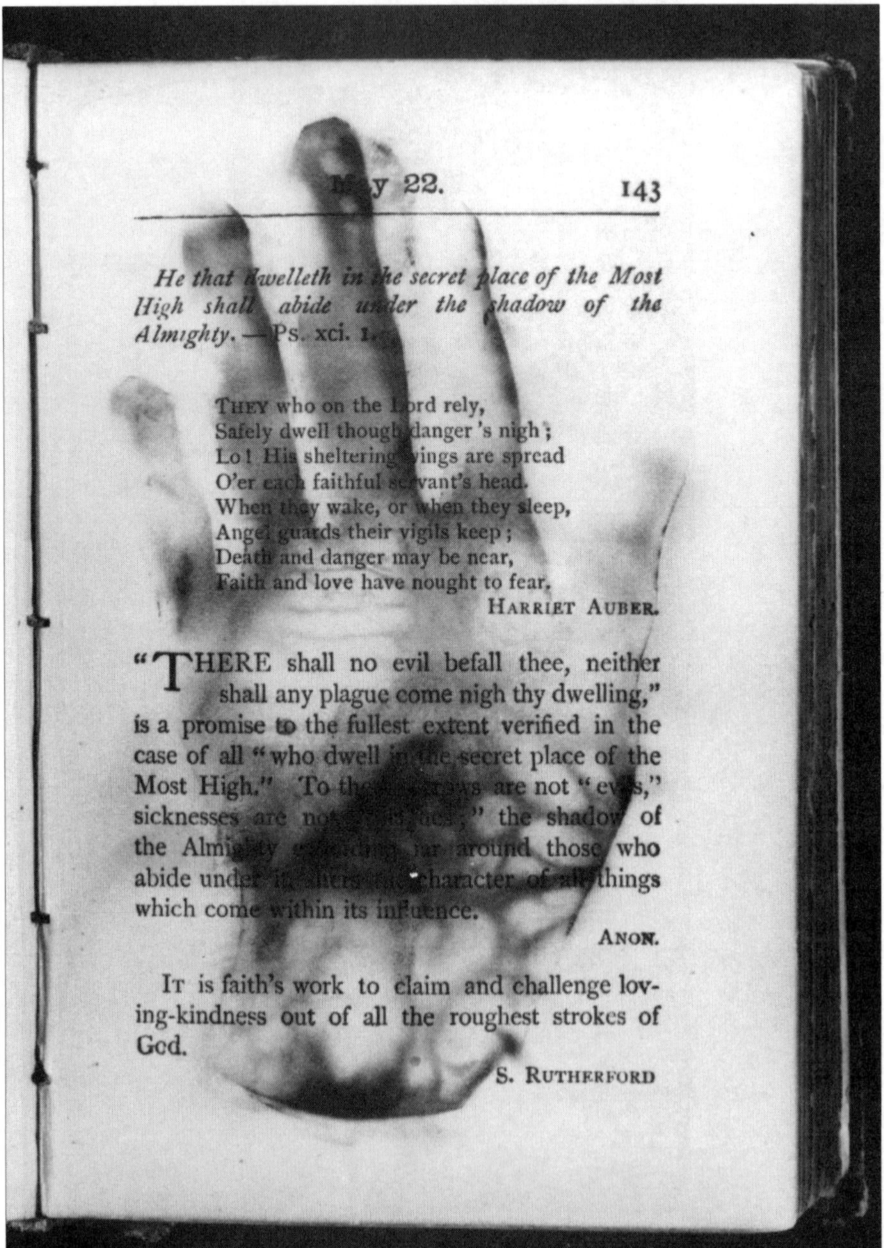

He that dwelleth in the secret place of the Most
High shall abide under the shadow of the
Almighty. —Ps. xci. 1.

THEY who on the Lord rely,
Safely dwell though danger's nigh;
Lo! His sheltering wings are spread
O'er each faithful servant's head.
When they wake, or when they sleep,
Angel guards their vigils keep;
Death and danger may be near,
Faith and love have nought to fear.

HARRIET AUBER.

"THERE shall no evil befall thee, neither shall any plague come nigh thy dwelling," is a promise to the fullest extent verified in the case of all "who dwell in the secret place of the Most High." To them sorrows are not "evils," sicknesses are not "plagues;" the shadow of the Almighty, stretching far around those who abide under it, alters the character of all things which come within its influence.

ANON.

IT is faith's work to claim and challenge loving-kindness out of all the roughest strokes of God.

S. RUTHERFORD

Figure 9: "Burning handprints"—scorched into pages of books or onto consecrated cloths—are attributed to spirits in purgatory. This example—the branded page of a nineteenth-century book of meditations—was actually made by the author.

Figure 10: Immunity to fire is a form of invincibility claimed by some Pentecostal Christians. This simple demonstration, of a hand being licked by flames from a kerosene-soaked torch, was actually made by the author. (Photography by Robert H. van Outer.)

Figure 11: An early photo of the grotto at Lourdes. To the left can be seen the many crutches left by those pilgrims who have been "cured."

Figure 12: Mary Baker Eddy (1821–1910) is shown here in 1880 holding what is perhaps a copy of her book, *Science and Health with Key to the Scriptures.* (Photo from *According to the Flesh* by Fleta C. Springer [Coward-McCann, 1930].)

Figure 13: The midnight vigil for the Mother of Jesus at Cold Spring, Kentucky, in 1992 was obviously inspired by alleged visitations of the Virgin at Medjugorje, Yugoslavia. (This case is discussed in the Afterword.)

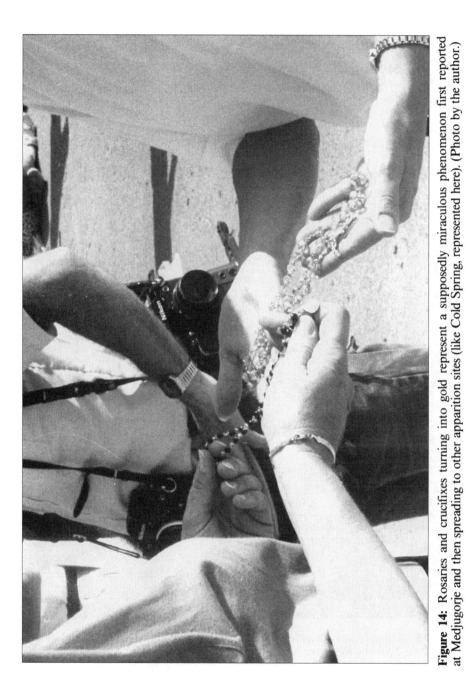

Figure 14: Rosaries and crucifixes turning into gold represent a supposedly miraculous phenomenon first reported at Medjugorje and then spreading to other apparition sites (like Cold Spring, represented here). (Photo by the author.)

Figure 15: A mysterious Polaroid photograph depicting the "Golden Door"—supposedly "the doorway to heaven"—was made by a pilgrim to Cold Spring, Kentucky, in 1992.

Figure 16: An experimental "Golden Door" photograph—made with a Polaroid One Step camera aimed at a 50-watt halogen lamp—demonstrates that the "doorway" is simply the shape of the camera's aperture. (Photo by Dale Heatherington.)

Figure 17: A statue of Saint Francis of Assisi, history's first recorded stigmatic, outside a church named in his honor in Santa Fe, New Mexico. Here, the saint's palms are turned to display the wounds that "miraculously" appear in evocation of the crucifixion of Christ. (Photo by the author.)

other hand. Later that same evening, he alternately applied each hand again to the acetylene flame for slightly longer periods. Once this saint, when in a relatively calm mood, turned to a coal fire for an hour's duration, picked up a flaming "stone coal" the size of a hen's egg and held it in the palms of his hands for sixty-five seconds while he walked among the congregation. As a control, the author could not touch a piece of burning charcoal for less than one second without developing a painful blister.[91]

Rogo responded to this description by stating, "There is simply no medical explanation for this type of 'miracle' which is known to just about every religion in the world."[92] What Rogo and Schwarz seem not to know is that there is indeed an explanation—not medical but instead attributable to the bag of tricks of any of history's canny fire handlers.

For example, in seventeenth-century England, a fire-eater named Richardson appeared to dine on various fiery materials. He munched glowing coals, drank flaming liquids, and otherwise attempted to prove he was unharmed by fire. In the next century Robert Powell performed similar stunts at British fairs, and in the first part of the nineteenth century an Italian woman named Signora Josephine Giardelli was exhibited in London as "The Fireproof Female." It was advertised that

> She will, without the least symptoms of pain, put boiling melted lead in her mouth, and emit the same with the imprint of her teeth thereon; red-hot irons will be passed over various parts of her body; she will walk over a bar of red-hot iron with her naked feet; will . . . put boiling oil in her mouth![93]

Giardelli was rivaled by Ivan Chabert, known as the French "Incombustible Phenomenon." He, too, ate burning materials. As *The Times* of London reported in 1826:

> . . . he refreshed himself with a hearty meal of phosphorus . . . he washed down this infernal fare with solutions of arsenic and oxalic acid . . . he next swallowed . . . several spoonsful of boiling oil, and, as a dessert . . ., helped himself with his naked hand to a considerable quantity of molten lead . . . the exhibitor offered to swallow Prussic acid, perhaps the most powerful of known poisons, if any good-natured person could furnish him with a quantity of it.

But it was Chabert's stunt with a fiery oven that created the greatest sensation. He entered the oven (actually an iron chest about six by seven feet) which had been heated to some 600 degrees Fahrenheit, carrying a thick steak and a leg of lamb. Closing the doors behind him, he remained there, talking to the audience through a thin tube, while the meat cooked. Then he flung open the door and stepped out in triumph.[94]

Since this is not a textbook on conjuring, I will forego an extended explanation of such tricks and instead refer the interested reader to several excellent books on legerdemain that contain discussions of how such apparent miracles are performed.[95] It is obvious, however, that the feats of the Pentecostals that awed the credulous Schwarz are tame by comparison with those of Richardson, Powell, Giardelli, Chabert, et al., and do not require invocation of the miraculous. One of Schwarz's photographs, for example, depicting a makeshift kerosene lamp being held to the foot of one sect member, reveals that the sole of the foot is placed *beside* the flame, not *over* it. Also recall Schwarz's statement that one "saint" actually "moved" his hand through a flame, a feat easily performed (Figure 10). As to holding the hot coal in the hand, such a stunt—easily accomplished[96]—is just another trick.

A friend of mine—of sufficient age to recall when kerosene lamps were still the common means of lighting in rural churches—related to me an amusing incident concerning fire immunity. She was attending a "Holy Roller" service wherein certain bold worshipers were performing a test of fire. They removed the hot glass chimneys from the lamps and—"quite gingerly!"—tossed them from hand to hand and passed them to each other, moved their hands through the flames, and so on—all to the growing anger of a local minister who had come to satisfy his curiosity about the radical sect. Finally, he leaped forward to seize a lamp and duplicate the effects, demonstrating that they were nothing more than stunts that anyone could perform. The Pentecostals rushed to stop the minister and the service was transformed into a bout of theological acrimony that— to some young onlookers at least—was most entertaining.[97]

It perhaps should be mentioned here that some wonderworkers—not Pentecostals, but certain religious mystics from the Orient—attempt to prove their resistance to fire by walking barefoot across red-hot embers. Such "firewalking" feats are possible because wood does not conduct heat well and because the time of contact is kept quite brief. Experiments show that it is possible to make a short walk across hot coals or a longer walk over cooler embers. (Ripley's "Believe It or Not" claimed one firewalker strode the length of a twenty-foot trench heated to 1400 degrees Fahrenheit. Actually the trench was divided at the middle by a crosswise section of dirt where the walker paused briefly. Thus his performance consisted of two short walks of ten feet each, not a single twenty-foot walk.) Physicist Bernard Leikind has actually walked on fire to demonstrate that no magical power is involved.[98]

Rogo also cites some instances of fire immunity allegedly performed by St. Francis of Paola (1416–1507), notably the claim that in 1435 St. Francis walked into a furnace used on a monastery construction site. The furnace was being used to make lime for mortar, and several of its stones had become dislodged, threatening to cause the structure to collapse. St. Francis waited until the workmen had gone to lunch, then stepped into the blazing furnace, assessed the damage, and exited unscathed, whereupon "the furnace's imperfections were repaired instantaneously."[99] Except for some alleged eye-witnesses to the reputed miracle, Rogo stated that he would have been willing to "just dismiss this story as an apocryphal tale."[100] But there have always been "eyewitnesses" to come forward when some popular figure was being considered for canonization, and St. Francis's reputed feat seems like many other reputed saints' miracles: As theologian A. E. Garvie states, "the character of most of these miracles is such as to lack probability."[101]

There is one other feat of immunity associated with Pentecostal fundamentalists that should be mentioned. It is attributed to the notorious preacher Glen Summerford, whom we discussed in connection with snake handling and drinking strychnine. According to an article in the *New York Times*, Summerford also routinely "touches live electrical wires"—a statement given without any explanation of the conditions involved.[102] Obviously, while it would be easy to fake such a feat, even that would not be necessary. Under proper conditions one can indeed touch electrical wires with relative impunity,[103] and only the naive are impressed by such a demonstration.

I leave it to others to interpret correctly the Gospel passages that have resulted in ridiculous demonstrations with snakes and fire. But surely simple faith is not expected to transform a Christian into an invincible being from the comic-book planet Krypton. Neither, one suspects, is it intended to leap all bounds of reason.

Select Bibliography

Baker, Robert A. *Hidden Memories: Voices and Visions from Within.* Buffalo, N.Y.: Prometheus Books, 1992. An excellent discussion of glossolalia and various prophetic visions—all part of an exhaustive analysis of cryptomnesia or "hidden memories."

Baker, Robert A., and Joe Nickell. *Missing Pieces: How to Investigate Ghosts, UFOs, Psychics, and Other Mysteries.* Buffalo, N.Y.: Prometheus Books, 1992. A handbook on how to investigate allegedly paranormal phenomena, including claims of prophecy (from which the discussion in this chapter was adapted).

Compolo, Tony. *How to Be Pentecostal without Speaking in Tongues.* Dallas, Tex.: Word Publishing, 1991. A defense of Pentecostalism and its doctrine of charismatic gifts, such as speaking in tongues and prophecy, that also disparages the extravagant claims and outright trickery of some evangelists.

Gardner, Martin. "Glossolalia." *Free Inquiry* 9.2 (Spring 1989): 46–48. A lively discussion of the topic of speaking in tongues by one of the nation's foremost science writers and critics of superstition.

Gibson, Walter B. *Secrets of Magic: Ancient and Modern.* New York: Grosset & Dunlap, 1967. An explanation of classic magical secrets, including tricks of fire eaters and fire walkers.

Larue, Gerald A. "The Cult of the Serpent." Chapter [12] of *The Supernatural, the Occult and the Bible.* Buffalo, N.Y.: Prometheus Books, 1990. A discussion of the role of the serpent in both the Old Testament and the Christian Scriptures, with a brief description of snake handling sects that derive their justification from the latter.

Notes

1. Michael Harper, *Gifted People: Discovering Your Supernatural Gifts and Learning How to Use Them* (Ann Arbor, Mich.: Vine Books, 1990), pp. 25–28, 38.

2. Ibid., p. 28.

3. Ibid., pp. 44–101. See also Acts 1:5, 2: 1–4; Mark 16: 17–18.

4. Merle Severy, ed., *Great Religions of the World* (Washington, D.C.: National Geographic Society, 1971), pp. 380–81; Tony Campolo, *How to Be Pentecostal without Speaking in Tongues* (Dallas, Tex.: Word Publishing, 1991), p. 17.

5. Compolo, *How to Be Pentecostal,* p. 7.

6. William A. Henry III, "God and Money Part 9," *Time,* July 22, 1991, p. 28; "The Wrath of 'Maximum Bob,'" *Time,* November 6, 1989, p. 62.

7. Pat Guy, "Robertson a Businessman behind Pulpit," *USA Today,* undated clipping.

8. Harper, *Gifted People,* pp. 10–11.

9. Campolo, *How to Be Pentecostal,* p. 23.

10. Ibid.

11. Popoff is referred to, without actually being named, in Campolo, *How to Be Pentecostal,* pp. 11–13. See also Robert A. Steiner, "Exposing the Faith-Healers," *The Skeptical Inquirer* 11.1 (Fall 1986): 28–31.

12. Isaac Asimov, *Asimov's Guide to the Bible,* vol. 2, *The New Testament* (New York: Equinox Books, 1969), p. 338.

13. Ibid.

14. "Tongues, Gift of," *Encyclopaedia Britannica,* 1960 ed.

15. Robert A. Walker, *Hidden Memories: Voices and Visions from Within* (Buffalo, N.Y.: Prometheus Books, 1992), pp. 250–53. Several similar examples are given.

16. Ibid., p. 251.

17. Quoted in Susy Smith, *The Conversion of a Psychic* (Garden City, N.Y.: Doubleday, 1978), pp. 69–70.

18. Ibid., p. 251.

19. Ibid., p. 250.

20. Harper, p. 92.

21. Quoted in Baker, p. 251.

22. Ibid.

23. Campolo, *How to Be Pentecostal,* p. 32.

24. Smith, *The Conversion of a Psychic,* p. 68.

25. Baker, *Hidden Memories,* p. 251.

26. Ibid., p. 254.

27. "Speaking in Tongues 'Linguistic Nonsense,' Says U of T Professor," *The Toronto Star,* August 26, 1972; William Samarin, *Tongues of Men and Angels* (New York: Macmillan, 1972), p. 70.

28. Martin Gardner, "Glossolalia," *Free Inquiry* 9.2 (Spring 1989): 48.

29. Ibid.

30. Asimov, *Asimov's Guide to the Bible,* vol. 2: 338; "Prophet," *Encyclopaedia Britannica,* 1960 ed.

31. Campolo, *How to Be Pentecostal,* p. 39.

32. Owen S. Rachleff, *The Occult Conceit* (Chicago: Cowles, 1971), pp. 136–37.

33. Ibid., p. 137.

34. Carol C. Calkins, ed., *Mysteries of the Unexplained* (Pleasantville, N.Y.: Reader's Digest Association, 1982), p. 13.

35. Asimov, *Asimov's Guide to the Bible,* vol. 2: 229.

36. Daniel Cohen, *The Encyclopedia of the Strange* (New York: Dorset, 1985), pp. 143–50.

37. James Randi, "Nostradamus: The Prophet for All Seasons," *The Skeptical Inquirer* 7.1 (Fall, 1982): 30–37; Terrence Hines, *Pseudoscience and the Paranormal* (Buffalo, N.Y.: Prometheus Books, 1988), pp. 39–42.

38. Rachleff, *The Occult Conceit,* p. 138.

39. See Joe Nickell, *Wonder-Workers! How They Perform the Impossible* (Buffalo, N.Y.: Prometheus Books, 1991), pp. 48–49.

40. P. Phillips, ed., *Out of This World: The Illustrated Library of the Bizarre and Extraordinary,* vol. 9 ([England]: 1978), p. 66.

41. Fort Worth (Texas) *Star-Telegram,* April 5, 1968.

42. Milbourne Christopher, *ESP, Seers & Psychics* (New York: Thomas Y. Crowell, 1970), p. 79. See also "Jeane Dixon Predicts . . .," *Chicago Tribune,* June 23, 1968.

43. Ibid., pp. 80–81.

44. Ibid., pp. 81–83.

45. G. M. Behe, "The *Titanic:* A Disaster Forseen?" *Fate,* June 1990, pp. 44–50; Cohen, *The Encyclopedia of the Strange,* pp. 227–80.

46. Cohen, *The Encyclopedia of the Strange,* p. 280.

47. Kendrick Frazier and James Randi, "Prediction after the Fact, Lessons of the Tamara Rand Hoax," *The Skeptical Inquirer* 6.1 (Fall 1981): 4–7; Hines, *Pseudoscience and the Paranormal,* pp. 43–44.

48. Thomas Goltz, " 'Doomsday' Church Wears Out Its Welcome in Montana Town," *The Atlanta Journal and Constitution,* April 29, 1990.

49. Michael Norman, "Seeking Signs in Headlines," Cleveland *Plain Dealer,* January 20, 1991.

50. Charles Mackay, *Extraordinary Popular Delusions and the Madness of Crowds* (1841; reprint New York: Harmony Books, 1980).

51. Gerald A. Larue, *The Supernatural, the Occult, and the Bible* (Buffalo, N.Y.: Prometheus Books, 1990), p. 212. See also "Mark," *Encyclopaedia Britannica,* 1960 ed.

52. Larue, *The Supernatural, the Occult, and the Bible,* p. 212.

53. "Realm of the Serpent," ABC documentary, March 8, 1992; Jim Yardley, "Mark of the Serpent" and "Poison and the Pulpit," *The Atlanta Constitution,* February 9, 1992.

54. "Snake-Handling Cult Claims Another Victim," *The Secular Humanist Bulletin* 8.1 (Spring 1992): 7; D. Scott Rogo, *Miracles* (New York: Dial Press, 1982), p. 5.

55. "Snake-Handling Cult Claims Another Victim," p. 7.

56. Gayle White, "They Take Up Serpents with Faith 'Good Enough to Die By,' " *The Atlanta Constitution,* April 16, 1990.

57. Dennis Covington, "Alabama Trial Involves Snakes and Bit of Faith," *The New York Times,* February 15, 1992.

58. Larue, *The Supernatural, the Occult, and the Bible,* p. 212.

59. "Testimony," *The Dictionary of Beliefs* (East Grinstead, England: Ward Lock Educational, 1984), p. 187.

60. Larue, *The Supernatural, the Occult, and the Bible,* p. 212.

61. Yardley, "Poison and the Pulpit."

62. White, "They Take Up Serpents."

63. Ibid.

64. Ibid.

65. Alexandra Parsons, *Amazing Snakes* (New York: Alfred A. Knopf, 1990), p. 15.

66. Chris Mattison, *A–Z of Snake Keeping* (New York: Sterling Publishing Co., 1991), p. 56.

67. Ibid., p. 57.

68. Bianca Lavies, *The Secretive Timber Rattlesnake* (New York: Dalton, 1990), pp. [4–5].

69. Russell Freedman, *Killer Snakes* (New York: Holiday House, 1982), p. 33.

70. Ibid., p. 32.

71. Hobart M. Smith and Edmund D. Brodie, Jr., *A Guide to Field Identification: Reptiles of North America* (New York: Golden Press, 1982), p. 10.

72. Joel Hartley, M.D., *First Aid without Panic* (New York: Hart Publishing Co, 1975), pp. 139–40.

73. Smith and Brodie, *A Guide to Field Identification,* p. 9.

74. Lowell J. Thomas and Joy L. Sanderson, *First Aid for Backpackers and Campers* (New York: Holt, Rinehart and Winston, 1978), p. 45.

75. Smith and Brodie, *A Guide to Field Identification,* p. 10.

76. Yardley, "Poison and the Pulpit."

77. Smith and Brodie, *A Guide to Field Identification,* p. 10; Bry Benjamin and Annette Francis Benjamin, *In Case of Emergency* (Garden City, N.Y.: Doubleday, 1965), p. 117.

78. Thomas and Sanderson, *First Aid for Backpackers and Campers,* pp. 42–47. See also Benjamin and Benjamin, *In Case of Emergency,* pp. 114–18; Hartley, *First Aid without Panic,* pp. 139–43.

79. Raymond L. Ditmars, *Reptiles of the World* (New York: Macmillan, 1959), p. 125.

80. Yardley, "Poison and the Pulpit."

81. White, "They Take Up Serpents."

82. Ibid.

83. Yardley, "Mark of the Serpent."

84. *Webster's New International Dictionary,* 2d ed. (Springfield, Mass.: G.

& C. Merriman Co., 1955). See also "Strychnine," *Encyclopaedia Britannica,* 1960 ed., and *Encyclopaedia Americana,* 1990 ed.

85. "Strychnine," *Encyclopaedia Britannica,* 1960 ed.

86. Yardley, "Poison and the Pulpit."

87. Ibid.

88. "Strychnine," *Encyclopaedia Britannica,* 1960 ed.

89. Ditmars, *Reptiles of the World,* p. 125.

90. D. Scott Rogo, *Miracles* (New York: Dial Press, 1982), p. 5.

91. Dr. Berthold Schwarz, quoted in Rogo, *Miracles.*

92. Rogo, *Miracles,* p. 6.

93. From Joe Nickell, *Wonder-Workers!* (Buffalo, N.Y.: Prometheus Books, 1991), p. 14.

94. Ibid., pp. 14–15.

95. See Milbourne Christopher, *Panorama of Magic* (New York: Dover, 1962), pp. 2, 36–40; Edwin A. Dawes, *The Great Illusionists* (Secaucus, N.J.: Chartwell Books, 1979), pp. 57–60; Walter Gibson, *Secrets of Magic: Ancient and Modern* (New York: Grosset & Dunlap, 1967), pp. 41–43.

96. Ibid. (n. 95); see also Minnie Vaid-Fera, "On the Trail of the Godmen," *Imprint,* October 1987, p. 62.

97. Interview with Ida Mae Elam, West Liberty, Ky., June 23, 1992.

98. Gibson, *Secrets of Magic,* pp. 92–94; Bernard J. Leikind and William T. McCarthy, "An Investigation of Firewalking," *The Skeptical Inquirer* 10.1 (Fall 1985): 23–34.

99. From a biography of the saint, quoted by Rogo, *Miracles,* p. 4.

100. Rogo, *Miracles,* p. 4.

101. "Miracles," *Encyclopaedia Britannica,* 1960 ed.

102. Covington, "Alabama Trial Involves Snakes and a Bit of Faith."

103. Interview with John A. May, an electronics engineer, June 24, 1992.

6

Faith Healing

Claims for the efficacy of faith healing—the belief that cures of diseases and other ailments can be effected by divine intervention (invoked by prayer, the laying on of hands, or the like)—are among the claims of the miraculous that are most widely reported and taken most seriously. This should come as no surprise since illness—including chronic, painful, and fatal conditions—has always plagued mankind.

The ancient Egyptians worshiped various gods, including the ibis-headed Thoth, who could be appealed to for healing—typically with the priests playing the role of intermediaries.[1] In Mesopotamia, angry gods were believed to cause many ailments, and a sufferer was in an especially bad predicament if he was unsure just which deity he had offended! One such petitioner—whose prayer was discovered in the library of the Assyrian king Ashurbanipal (668–633 B.C.)—exhorts:

> May the god whom I either know or do not know be at peace with me. May the goddess whom I either know or do not know be at peace with me.

Begging for mercy, he wonders,

> How long, O my goddess whom I either know or do not know, will it be before your heart be at peace?[2]

The ancient Greeks also appealed to their gods for healing. The temple of Aesculapius—the god of medicine, who was assisted by the "boy genius" or divine healer, Telesphorus—was especially important in this regard, but the cult eventually yielded to Christianity.[3]

As demonstrated in the Old Testament, the ancient Jews universally recognized Yahweh (Jehovah) as the single cause of sickness and disease. If Israel should sin, Yahweh threatened not only plagues and pestilence but also "consumption and the burning ague that shall consume the eyes" (Lev. 26: 16–26). Conversely, Yahweh was also the sole source of healing and restoration. Prayers to Yahweh could effect magical healing, although they might be accompanied by folk medical treatment. For example, King Hezekiah was cured of a supposedly fatal illness—an ulcerous boil—by means of a fig poultice and prayer (2 Kings 20:1–11). Similarly, invocation of the power of Yahweh, together with a ritualistic washing in the Jordan River (performed seven times to tap the potency of a magical number) cured Naaman the Syrian of his leprosy. (Actually, what was termed "leprosy" in the Bible was probably often psoriasis, a disease known to be responsive to a reduction of stress.) Again, gazing upon a brass serpent—placed upon a pole at the direction of Yahweh—could cure Israelites bitten by serpents during the Exodus from Egypt.[4]

Interestingly, however, as Gerald Larue observes:

The Book of Job is a forthright refutation of the theological doctrine of the relationship between sin and suffering. The author of the book carefully set the stage. Job is portrayed as a righteous man. This is affirmed by Yahweh, Satan, and the author. He did nothing to offend Yahweh. He broke no religious rules. He had been faithful in observing cultic rites. His terrible afflictions were caused not by sin but by a cruel wager between Yahweh and Yahweh's son, Satan.

Yahweh had boasted of Job's loyalty and righteousness. Satan suggested that the pious behavior could be explained by the blessings and rewards with which God had favored Job. In other words, Job was pious because piety paid off in material goods. Yahweh decided to put Job to the test. Would this righteous man curse the deity when he lost all his goods and when his health was impaired? Job's material wealth and his family, with the exception of his wife, were wiped out. His body was afflicted with hideous sores. No sin or violation of the divine will was involved, and Job did not curse Yahweh.

Moreover,

The conclusion of the story provided Job with little reassurance and no understanding. God announced that the counselors were wrong. Job was not being punished for his sins (indeed, how could he be, inasmuch as he was righteous?). Job never learned why he suffered. The cruel and unethical wager that resulted in brutal treatment by his God remained a divine secret (to Job at least; it was revealed, of course, to the readers of the story). Wealth and health were restored to Job and he acquired a new family.[5]

In Christianity, Jesus became a source of restorative power, bringing a healing ministry and effecting miraculous cures of both mind and body wherever he went. Not counting duplicate or parallel accounts, the gospels record more than forty healing acts—representing in some instances the cure of an individual, and in others the healing of entire groups. Jesus also gave his disciples the power of healing, saying of those who believe that "they shall lay hands on the sick, and they shall recover" (Mark 16: 15–18).

This was the authority for the healing tradition in early Christianity. Subsequent practices of the Roman Catholic and Eastern Orthodox churches employed various amulets and relics to effect cures, while the Protestant reformers eschewed all such practices. To Calvin and Luther the age of faith healings ended with the death of the apostles, and that view has prevailed in churches associated with those reformers.[6] In fact, in 1962, the United Lutheran Church appointed a commission of doctors and theologians to investigate faith healing as it was performed by certain practitioners. In their report, the investigators charged that for money and power faith healers exploited the desperate, ignored proven scientific treatments, and blamed their failures on the sick people's lack of sufficient faith.[7]

Nevertheless, "miraculous" healing practices continue in the Catholic and Orthodox faiths and have been revived among certain Protestants by the charismatic movement—especially Pentecostals.

How Faith Healing "Cures"

Healing occurs naturally in the body. Wounds routinely mend, broken bones knit, infections respond to the body's immune system, and so on. While this natural process may be assisted—cuts may be cleaned and bound, fractures splinted, a fever reduced with a cool sponge bath or medication—quite often the body's own self-healing mechanisms will respond effectively. It has been estimated that up to 75 percent of patients would get better even if they received no medical treatment.[8]

Indeed, some serious ailments, including certain types of cancer, may undergo what is called "spontaneous remission." That is, they may go away entirely or, as is sometimes the case with multiple sclerosis, for example, they may abate for periods ranging from a few months to several years. Although the nature of such remissions is still not fully understood by medical science, the fact of their unpredictable occurrence is well documented. If a remission or regression occurs any time after a faith healer has performed his ritualistic ministrations, it may be falsely attributed to the healer's intervention.[9]

So may illnesses that have been misdiagnosed or simply misreported—occurrences less uncommon than are popularly believed.[10] In one case a girl's "inoperable, malignant brain-stem tumor" was supposedly confirmed by two CT scans and attested by doctors at Johns Hopkins University. Actually, medical investigator Dr. Gary P. Posner discovered that the "dark mass" in the CT scan was merely an imperfection of the scanning process, that the girl's physicians had not suspected a tumor at all, and that subsequently the "miracle" was an invented one.[11]

Psychosomatic illnesses—those which demonstrate the interrelationship of mind (*psyche*) and body (*soma*)—are most amenable to "miraculous" healing. An impressive variety of such ailments, ranging from back pains to hysterical blindness, are known to be highly responsive to the power of suggestion, whether it takes the form of faith healing, chiropractic or acupuncture treatments, so-called hypnosis, or placebo medications—the main requisite for curative effects being the patient's belief in the practitioner's assurances.[12]

Even illnesses that have distinct physical causes may also be partially responsive to what is called "mental medicine." For example, techniques of meditation and "visualization"—in which the patient is encouraged to focus mentally on his or her condition and envision its cure (e.g., that a tumor is disappearing)—have been used in conjunction with traditional medicine to treat such conditions as high blood pressure, gastrointestional disorders, arthritis, and cancer.[13] Just as physical ailments can be exacerbated by worry and other forms of stress, positive attitudes seem to enhance the body's healing capacities.[14]

Pain is especially responsive to suggestion—just as it is to the physiological effects of excitement. (For example, there are numerous well-documented cases of injured persons acting as if unharmed in emergency situations.) Various studies show that such pain reduction is due to the body's release of substances known as endorphins. As psychologist Terence Hines states in his *Pseudoscience and the Paranormal,* "The placebo effect and the temporal variability of pain in any painful disease work together to produce a powerful illusion that a faith healer or a quack has effected a 'cure.' "[15]

How such processes can seem to effect a miracle—and the tragic consequences that may result—are illustrated by a case investigated by William A. Nolen, M.D., author of *Healing: A Doctor in Search of a Miracle.* At a "Miracle Service" held by the late Kathryn Kuhlman, the evangelist shouted, "Someone here is being cured of cancer." In response, Mrs. Helen Sullivan (a pseudonym) left her wheelchair and hobbled onto the stage. According to Nolen:

> Mrs. Sullivan had, at Kathryn Kuhlman's suggestion, taken off her back brace and run back and forth across the stage several times. Finally, she walked back down the aisle to her wheelchair, waving her brace as she went, while the audience applauded and Kathryn Kuhlman gave thanks to the Lord.[16]

In fact no miracle—not even a cure—took place. When Dr. Nolen investigated by following up on the case and interviewing Mrs. Sullivan two months later, she told him she had attended the "Miracle Service" in expectation of a cure. She went on to state:

> At the service, as soon as she [Kathryn Kuhlman] said, "Someone with cancer is being cured," I knew she meant me. I could just feel this burning sensation all over my body and I was convinced the Holy Spirit was at work. I went right up on the stage and when she asked me about the brace I just took it right off, though I hadn't had it off for over four months, I had so much back pain. I was sure I was cured. That night I said a prayer of thanksgiving to the Lord and Kathryn Kuhlman and went to bed, happier than I'd been in a long time. At four o'clock the next morning I woke up with a horrible pain in my back. It was so bad I broke out in a cold sweat. I didn't dare move.[17]

X-rays revealed that a cancer-weakened vertebra had collapsed due to the strain placed on it during the demonstration. Two months later, Mrs. Sullivan died.[18]

Nolen investigated many similar "cures" without finding a single miracle. In the excitement of an evangelical revival, the reduction of pain due to endorphin release often causes people to believe and act as if they have been miraculously healed, whereas later investigation reveals their situation is as bad—or even worse—than before. It is the illusion, however, and not the reality that is witnessed by thousands and cited as "proof" of miraculous cures.

As a consequence, one should regard testimonials from those who have allegedly been cured with appropriate skepticism. States Hines:

> One can find testimonials attesting to the effectiveness of almost anything. In the early part of this century, before government regulation of advertising claims for medicines, it was common for manufacturers to claim that their particular brand of "snake oil" would cure "consumption," as tuberculosis was known then. They would provide genuine and sincere testimonials from people who had actually used their medicine and felt themselves to be cured. These people would later die of tuberculosis, because the remedies were in fact worthless.

Hines adds:

> My own favorite testimonial touts a cure for cancer and cataracts so bizarre that it's difficult to believe it's not a joke. *Time* magazine, in its October 24, 1977, issue, reported that then Indian Prime Minister Morarji Desai attributed his vigor at age eighty-one to drinking a cup of his own urine each morning. He said "it was a cure for cancer and cataracts; he claimed to have cured his own brother of tuberculosis" with urine. This item promptly brought another testimonial to the effectiveness of "urine therapy," which was published in *Time*'s "Letters" column in the November 14, 1977, issue. One Harish Jirmoun of New Bern, North Carolina, reported that he had adopted the custom of drinking his own urine and "have faithfully maintained it for the past twelve years, gaining a sense of vigor that few of my contemporaries (I am 74) can match." It is safe to say that if testimonials play a major part in the "come on" for a cure or therapy, the cure or therapy is almost certainly worthless. If the promoters of the therapy had actual evidence for its effectiveness, they would cite it and not have to rely on testimonials.[19]

Finally, some of the most dramatic evidence offered by faith healers is actually the result of trickery—conscious deception on the part of the alleged miracle worker. As we shall see, fraud performed in the guise of holiness is much more common than many people are willing to believe.

"Healing," Hoopla, and Hoaxes

The Rev. Peter Popoff is director of an Upland, California, based religious empire that is estimated to rake in between ten and twenty million tax-free dollars a year. He claims that as a child he witnessed his father transform water into wine for a wartime communion service in Berlin. Now Popoff *fils* works miracles—or so many are led to believe.

An "Anointed Minister of God," the evangelist combines his gift of healing with demonstrations of another of the Pentecostal gifts enumerated in 1 Corinthians—that of the Word of Knowledge. This "gift" consists of one receiving, directly from God, special messages that are then to be imparted to others. Usually such messages cannot be verified as having emanated from a divine source, so the typical procedure seems to be to credit those that coincide with one's views and discount those that do not. States one Pentecostal writer:

> I have people come up to me regularly with such messages just before or after I preach. Personally, I must admit that I am usually put off by most of these "gifted" people and discount what they tell me. However, I have to learn to be careful. After all, I may be cutting myself off from a revelation that I very much need.[20]

But Popoff's gift was openly demonstrated, taking the form of "calling out" audience members for healing and telling them their diseases, naming their doctors, stating their addresses, and providing similar information—all promptly verified by the individuals concerned. Popoff specifically claimed the information came directly from God.

For example, at a service in Anaheim, California, on March 16, 1986, Popoff called out: "Virgil. Is it Jorgenson? Who is Virgil?"—whereupon a man in the audience identified himself as Jorgenson. Then Popoff continued: "Are you ready for God to overhaul those knees?" As the man reacted to Popoff's amazing knowledge about him, the evangelist continued: "Oh, glory to God. I'll tell you, God's going to touch that sister of yours all the way over in Sweden." Popoff then took the "healed" man's cane. Breaking it over his knee, Popoff stood by as the man walked about unaided, giving praise to both Popoff and God.[21]

Popoff's alleged gift was soon revealed as blatant trickery. The noted magician and paranormal investigator, James "the Amazing" Randi—wondering at the alleged healer's wearing of an apparent hearing aid—began to suspect that the device might actually be a tiny radio receiver and that someone was secretly broadcasting the information that was alleged to come from God.

As it happened, the evangelist's wife, Elizabeth Popoff, was obtaining the relevant information from so-called prayer cards that attendees filled out before the service. As Randi learned by smuggling in an electronics expert with computerized scanning equipment, Mrs. Popoff broadcast the information to her husband from backstage. Her first recorded message was intended only for his ears: "Hello, Petey. I love you. I'm talking to you. Can you hear me? If you can't, you're in trouble. . . ."[22] The session with the spectator named Jorgenson (actually investigator Don Henvick!) sounded like this when Mrs. Popoff's secret broadcasts were also heard:

Elizabeth Popoff transmits to Peter Popoff:
    "Virgil Jorgenson. Virgil."
    Peter Popoff calls out "Virgil."
    Elizabeth: "Jorgenson."
    Peter (inquiringly): "Is it Jorgenson?"
    Elizabeth: "Way back in the back somewhere. Arthritis in knees. He's got a cane."
    Peter: Are you ready for God to overhaul those knees?"
    Elizabeth. "He's got arthritis. He's praying for his sister in Sweden, too."
    Peter: "Oh, glory to God. I'll tell you, God's going to touch that sister of yours all the way over in Sweden."

Many similar "calling out" sessions of the service were also intercepted and recorded.

Randi played a videotape of one of the sessions in before-and-after fashion on Johnny Carson's "Tonight Show." This was so that viewers could appreciate the original effect of Popoff's apparent gift of knowledge, followed by the revelation provided by the secret broadcast. Popoff reacted first by denying everything; his ministry later charged that the videotapes had been "doctored" by NBC. Finally, he admitted to use of the "communicator" device (the radio receiver) but attempted to deny any intention to deceive. In fact, however, Randi had videotaped documentation to the contrary.[24]

Randi's investigation uncovered other deceptions—notably those by Dallas-based faith healer W(alter) V(inson) Grant. Grant dresses in tailored suits and wears monogrammed shirts and expensive jewelry. Although he is apparently unable to cure his own stammer, he claims to give the blind sight and make the lame walk.

As reported by Randi, one of Grant's deceptions was similar to Popoff's, except that instead of the "hearing aid" he used a more primitive method. Members of his staff chatted with attendees before the healing service began in order to gather the necessary information. This was transferred to "crib sheets" that were placed on Grant's podium so he could perform the "calling out" stunt. (After one of Grant's services in Fort Lauderdale, Florida, Randi searched the nearby trash dumpsters and found one of the crib sheets, reproducing it in his book.)[25]

Another Grant trick is to "heal" someone in a wheelchair who then leaps out of the chair and pushes Grant down the aisle in it triumphantly. The crowd invariably cheers. It is an old stunt, one apparently originated by Kathryn Kuhlman (mentioned earlier). Explains Randi:

> When I looked into this trick, I was immediately struck by two facts: First, disabled persons who spend much of their lives in a wheelchair naturally equip it for their specific needs, and Grant *never* summoned from a wheelchair any person who had personalized the device. Second, almost all of those who rose up "healed" did so from one color, model, and make of wheelchair; even Grant's slick, expensive four-color magazine, *Dawn of a New Day,* showed those same wheelchairs in the illustrations, every issue.

Randi interviewed one person whom Grant had supposedly healed of cancer earlier in the day.

> He'd been told by the evangelist, "Get up out of that wheelchair and walk!" and he'd done so, vigorously. Questioning revealed that his cancer was no impediment to his walking ability. In fact, we interviewed him at his home, where he lived in a fourth-floor walk-up whose stairs he had to negotiate several times a day! Why had he been in the wheelchair? Because, he said, his pastor had told him to sit in it when he arrived at the auditorium. The chair was supplied by an usher. He'd never been in a wheelchair before in his life.[26]

One of Grant's most sensational feats is what Randi dubs " 'the leg-stretching' miracle," explaining:

> At every crusade meeting, Reverend Grant announces that a subject has "a short leg" that needs to be adjusted. He brings the person on stage, and seats him on a chair facing across the stage but slightly turned to the audience. He lifts both legs up, parallel to the floor. At this point, the spectators see that one leg (the one nearest them) appears shorter by about two inches, judged by the relative positions of the heels of the shoes or boots. During some heavy incantations, with Grant holding both feet resting upon his one hand, the short leg seems to lengthen to match the other one.

As Randi continues:

> The stunt is similar to one that is still a carnival mainstay. "The Man Who Grows" is the name of the act. In this performance, a man is revealed onstage who seems to fit his clothes well enough. He is seen to go into a "trance" and appears to grow by seven or eight inches, by which time his sleeves are far too short and his pants to half-mast as well. The gimmick is simple: The man is dressed in a too-small suit, and only has to "scrunch down" while in a standing position. The suit appears to fit him at this point, but as he straightens up and swells out his chest, the bad fit becomes apparent. It is a striking illusion, often enhanced by a popping belt buckle and falling shirt buttons thrown in for further effect.
>
> Grant's trick is even simpler. His subject must be wearing loose shoes; cowboy boots are far better. As the subject sits, Grant merely places his hand beneath the feet, twisting his hand so that one shoe is pulled slightly off the foot (the farther one) and the other shoe is pressed tightly against the sole (the nearer one). By reversing the twist, the farther shoe is pushed on against that sole and the two shoes—as well as the two feet!—are now seen to be the same length.[27]

Randi provides photographs that confirm his analysis.[28]

Although Grant sometimes used a member of the audience for the leg-lengthening trick, on at least one occasion he used what in carney talk is known as a "shill." This was discovered by Terence Hines, who—at Randi's suggestion—enlisted as one of Grant's volunteer ushers. He discovered that one man used for the leg stunt was actually a member of Grant's staff. After the man was "healed," states Hines: "Another huge cheer went up, and Grant's latest miracle cure walked, without limping, offstage. Of course, he hadn't limped when he came onstage, but I suspect this was not widely noticed."[29]

Hines tells of another Grant deception he witnessed. Approaching one woman, the evangelical healer inquired how long she had been blind. "Partially," she corrected him, but he ignored her and, addressing the audience, asked if they had faith that Jesus could cure her. "Yes!" shouted the crowd, whereupon Grant, holding up several fingers, asked the woman, "How many?" As Hines reports: "She promptly gave the correct answer— not surprisingly, since she was only partially blind. But Grant was given credit for yet another miraculous cure."[30]

As part of Randi's investigation, skeptic Don Henvick donned suitable disguises and adopted various pseudonyms to attend the services of several faith healers. As "Abel McMinn" he was healed of a nonexistent prostate condition by W. V. Grant. As "Tom Hendrys" he was cured of nonexistent alcoholism by the Rev. David Paul. And as "Bernice Manicoff"—suitably coiffed and garbed—he was "cured" of uterine cancer by Peter Popoff![31]

Actually Henvick out-conned Popoff several times. After some previous "healings" by Popoff, Henvick shaved his beard and mustache, thinned his hair, dyed the remainder gray, and limped about with a cane. Says a fellow investigator:

> It was this superb skill in out-conning the con artist and his wonderful acting ability that got Don "Virgil Jorgenson" Henvick shown on the televised Popoff show for three weeks running. He was now on his way to be "healed" again.[32]

Another who was appropriately deceived by Henvick was Grace Di-Biccari, a former beautician and singer turned faith healer, who uses the stage name "Amazing Grace." According to magician Robert A. Steiner, a member of the Randi investigative team who appeared with Sister Grace (as she is also styled) on a television program:

> When I first came out, I asked for and received clear assurance from Grace that she had the Gift of Knowledge, that her information came directly from God, and that God never makes a mistake.
>
> I then produced my secret weapon. The first person she had chosen to "heal" was (Are you ready?) Don Henvick. By exposing the fact that

Grace healed him under an assumed name of a nonexistent ailment, I was able to show that her claim was false, that her information does not come from God.[33]

At least one faith healer, the Rev. Willard Fuller of Palatka, Florida, specializes in remedying dental conditions. Calling himself "The Psychic Dentist," Fuller causes fillings to appear spontaneously, turns silver crowns to gold, straightens crooked teeth—even miraculously produces new teeth —or so he claims, in Jesus' name. Unfortunately, Fuller refuses to supply skeptics with the identities of some who were allegedly healed, such as a woman whom he claimed "re-grew an entire new set of teeth."[34]

One dentist examined twenty-eight people prior to their "healing" by Fuller, then re-examined those who claimed to be healed. In one instance, "gold fillings miraculously bestowed turned out instead to be tobacco stains." In another instance, a woman who reported miraculously receiving a new silver filling changed her mind when confronted with pictures taken before the service. She then "readily admitted that she had forgotten that the filling was there."[35]

Interestingly, Rev. Fuller, who was convicted in Australia of fraud and practicing dentistry without a license,[36] has no fewer than six missing teeth himself, while the remainder are "badly stained and contain quite ordinary fillings"![37]

Several self-proclaimed healers have discovered that the "laying on of hands" spoken of in the Bible in not necessary, and that they can heal easily from a distance. Oral Roberts, for example, began as a tent-show healer with "God-anointed hands," but he eventually worked his "miracles" via radio, television, recordings, and other media while operating his ministry from a $500 million "City of Faith" complex and business conglomerate in Tulsa, Oklahoma. Roberts has claimed countless healings, as well as frequent resurrections from the dead! However, he has refused repeated requests—including one from a Church of Christ in 1955 and another by James Randi in 1986—to submit convincing proof that any miracle healing ever took place. (In 1992 Roberts sold his City of Faith medical complex and joined his son on television—said one writer, "as if the two evangelists were carnival barkers with Jesus their top attraction.")[38]

Fundamentalist Pat Robertson—due to his high media profile and his presidential aspirations—is another whom Randi challenged to prove his claims. A typical Robertson TV performance involved him bowing his head to receive a "Word of Knowledge" from God, then proclaiming miraculous healings and other miracles for anonymous beneficiaries. For example, on one occasion Robertson stated:

> There is a woman in Kansas City who has sinus. The Lord is drying that up right now. Thank you, Jesus. There is a man with a financial need—I think a hundred thousand dollars. That need is being met right now, and within three days, the money will be supplied through the miraculous power of the Holy Spirit. Thank you, Jesus! There is a woman in Cincinnati with cancer of the lymph nodes. I don't know whether it's been diagnosed yet, but you haven't been feeling well, and the Lord is dissolving that cancer right *now!* There is a lady in Saskatchewan in a wheelchair—curvature of the spine. The Lord is straightening that out right now, and you can stand up and walk![39]

However, Randi insists that "Robertson has refused to produce *one case* of his that will stand examination."[40] (Interestingly enough, Robertson's Christian Broadcasting Network and 700 Club also lack accountability. According to a *USA Today* report, those "charitable" organizations "flunk accountability and spending standards" maintained by the Better Business Bureau.[41])

Televangelist Robert "Bob" Tilton, of Dallas, Texas, who speaks in tongues, has a clever way of helping people engage his special power over long distances. As I learned firsthand, Tilton responds to requests for information about his ministry by sending a "miracle package." This consists of a special form on which to trace one's hand and to write one's prayer requests; a red "Miracle Prayer Cloth" (a postcard-size swatch of cheap fabric); a tiny package of "Anointing Oil"; and other items, including a booklet, life-size poster of Tilton, and envelopes for sending money. Tilton promises, "I'm going to lay my hand on top of your hand that you trace, and I'll begin to pray over your cloth." He avows:

> When you receive this cloth back from me, no longer will this be common red cloth, but it will become a PRAYER OF AGREEMENT MIRACLE-WORKING, HEALING CLOTH . . . every fiber will be saturated with the very Presence and Power of God, according to Acts 19: 11–12.

In the meantime, one can place one's hand on the photo of Tilton's hand on the poster—"our miracle point of contact"—as a reciprocal gesture "to break the principalities and the powers of darkness that may be hindering your miracle answer." Then,

When you receive the enclosed Miracle Cloth back from me, open the enclosed special package of oil and anoint the point of your need. . . . Anoint yourself or a loved one with this Prayer of Agreement Miracle Oil as you agree with me for your toughest needs to be met by God. Let the Holy Spirit lead you in applying this Miracle Anointing Oil and Miracle Cloth in faith to pictures of your loved ones, to your billfold, to the doorposts of your home, to your body. However He shows you, apply this Miracle Cloth and Anointing Oil in faith for special miracles.

Of course, one must be "obedient to God in sowing your finances into His Kingdom" (translation: SEND MONEY) and include with the cloth one's "best gift to God" (that is, GIVE ALL THE CASH YOU CAN SPARE). Over a three-week period, one is to use a second envelope to "put in a little extra seed" and a third "to send God a thanksgiving offering toward your vow in expectancy of your miracle" (in other words, KEEP THE MONEY COMING). Also, "Remember to send God a sweet-smelling sacrifice . . . an offering in faith to Him of $100, $35, $50, $15, $1000 or more" (i.e., SEND WHATEVER YOU CAN SCRAPE TO-GETHER TO GOD—IN CARE OF BOB, OF COURSE). Tilton quotes James 2:20: "Faith without corresponding actions is dead" (interpretation: IF YOUR MIRACLE DOESN'T OCCUR, YOU DIDN'T SEND ENOUGH CASH).[42]

Tilton's "Success-N-Life" television show makes similar requests, asking viewers to send in "prayer requests" and $1000. In return, Tilton promises to bless the letters and (according to *USA Today*) "through God, deliver to the true believer miracle cures and material wealth."

However, an exposé by investigative reporters showed that Tilton simply tosses the letters into the trash, after extracting the money. (Tilton responded that he did pray over the letters—in piles of 200,000 at a time.) Further investigations were soon in progress—by the FBI, IRS, U.S. Postal Service, the Texas Attorney General, and others—but in one court battle Tilton successfully blocked demands to turn over most of the financial records of his $65 million Word of Faith ministry.[43]

Tilton conceded that his church lost 1,000 of its approximately 8,000 members in the wake of news reports about the investigations, and his mail-order fount of donations from the gullible may now gush less freely. Tilton claims he is being "persecuted." As he told his congregation,

It's faith on trial. It's spiritual wickedness in high places. . . . If you want to get right down to the persecution this church is having, the root of it is religion.

Meanwhile, the "persecution" continued. Two Oklahoma widows were each suing Tilton for $40 million, saying that he repeatedly sent form letters promising to heal their husbands—long after the men had died.[44]

Although thus far we have considered Protestant faith healers, some would-be miracle workers are Catholic and have the cautious approval of the Vatican. One is Father Ralph DiOrio, a Massachusetts-based charismatic who follows in the footsteps of the late Kathryn Kuhlman. In fact, he dedicated himself to healing on the day of Kuhlman's death, and it was on the anniversary of her birth that he first attempted a cure. Since then, DiOrio has claimed hundreds of miraculous healings—healings which he claims are documented by a "medical team" from his organization, the Apostolate of Prayer for Healing Evangelism in Leicester, Massachusetts. Alas, DiOrio failed to respond to James Randi's request for evidence that would verify the priest's claims.[45] DiOrio was defended, however, by a bishop's representative, the Rev. George Lange, who told a reporter:

Everyone wants to know whether [Father DiOrio's] cures are real or not. I say that they are. Sure, some are psychosomatic, and some hysterical, and some can be explained through natural reason. I don't have any problem with that, because they're still real. There's no great reason to prove them because when a doctor provides the means of healing, you feel God is working through him. God is working throughout a person's life. It's not that important to prove that it's extraordinary or divine intervention.[46]

What an equivocal defense that is! Unfortunately, such evasions and rationalizations are all too typical of faith-healing evangelists and their apologists.

Lourdes

Notwithstanding Father DiOrio and other charismatic Catholic faith healers, when most people link cures with Catholicism they doubtless think first of Lourdes—the French shrine popularly credited with countless healing miracles since the middle of the last century. Today, Lourdes still attracts more supplicants—millions each year—than any other healing site in the world.

The shrine originated, almost predictably it seems, as part of "an extraordinary revival of the pilgrimage" that took place in the nineteenth century.[47] It began with an alleged apparition, witnessed, like so many others,[48] by a peasant. In this case the seer was the illiterate daughter of a miller at Lourdes, a town in the foothills of the Pyrenees.

On February 11, 1858, Bernadette Soubirous, age fourteen, was gathering firewood along the river bank with her sister and a friend. Suddenly she heard a rustling in the hedge above a nearby grotto (a cave called Massabeille) and looked up to see "something white" in the form of a young girl. Neither of the other girls saw or heard anything.

On Sunday, February 14, after High Mass, Bernadette returned to the grotto accompanied by several other young girls. They all knelt and were saying the rosary when the figure appeared for the second time—again only to Bernadette. On a third occasion (February 18), she claimed the apparition requested her to visit the grotto for each of fifteen days. Now, watched by up to a thousand or more people, Bernadette would stand stiffly, occasionally smiling or moving her lips as if she were actually communicating with an invisible being. When Bernadette was ready to leave, she would usually indicate the fact by making a sign, whereupon those who gathered around would kneel in unison.

Moreover, as shown by contemporary sources, those who came to the grotto or who sought Bernadette out elsewhere "already saw and treated her as if she were a saint." Indeed:

> When she held up her rosary during one of the earlier episodes of the apparition sequence, those in the crowd who had rosaries held them up also. When she left the grotto, many people tried to kiss her, and many who could not do so reportedly scraped up earth from her path and kissed this instead. Bernadette had become for the masses, the local paper concluded, "the interpreter if . . . not the image of a superior power."[49]

Originally, Bernadette had referred to the figure as *aquerò,* meaning "that one," describing her as being about her own age, clothed in a white dress having a blue waistband, and carrying on her arm a rosary. Some seemed to think Bernadette had seen a ghost, and at least one woman suggested the description fit that of a recently deceased girl named Elisa Latapie.[50]

According to one scholarly source, commenting on the historical records pertaining to the events, "It is not clear from the documents just who first concluded that *aquerò* was the Virgin Mary.[51] However, within a matter of days everyone was equating the figure with Mary, including, implicitly, Bernadette.

On February 25, Bernadette crawled on her knees to the back of the grotto where she dug some muddy water, later explaining that she had been directed to drink and wash there. Soon miraculous cures were being credited to the spring and people began to carry away bottles of the water. On March 2, as an estimated 1,600 people watched, the captivating teenager claimed to have been given her mission: to tell the priests that a shrine was to be built on the site and that people were to visit it in procession.

By this time the curé of the parish, Dominique Peyramale, had had enough of what he considered an outrageous hoax. He called Bernadette a liar, and demanded that she ask the entity to provide her name and also to give a sign: to cause a rosebush in the grotto to bloom. Finally, on March 4, came the final day of the prescribed period. According to the book, *Encountering Mary,* by Sandra L. Zimdars-Swartz:

> Estimates of the crowd . . . ranged from five thousand to twenty thousand people. Many had come that day, it seems, in anticipation of a miracle, for a rumor was circulating that Bernadette had predicted "a revelation of the Virgin" on that day. Many apparently also expected that everyone present on the occasion would be able to see and hear the Virgin themselves. Others hoped that in response to Peyramale's request, *aquerò* would reveal her name and that the rose bush would bloom. A reporter for one of the major newspapers was not very favorably impressed by the piety and credulity of the crowd that day. He noted that all streets, paths, mounds and fields from which one could see the "mysterious grotto" were literally covered with people. Above the din of the crowd, he said one could sometimes hear piercing cries, dares, insults, invocations, and prayers. In the swarm of humanity there was a woman worried about her crinolines being crushed by peasants and a man ready to avenge himself for having his foot stepped on. The trees were full of urchins gamboling about like monkeys, and the police were powerless to keep order. Such was the conduct of the people, he observed, when Bernadette finally appeared and the cry was heard, "There is the saint! There is the saint!"[52]

The sign requested by Peyramale, not surprisingly, failed to appear. Nevertheless *rumors* of great miracles spread through the credulous throng. Bernadette's having stopped on her way to the grotto to embrace a *partially* blind girl, was transformed into a miracle: Bernadette had supposedly breathed on the girl's eyes and restored her sight (like Christ in Matt. 9:27-30). Another tale related how Bernadette had healed a child's paralyzed arm (cf. Mark 3:1-5). Again, some said a dove had hovered over her head during her ecstatic vision (an evocation of Matt. 3:16). Zimdars-Swartz states:

> But not all of the "signs" followed the New Testament models quite so closely. An especially bizarre rumor concerned the fate of a peasant from the valley of Campan who had boasted that he was not fooled by these scenes of hallucination. That very evening, it was said, through the agency of the young seer, the sins of this irreverent man had been changed into serpents, the serpents had devoured him on his way home, and no trace was ever found of him thereafter. According to another version of the story, though, some of this man's skin had been left behind, which was found and put on display in Lourdes at the historical museum. This story shows clearly the degree to which popular imagination had been stimulated by the events at Lourdes and the dramatic ways in which nascent belief was being reinforced.[53]

At the same time, the Lourdes legend-makers began to circulate tales of miracles in Bernadette's youth. One such story told how the girl, who had been tending sheep, had encountered a rain-swollen stream. Supposedly, the waters had parted to allow Bernadette and her flock to pass safely through. Less flattering rumors were also circulating, including one that Bernadette's parents were collecting a fifteen-centime fee from each of her daughter's visitors.

Bernadette returned to the grotto on the Feast of the Annunciation (March 25) whereupon, she claimed, the figure identified herself, stating, "I am the Immaculate Conception." This was only four years after the doctrine of Mary's Immaculate Conception became an official, obligatory dogma of the Catholic Church. It is often argued that Bernadette would have known nothing of this, but in fact, "by 1854 this was already a very popular doctrine, supported and advanced by many prophecies, apparitions, cures, devotional cults, and pious tracts."[54]

Actually, since the term refers not to Mary or to her identity but to her supposed freedom from original sin when she was conceived, the statement "I am the Immaculate Conception" is a logical/grammatical inaccuracy. The skeptical Peyramale was quick to note the telltale error—one less to be expected from "the Mother of God" than from an untutored schoolgirl. Thereupon Bernadette quickly amended the statement to "I am the Virgin of the Immaculate Conception."

Bernadette reported only two additional appearances of the Virgin at the grotto, but the site was already becoming an established shrine, despite the efforts of local officials to discourage the hysteria and disparage the "propaganda" claiming miraculous properties for the grotto's water. Now other alleged visionaries came forth, including (as they were described by the police commissioner) a "bad woman devoted to drink"; a prostitute with "disgusting morals"; and some fifty others, including many schoolchildren. In the meantime a zinc basin fitted with three spigots was installed at the spring and claims of cures and healings attributed to the supposedly magical water proliferated.[55]

As for Bernadette, two years after her alleged visions, arrangements were made for her to board at a hospice school where she remained until 1866. Then she went to Nevers to join the religious order that had cared for her the previous six years, and she spent the remainder of her life there as a nun with the appellation Marie Bernard.

Ironically, all her life Bernadette endured ill health. As a child she had had asthma, and she later suffered for many years from tuberculosis of the bone in the right knee as well as numerous attendant complications. She was bedridden for the last years of her life. When Bernadette died on April 16, 1879, she was only thirty-five years old; the "healing" waters of Lourdes had never been for her. Nevertheless, she was canonized a saint in 1933 and, as we saw in Chapter 4, her "incorruptible"—if emaciated—body, complete with wax mask, remains on view in a chapel bearing her name at Nevers.[56]

And what of the miraculous cures that are claimed at Lourdes? Millions of pilgrims annually visit the massive basilica that has replaced the vision-inspired chapel. The injured, the crippled, the blind and deaf, the sick and dying—all wait in line to enter the sacred grotto, some to be bathed in its cold mountain waters, others to take home water from the holy spring. (See Figure 11.) Despite "multitudinous failures" over the years, the crowds continue to prove the truth of the statement that "one apparent cure will efface the memory of a hundred failures."[57]

Since its founding in 1884, the Lourdes Medical Bureau has been investigating and certifying miracles attributed to the shrine. The bureau's doctors attempt to screen out cases involving non-life-threatening illnesses, recoveries that are not permanent, and cures that may actually be attributable to medical treatment. Only if the case is determined to represent a medical mystery is it then referred to an international committee to determine whether or not a miracle occurred. Of course the committee—composed entirely of Catholic doctors from countries that send countless pilgrims to Lourdes—might be assumed to be less skeptical than one composed of secular physicians. Even so, only rarely are cases officially authenticated as miraculous—sixty-four as of 1984. In contrast, 6,000 other allegedly miraculous cases were rejected.[58]

As might be expected, cases that the Lourdes bureau finds "medically inexplicable" may be found otherwise by independent medical investigators. For example, a scrutiny of many Lourdes "healings" was conducted in 1957 by Dr. Donald J. West, a British psychologist, who concluded that none could be considered medically inexplicable, let alone miraculous. He observed that virtually all were diseases that were susceptible to psychosomatic influences—cancer and tuberculosis among them—and that, therefore, many of the Lourdes cures could actually be attributed to the positive feelings that result from patients' pilgrimages.[59]

The "miraculous" label in more recent cases certified by the committee in 1978 has also been criticized. An example was a patient diagnosed as suffering from "recurring organic hemiplegia with ocular lesions, due to cerebral circulatory defects." Actually, specialists in the United States concluded that if there was any organic illness, the more likely possibility was multiple sclerosis—a disease known to show spontaneous remissions. Three additional post-1954 healings certified as miraculous were also cases of multiple sclerosis.[60]

A 1963 certification of a miracle cure by the committee concerned a young woman with Budd-Chiari syndrome—a condition characterized by blockage of the veins in the liver. The committee did conclude in reaching its decision that they were insufficiently aware of the possibility of natural remission in Budd-Chiari syndrome, but they nevertheless certified that the woman's apparent healing was miraculous. In fact, seven years after the "miraculous" certification, the woman died; the cause of death was Budd-Chiari syndrome.[61] Such cases demonstrate that even the Lourdes "miracle cures" that pass the committee, and that are touted by many rank-and-file Catholics as evidence of divine intervention, may actually be nothing more than the result of poor investigation. Indeed, a critical article on Lourdes in the *Encyclopaedia Britannica Medicine and Health Yearbook* quoted U.S. doctors who examined one 1976 certification and pronounced it "vague" and "obtuse," labeling the documents as "a lot of mumbo jumbo" and as "unscientific and totally unconvincing."[62]

On the other hand, as Terence Hines observes:

> A major source of the fame of Lourdes is not the certified miracle cures but the thousands of personal reports of people who went there and "got better." The shrine is lined with the discarded canes and crutches of those who could walk without them after their visit. However, the trip to Lourdes and the ceremonies performed there serve to build great excitement and hope in the pilgrims. [*The Encyclopaedia Britannica 1982 Medicine and Health Yearbook*] describes the "electricity in the air as the huge crowd [of pilgrims] moves from the bank of the river to the grand upper basilica, singing in unison." This is just the type of exciting and physiologically stressful stimulus that causes release of pain-reducing endorphins. . . . Those who come to Lourdes finding it difficult but not impossible to walk with crutches or a cane will thus experience a reduction in their level of pain, perhaps enough to allow them to walk unaided, at least for a while. When the pain returns, at least the period of relative freedom from pain will be accepted as a miracle. After all, the biochemistry of pain reduction via endorphin release is far from common knowledge. The pain's return will be explained as due to failure to pray enough, or to some other mystical cause. The French writer Anatole France made a telling and pungent comment upon visiting Lourdes in the late nineteenth century and seeing all the abandoned crutches and canes: "What, what, no wooden legs???"[63]

Some of the cases of attempted healings at Lourdes are heart-rending. Such a case was that of a seven-year-old boy from St. Joseph, Michigan, named Randy Eckman. In 1956 his neighbors raised the money to permit his mother, a Lutheran, to take Randy to Lourdes to cure his leukemia since doctors had given the child only a year to live. The *Chicago Sun-Times* featured a series of articles on the pilgrimage. Afterward, Randy's mother claimed her son had made a 100-percent improvement. He even returned to school, whereupon the *Sun-Times* headlined "Randy Romps His Age after Shrine Trip." With tragic irony, however, on February 5, 1957, exactly one year after the little boy had departed for Lourdes, he was baptized as a Catholic and died. The *Sun-Times* placed the story in an inconspicuous spot on an inside page.[64]

Despite similar cases of failed expectations, and what *Time* magazine reported as "a holy-water shortage" at the grotto in 1990 that led to "rationing the blessed potion,"[65] Lourdes still flourishes. Pilgrims continue to flock there, enriching the town annually by about $400 million. Although Lourdes is still relatively small, it has an international airport, 400 hotels, and countless gift shops that sell images of the Virgin Mary and amulets containing Lourdes water. Although, as one skeptic observes, the townsfolk "are no healthier than residents in surrounding villages, despite their proximity to the magical waters,"[66] they are certainly richer.

Lourdes water is also sold in the United States, imported by the Lourdes Center in Boston, Massachusetts. The center's newsletter is replete with testimonials to the amazing healing powers of the water. The Missionary Oblates of Mary Immaculate in Bellville, Illinois, offer a unique opportunity as well:

> Designed to enhance times of personal prayer, this LOURDES MEDAL-LION CANDLE and LOURDES WATER set is a beautiful memento of The Lourdes apparations [*sic*].
>
> The LOURDES MEDALLION CANDLE, imported from France, contains wax from candles previously burned before the Sacred Grotto in Lourdes. . . . Inset into the front of the candle is a 2⅜-inch goldtone metallic [cheap imitation gold] medallion with the richly detailed, bas-relief images of Our Lady and St. Bernadette. . . .
>
> Included with each candle is a container of LOURDES WATER from the famous spring. . . . The imported, unbreakable container, 2¾ inches in height, depicts the apparation [*sic*] of Our Lady of Lourdes in bas-relief.

(That is, the bottle is cheap molded plastic.) This set will be sent to anyone who "can help with a gift of $12." In addition one can fill out a "prayer petition" which will be "prayed for in two Mass Novenas. . . ." And "your prayer petitions will also remain sealed in the Prayer Capsule at the Lourdes Grotto" for a specified time, "thus assuring that your needs will be prayed for" during the year. Says an advertising brochure: "While this water is not magical, it is often the sign of God's healing, loving presence through Mary's intercession." Included is a testimonial from "D. N., Arizona," telling how her prayer petition worked "a miracle" by curing her grandson of a speech impediment.[67]

Attributable in part to the success of Lourdes, other "curative" waters are (so to speak) springing up elsewhere. Perhaps the most recent is at Tlacote, Mexico, where ranch owner Jesus Chain Simon claims his well water can cure any disease, including AIDS. Simon allegedly discovered the well's wondrous healing properties when his seriously ill dog fell into the well, drank the water, and was instantly cured. Since then, Simon says, over three million pilgrims from Mexico, the United States, Canada, and several European countries have visited the Hacienda Tlacote to drink the water, often standing in the 95-degree heat in lines almost a mile long.[68] According to one newspaper report on Simon's claims, "Some call him a charlatan, others a saint."[69] Another article states:

> Simon doesn't have too much time anymore for visitors. He says that the healing power of his water is growing so that whereas a few weeks ago a few pints were needed to heal a sickness, now only a few swallows are necessary.
>
> This being the case, he adds, he no longer is going to be giving the water away for free but, as a blessing to humanity, will start selling it.
>
> Price: $200 per pint.[70]

Scientists said the well yielded only ordinary water but noted that it was safe to drink.[71]

A different verdict was rendered in the case of water on the Rockdale County, Georgia, property of Nancy Fowler, a woman who—according to the *Atlanta Constitution*—"claims to see recurring apparitions of the Virgin Mary." Mrs. Fowler stated that her well water was blessed when Jesus Christ himself appeared to her. However, a sample of the water was found to be contaminated with coliform bacteria and therefore "unsatisfactory for drinking." The Rockdale County Health Department asked the visionary to post a sign at the well to warn people of the possible danger.[72]

Then there is the "Lourdes of Bronx"—as the *New York Times* dubbed it—where curative water flows from a rocky replica of the French grotto. The fake spring is only piped city water, but the parish priest blesses the water annually in a special rite. The parish business manager says of some people's claims of miracles at the local shrine: "I can't prove anything but the faith they had in the Lord and themselves. I do know there is something here you can't touch, see or feel. But there is something here."[73]

Prophets of Healing

No discussion of faith healing would be complete without mentioning Christian Scientists—adherents of the sect known as Church of Christ, Scientist. Their name declares their belief: they are followers of Christ the healer, and their faith is "scientific" in the supposed "demonstrability of its effectiveness."[74] They therefore reject medical treatment.

The founder, first practitioner, and first teacher of Christian Science was Mary Baker Eddy (1821–1910). The youngest of six children of Mark Baker (a justice of the peace and Congregational Church deacon) and Abigail Ambrose Baker, Mary was born at Bow, near Concord, New Hampshire. She attended ordinary schools, then an academy at Tilton, and was also privately tutored. After her first husband's death, with an infant son to care for, Mary taught school off and on for nine years. In 1853 came her ill-fated marriage to her second husband, which resulted in his desertion after ten years and her divorcing him after ten more. Four years later (in 1874) she married Asa Gilbert Eddy who became her first serious convert to Christian Science.[75]

In her youth, Mrs. Eddy had shown a deep interest in religion, and a pastor who had tutored her described her as "an intellectual and spiritual genius." Her interest in spiritual healing supposedly began at twelve when prayer seemed to cure a fever. She regarded her "discovery" of Christian Science as occurring in 1866 when she was injured—supposedly critically— by a fall on an icy street. On the third day of what seemed to her a slow recovery, Mrs. Eddy asked for the Bible and read a passage about Christ curing a man of palsy (Matt. 9:2), whereupon she immediately recovered.

However, young Mary's condition may have been less critical than supposed and her recovery something less than implied. A look at her childhood reveals a pampered, spoiled child who learned to get her own way by feigning various illnesses and seizures. According to one biographer,

> . . . Mary Baker's "fits," as outsiders rather crudely called them, are still a household word among her old friends. They frequently came on without the slightest warning. At times the attack resembled a convulsion. Mary pitched headlong on the floor, and rolled and kicked, writhing and screaming in apparent agony. Again she dropped limp and lay motionless. At other times, like a cataleptic, she lay rigid, almost in a state of suspended animation. The family worked over her, but usually in vain. Mark Baker,

standing upright in his wagon and lashing his horses, would drive for Dr. Ladd, the family physician. An old neighbor remembered him driving thus and shouting all the way: "Mary is dying!" The family actually believed that she was. For years they expected that Mary would end her days in one of her hysterical attacks, and went to every extreme to prevent them. As a precautionary measure they gave in to all the girl's whims. . . . Dr. Ladd occasionally diagnosed them as "hysteria mingled with bad temper"; but at other times he took them seriously. He regarded the girl as an interesting pathological case. Becoming much interested in mesmerism at about that time, he practiced up on Mary Baker. He found her a sensitive subject. He discovered that, by mental suggestion, he could partly control her. "I can make that girl stop in the street any time, merely by thinking," he would tell his friends, and he frequently demonstrated that he could do this.[76]

Nevertheless, Mary decided her "healing" had been divine, and she then began to study the subject of Christian healing, saying, "The Bible was my textbook." In a pamphlet, *The Science of Man,* copyrighted in 1870, Mary stated dramatically: "In the nineteenth century I affix for all time the word *Science* to *Christianity*; and *error* to *personal sense*; and call the world to battle on this issue." There followed several other books, notably the Christian Science textbook, *Science and Health with Key to the Scriptures,* first published in 1875. (See Figure 12.) Mrs. Eddy formed a Christian Science association the following year, and in three more years she and several followers organized a fledgling church. In 1892, she and selected followers founded the mother church of today's Christian Science religion, the First Church of Christ, Scientist, in Boston.

Mrs. Eddy defined Christian Science as "divine metaphysics" and "the scientific system of divine healings." She maintained it was "the law of God, the law of good, interpreting and demonstrating the divine Principle and rule of universal harmony."[77] Christian Science's most important teaching is the distinction between that which is real (God, health, truth) and that which is apparent but unreal (hell, illness, falsehood). As Mrs. Eddy explained:

All reality is in God and His Creation, harmonious and eternal. That which He creates is good, and He makes all that is made. Therefore, the only reality of sin, sickness or death is the awful fact that unrealities seem real to human, erring belief, until God strips off their disguise. They are not true, because they are not of God.[78]

However, Christian Science does not ignore the "unreal" but rather seeks to overcome it with spiritual understanding, law, and power. Since sickness is one such unreality, it is to be conquered by means of Christian healing.[79]

In adherence to church dogma, devout members of the sect reject all forms of medical treatment—including drugs and instruments such as thermometers, as well as even such simple measures as ice packs or back rubs. Instead, members depend on faith healers called *practitioners* whose training consists of a brief period of religious tutelage and whose treatment is limited exclusively to praying. This may be done in person or by telephone, and the practitioners charge for their time. Although the praying is clearly a religious practice, the IRS permits the charges to be deducted as a medical expense for income tax purposes, and some medical plans (e.g., Blue Cross-Blue Shield in many states) cover such expenses.[80]

These practices—termed "bizarre" by critics[81]—have necessarily resulted in numerous deaths, including those of many children who would surely have survived if medical treatment had not been withheld. An article in the *New England Journal of Medicine*, written by a former Christian Scientist who herself lost a child to the sect's dogma, tells how the church defends parents' "right" to withhold medical treatment from their children. The church insists that parents should not be charged with child abuse if their children die as a consequence, and many state laws intended to protect children from abuse nevertheless contain exemptions for religious practices like those of the Church of Christ, Scientist. The church lobbies forcefully against any attempt to remove such exemptions.[82]

A 1990 *New York Times* headline "Christian Scientists Get Probation in Death of Son" reported the results of one tragic case of the sect's intransigence. The courtroom drama was played out in Boston, where the Church of Christ, Scientist, is headquartered. Church officials emphatically defended the sect's tenet on spiritual healing as an alternative to medical treatment and staunchly supported the two defendants in the case, Ginger and Paul Twichell. The Twichells' two-year-old son Robyn died after a five-day illness in 1986—an illness an autopsy revealed was a bowel obstruction that was surgically treatable.[83] The defense maintained that the couple's actions were dictated by deeply held beliefs. The prosecution countered: "The whole idea is to bring to the front: What is the required conduct of parents? We are advocates of children. We are not persecutors of religious beliefs."[84] At issue was the possible well-being of the Twichells' three other children, two of whom were born after Robyn died and the couple moved from Boston to Brentwood, New York. The trial resulted in a conviction for manslaughter and Judge Sandra Hamlin sentenced the Twitchells to ten years' probation, a condition of which was regular pediatric examinations for their remaining children. The Twitchells' attorneys filed an appeal, and a spokesman for the church stated, "The judge in effect tried to take the heart out of Christian Science."[85]

More recently the church found itself embroiled in quite a different controversy—this time over a book titled *The Destiny of the Mother Church* by Bliss Knapp. Although church officialdom deemed the book unsound shortly after it first appeared in 1948, in 1991 it was officially published and placed in Christian Science Reading Rooms everywhere. At issue was the book's portrayal of Mary Baker Eddy. Although she herself claimed to be no more than the inspired founder and leader of Christian Science, author Knapp claimed that Eddy's advent as a religious figure had been foretold by a prophecy of Isaiah ("Thy seed shall inherit the Gentiles"). Knapp also portrayed Eddy as virtually a second Jesus Christ. Some church members who were disillusioned by the book's publication charged it was done in a crass attempt to ease the church's financial crisis. At stake was a $90 million bequest from the Knapp family, the terms of which required publication of the book by 1993 or else the fortune was to go to Stanford University and the Los Angeles County Museum of Art.[86]

Strangely at odds with Knapp's "heavenly" portrayal is a documented indication of Mrs. Eddy's quite human limitations: the fact that her husband and first convert died only six years after the "science" was "discovered," occurring under conditions that are quite revealing. When her husband suddenly fell ill, a physician, Dr. Rufus K. Noyes, diagnosed organic heart disease, warning that Eddy might die at any moment. Mrs. Eddy was convinced, however, that her enemies were conspiring to harm him and that her husband must have been poisoned. She asked "Dr." Charles J. Eastman, a director of something called the Massachusetts Metaphysical College, to confirm her "diagnosis." Her husband soon died. A biographer explains:

> Whatever the warmth of their mutual regard, the Eddys' marriage had not really been a success. . . . And now that marriage had confronted her with the greatest embarrassment possible. How was one to reconcile Eddy's death with the pretensions of his wife's healing method? Mrs. Eddy chose the characteristic course of insisting on her own point of view, whatever the consequences and as publicly as possible. She called

in Dr. Noyes to perform an autopsy, certain that he would find evidence of foul play. He found the death to have been caused by serious disease of the aortic valve of the heart, even showing that organ to Mrs. Eddy to demonstrate his conclusion. She transformed his findings in a unique way. Since he had not found evidence of arsenical poisoning, she said, it proved that Dr. Eddy had been killed by metaphysical arsenical poisoning, which leaves no trace. "Dr." Eastman was happy again to concur with her diagnosis. . . .[87]

Such was the bizarre thinking of the Prophet of Christian Science.

Another great guru of mystical healing was Edgar Cayce (1877–1945), the "sleeping prophet." In an alleged "trance," Cayce gave medical readings to thousands of people who wrote for his help. His disciples point to some 14,000 case histories (housed in the library of the Association for Research and Enlightenment—a Cayce promotional institution founded by the prophet's son), wherein they find many supposedly accurate diagnoses of, and testimonials from, people who believed themselves cured. Yet as Martin Gardner observes:

> Most of Cayce's early trances were given with the aid of an osteopath who asked him questions while he was asleep, and helped later in explaining the reading to the patient. There is abundant evidence that Cayce's early association with osteopaths and homeopaths had a major influence on the character of his readings. Over and over again he would find spinal lesions of one sort or another as the cause of an ailment and prescribe spinal manipulations for its cure.[88]

In addition to osteopathy and homeopathy, Cayce's prescribed remedies derived from naturopathy, with some folk medicine and sheer inspiration thrown in.

> There were special diets, tonics, herbs, electrical treatments, and such medicines as "oil of smoke" (for a leg sore), "peach-tree poultice" (for a baby with convulsions), "bedbug juice" (for dropsy), "castor oil packs" (for [a priest with an epilepsy-like condition]), almonds (to prevent cancer), peanut oil massage (to forestall arthritis), ash from the wood of a bamboo tree (for tuberculosis and other diseases), and fumes of apple brandy from a charred keg (for his [Cayce's] tuberculous wife to inhale).[89]

An obviously fantasy-prone individual (as a child he had imaginary playmates), Cayce never attended school beyond the ninth grade but worked in a bookstore and was an avid, if eclectic, reader. He read the Bible annually, but soon became a thoroughgoing occultist. He was arrested and charged with fortune-telling fraud in New York, but was acquitted on the basis of "ecclesiastical" freedom.

Thus Cayce progressed—if that is the right word—from ascribing homeopathic and osteopathic causes to ailments, to linking them with the person's "Karma." He began to describe his subjects' previous incarnations and to "see" their "auras" from which he diagnosed character and health.[90]

But did Cayce possess clairvoyant diagnostic powers? James Randi finds in Cayce's readings "the myriad half-truths, the evasive and garbled language, and the multiple 'outs' that Cayce used." Randi explains:

> Cayce was fond of expressions like "I feel that . . ." and "perhaps"— qualifying words used to avoid positive declarations. It is a common tool in the psychic trade. Many of the letters he received—in fact, most— contained specific details about the illnesses for which readings were required, and there was nothing to stop Cayce from knowing the contents of the letters and presenting that information as if it were a divine revelation. To one who has been through dozens of similar diagnoses, as I have, the methods are obvious. It is merely a specialized version of the "generalization" technique of fortune-tellers.[91]

Although Cayce was never subjected to proper testing, ESP pioneer Dr. Joseph B. Rhine of Duke University—who should have been sympathetic to Cayce's claims—was unimpressed. A reading that Cayce gave for Rhine's daughter was notably inaccurate.[92] Frequently, Cayce was even wider of the mark, as when he provided diagnoses of subjects *who had died* since the letters requesting the readings were sent. Instead of perceiving their profoundly altered state, Cayce blithely rambled on in his typical fashion, in one instance prescribing an incredible nostrum made from sarsaparilla root, Indian turnip, wild ginseng, and other ingredients. As Randi says of Cayce's lapses in these instances, "Surely, dead is a very serious symptom, and should be detectable."[93]

The guru of another type of "miraculous" healing was neither the founder of a sect like Mary Baker Eddy nor a sleeping seer like Edgar Cayce. Instead, José Arigó of Brazil was considered by many to be the most remarkable practitioner of so-called psychic surgery.

Psychic surgery typically involves the alleged healer placing his bare hands directly into the body of the patient—without any incision—and removing the "diseased tissue" which is then "ritually destroyed." It should come as no surprise that such alleged surgery is nothing more than a sleight-of-hand trick, the destruction of the tissue merely being a means of preventing a histological analysis that would reveal the animal source of the tissue. Forensic tests of "tumors" and blood from one "operation" revealed they had come from a pig. In another case the "tumor" was a piece of chicken intestine and the accompanying blood that of a cow. A doctor who himself volunteered for a psychic operation later commented, "I did not feel his fingers inside, the blood I saw running on me was cold, and the gallstones he showed me were not gallstones." X-rays later proved that no gallstones had been removed.[94] Journalist Tom Valentine said of one psychic surgeon that he "usually wears short sleeves when he operates and often exposes his palms to viewers before beginning an operation to assure them he has nothing in his hands," just as a stage magician would.

The psychic simply pushes his fingers into the fleshy parts of the body; and when operating on the midriff of an obese person the hands can appear to be inside up to the wrists. This trick is not, of course, used in operations on non-fleshy parts of the body. In these cases the surgeon permits viewers to peer only through his cupped fingers. Valentine concluded:

One thing I learned from watching [a psychic surgeon] was that the eye can be fooled no matter how careful the viewer. I did not notice him protrude his fingers beneath a blanket near the area of operation. Yet, on movies, it is apparent.[95]

The fake blood may be contained in a sponge or be packaged in a small red balloon that is secretly palmed, broken under cover of the hands and a fold of the patient's abdomen, and then extracted in full view as if it were a piece of tissue. Other hiding places for blood and tissue include a magician's false thumb.[96]

Among the best-known psychic surgeons of the Philippines was Antonio "Dr. Tony" Agpaoa who, in late 1968, was arrested in San Francisco. A month later, on December 19, he was indicted by a Detroit grand jury on a charge of fraud in foreign commerce. The indictment stemmed from a Michigan steelworker's 1966 visit to Manila, where Agpaoa pretended to mend fractured bones in the man's neck. Later X-rays, however, revealed the bones were as before although the man (briefly relieved of pain by suggestion) had believed himself healed. Many sick people had actually mortgaged their homes just to make a pilgrimage to see "Dr. Tony," and he, too, had decided to make a pilgrimage—out of the country to avoid answering the charges.[97]

States writer Francis X. King, however:

> The work of some psychic surgeons is not so easy to explain. Remarkable among these was the Brazilian, José Arigo, whose body was, apparently, often taken over by the spirit of a deceased German physician, "Doctor Fritz."
>
> There seems to have been no question of sleight of hand being involved in the surgical operations carried out by Arigo in the period from 1950 to 1971. Wounds were left on his patients' bodies, which healed with unusual speed, but were undoubtedly genuine. The quickness of this healing was all the more remarkable in that Arigo—or "Doctor Fritz" used unsterilized instruments.[98]

"Dr. Fritz"—Arigo—also had another appellation, as indicated by the title of a credulous book by John Fuller, *Arigo: Surgeon of the Rusty Knife.*

Apparently "Dr. Fritz" usually did eschew blatant trickery, but James Randi cites at least one apparent exception mentioned by Fuller who claimed that Arigo once used his bare hands to remove a patient's liver. But, as Randi says: "Fuller spends no time at all trying to convince the reader of this feat, as if he were embarrassed by it all."[99] Arigo was also fond of a simple stunt—placing a knife blade (with a rounded tip) under a patient's eye—supposedly to demonstrate his magical power with the knife. However, Randi explains the simple stunt (one that anyone can perform if shown how) and publishes a photograph of himself demonstrating the feat.[100]

Most often, apparently, "Dr. Fritz" merely performed such simple operations as lancing a boil, removing a cyst, excising a lipoma (a tumor of fatty tissue) from just under the skin of a man's arm, and similar procedures. He also prescribed various potions and concoctions that obviously depended for their effectiveness on the placebo effect. His prescriptions were filled at the only pharmacy in town—run by the amateur doctor's brother.[101] By such means were Arigo's alleged "miracle healings"[102] actually performed.

One case of "psychic surgery" illustrates the false hope that victims of "miracle healings" are frequently subjected to. It concerned Andy Kaufman, who acted in the television series "Taxi." Kaufman traveled to the Philippines in the desperate hope of having his terminal cancer cured by one of the resident charlatans. Kaufman's girlfriend, who accompanied him on the pilgrimage, was convinced that no trickery was involved, explaining that she stood "not a foot away." Alas, Kaufman's reputed "cure" had no effect on his cancer, and he died.

Select Bibliography

Hines, Terence. "Faith Healing." Chapter 10 of *Pseudoscience and the Paranormal.* Buffalo, N.Y.: Prometheus Books, 1988. A concise discussion of the nature of disease, the techniques of faith healers, psychic surgery, and "healing" shrines.

Larue, Gerald A. "The Mysterious Power of Faith Healing." Chapter [10] of *The Supernatural, the Occult, and the Bible.* Buffalo, N.Y.: Prometheus Books, 1990. A consideration of faith healing in relationship to biblical traditions, including such topics as "Healing in the Christian Scriptures," "Mind-Body Relationships," "Modern Faith Healing," "New Age Healing," "Lourdes," "Oral Roberts's City of Faith," "Spiritual Healing in the Philippines," and other related topics.

Randi, James. "The Medical Humbugs." Chapter 9 of *Flim-Flam! Psychics, ESP, Unicorns, and other Delusions.* Buffalo, N.Y.: Prometheus Books, 1982. A report on psychic surgeons and Edgar Cayce by an internationally known paranormal investigator.

———. *The Faith Healers.* Buffalo, N.Y.: Prometheus Books, 1987. A devastating indictment of faith-healing charlatans and their tricks, based on an in-depth investigation by a team of researchers using such techniques as disguise, infiltration, and interception of secret messages.

Rogo, D. Scott. "Miraculous Healings." Chapter 11 of *Miracles: A Parascientific Inquiry into Wondrous Phenomena.* New York: Dial Press, 1982. A credulous look at faith healing at Lourdes, Kathryn Kuhlman services, and the like, concluding that "psychic forces" are involved, whether they are divine or not.

Silberger, Julius, Jr. *Mary Baker Eddy: An Interpretive Biography of the Founder of Christian Science.* Boston: Little, Brown and Company, 1980. Psychological insights into the life of the eccentric founder of a religion based on faith healing.

Zimdars-Swartz, Sandra L. *Encountering Mary: From La Salette to Medjugorje.* Princeton, N.J. : Princeton University Press, 1991. A phenomenological approach to the study of Marian apparitions, including those alleged by Bernadette Soubirous at Lourdes.

Notes

1. Gerald Larue, *The Supernatural, the Occult, and the Bible* (Buffalo, N.Y.: Prometheus Books, 1990), p. 116.

2. Quoted in Larue, *The Supernatural, the Occult, and the Bible,* pp. 117–18.

3. "Aesculapius, *Encyclopaedia Britannica,* 1960 ed.

4. Larue, *The Supernatural, the Occult, and the Bible,* pp. 122–26.

5. Ibid., pp. 129–30.

6. Ibid., pp. 131, 138.

7. Martin E. Marty and Kenneth L. Vaux, eds., *Health/Medicine and the Faith Traditions* (Philadelphia: Fortress Press, 1982), cited in Larue, *The Supernatural, the Occult, and the Bible,* pp. 138–39.

8. Terrence Hines, *Pseudoscience and the Paranormal* (Buffalo, N.Y.: Prometheus Books, 1988), p. 239.

9. Ibid.; Larue, *The Supernatural, the Occult, and the Bible,* p. 139.

10. See James Randi, "Lourdes Revisited," *The Skeptical Inquirer* 6.4 (Summer 1982): 4; James Randi, *The Faith Healers* (Buffalo, N.Y.: Prometheus Books, 1987), pp. 291–92; Rev. Robert D. Smith, *Comparative Miracles* (St. Louis, Mo.: B. Herder Book Co., 1965), p. 92.

11. Randi, *The Faith Healers,* pp. 291–92.

12. Hines, *Pseudoscience and the Paranormal,* pp. 238–39; Larue, *The Supernatural, the Occult, and the Bible,* pp. 139–43.

13. Robert A. Baker, *They Call It Hypnosis* (Buffalo, N.Y.: Prometheus Books, 1990), pp. 282–83.

14. Larue, *The Supernatural, the Occult, and the Bible,* pp. 142–43.

15. Hines, *Pseudoscience and the Paranormal,* pp. 238–39.

16. Quoted in Hines, *Pseudoscience and the Paranormal,* pp. 234.

17. Ibid., p. 235.

18. Ibid.

19. Ibid., pp. 236–37.

20. Tony Campolo, *How to Be Pentecostal without Speaking in Tongues* (Dallas, Tex.: Word Publishing, 1991), p. 38.

21. Robert A. Steiner, *Don't Get Taken!* (El Cerrito, Calif.: Wide-Awake Books, 1989), pp. 124–25.

22. Ibid., pp. 124–26. See also Robert A. Steiner, "Exposing the Faith-Healers," *The Skeptical Inquirer* 11.1 (Fall 1986): 28–31; Randi, *The Faith Healers,* pp. 141–49.

23. Steiner, *Don't Get Taken!* p. 126.

24. Randi, *The Faith Healers,* pp. 149–50. See also Greg Garrison, "Unmasking Fake Miracles," *Birmingham News* (Alabama), January 11, 1991.

25. Randi, *The Faith Healers,* pp. 124–27.

26. Ibid., pp. 105–106.

27. Ibid., pp. 128–30.

28. Ibid., photo section following p. 166.

29. Hines, *Pseudoscience and the Paranormal,* p. 242.

30. Ibid.

31. Steiner, "Exposing the Faith-Healers," p. 31.

32. Ibid., pp. 30–31.

33. Ibid., p. 31.

34. Quoted in Randi, *The Faith Healers,* p. 208.

35. Quoted in Hines, *Pseudoscience and the Paranormal,* p. 247.

36. Hines, *Pseudoscience and the Paranormal,* p. 247. See also Mark Plummer, "Current Investigations," *The Skeptic* (Australia) 6.2 (1986): 2–5.

37. Randi, *The Faith Healers,* p. 212.

38. Ibid., pp. 183–95. See also Clark Morphew, "City of Faith Buyers Face Moral Dilemma," *Lexington Herald-Leader* (Lexington, Ky.), July 11, 1992.

39. Quoted in Randi, *The Faith Healers,* p. 199.

40. Randi, *The Faith Healers,* p. 204.

41. Denise Kalette, "Watch Where You Make Donations," *USA Today,* February 3, 1992.

42. Quotes from Tilton are from the letter, brochures, etc., in his direct-mail "miracle package."

43. Debbie Howlett, "Televangelist Under Scrutiny," *USA Today,* March 27, 1992.

44. Ibid.

45. Randi, *The Faith Healers,* pp. 217–25.

46. Rev. George Lange, bishop's representative to the charismatic movement in Worcester, Massachusetts, quoted in Randi, *The Faith Healers,* p. 222.

47. "Pilgrimage," *Encyclopaedia Britannica,* 1960 ed.

48. Consider, in addition to Lourdes, the shrines at Guadalupe, Mexico; Fatima, Portugal; Medjugorje, Yugoslavia; and others, including La Salette, France. See Sandra L. Zimdars-Swartz, *Encountering Mary: From La Salette to Medjugorje* (Princeton, N.J.: Princeton University Press, 1991).

49. Zimdars-Swartz, *Encountering Mary,* p. 50.

50. Ibid., pp. 43–49.

51. Ibid., p. 49.

52. Ibid., p. 52.

53. Ibid., p. 53.

54. Ibid., p. 56.

55. Ibid., pp. 57–67.

56. John Coulson, ed., *The Saints: A Concise Biographical Dictionary* (New York: Hawthorn Books, 1958), pp. 85–86; Joan Carroll Cruz, *The Incorruptibles* (Rockford, Ill.: Tan Books and Publishers, 1977), pp. 288–89.

57. Keith Thomas, *Religion and the Decline of Magic,* quoted in Larue, *The Supernatural, the Occult, and the Bible,* p. 157.

58. Hines, *Pseudoscience and the Paranormal,* p. 249. See also Curtis D. MacDougall, *Superstition and the Press* (Buffalo, N.Y.: Prometheus Books, 1983), p. 495; Larue, *The Supernatural, the Occult, and the Bible,* p. 157.

59. D. Scott Rogo, *Miracles: A Parascientific Inquiry into Wondrous Phenomena* (New York: Dial Press, 1982), pp. 290–91. (Rogo cites Dr. West's book, *Eleven Lourdes Miracles,* 1957.)

60. Hines, *Pseudoscience and the Paranormal,* p. 249.

61. Ibid., p. 250.

62. James Randi, "Lourdes Revisited," *The Skeptical Inquirer* 6.4 (Summer 1982): 4.

63. Hines, *Pseudoscience and the Paranormal,* p. 250.

64. MacDougall, *Superstition and the Press,* pp. 493–94.

65. "Have Faith, Save Water," *Time,* October 1, 1990.

66. Larue, *The Supernatural, the Occult, and the Bible,* p. 158.

67. Advertising materials from the Missionary Oblates of Mary Immaculate, Belleville, Illinois.

68. " 'Miraculous' Well Water Draws Hordes to Mexico," *Rocky Mountain News,* February 13, 1992; Thomas Von Mouillard, "Throngs of Sick Wait for Days to Drink the 'Miracle Water' from Mexican Well," *Rocky Mountain News,* May 11, 1992.

69. " 'Miraculous' Well Water."

70. "Throngs of Sick."

71. Ibid.

72. Bill Osinski, "Woman Asked to Post Warning about Water at Apparition Site," *Atlanta Constitution,* February 15, 1992.

73. David Gonzalez, "At Lourdes of Bronx, Where Cooling Hope Flows," *New York Times,* May 27, 1992.

74. Merle Severy, ed., *Great Religions of the World* (Washington, D.C.: National Geographic Society, 1971), p. 381.

75. "Eddy, Mary Baker," *Encyclopaedia Britannica,* 1960 ed.

76. Georgia Milmine, "Mary Baker G. Eddy," *McClure's Magazine* 28 (1907): 236, quoted in Julius Silberger, Jr., *Mary Baker Eddy* (Boston: Little, Brown and Co., 1980), pp. 27–28.

77. From *Science and Health, with Key to the Scriptures* and *Rudimental Divine Science,* quoted in "Christian Science," *Encyclopaedia Britannica,* 1960 ed.

78. *Science and Health,* quoted in *Encyclopaedia Britannica,* 1960 ed.

79. "Christian Science."

80. Hines, *Pseudoscience and the Paranormal,* p. 248. See also Rita Swan,

"Faith Healing, Christian Science, and the Medical Care of Children," *New England Journal of Medicine* 309 (1983): 1639–41.

81. Hines, *Pseudoscience and the Paranormal*, p. 248.

82. Ibid. See also Swan, "Faith Healing," pp. 1639–41.

83. "Christian Scientists Get Probation in Death of Son," *The New York Times*, July 7, 1990; Monica Maske, "Care of Children Fuels Christian Science Debate," *The Sunday Star-Ledger* (Newark, N.J.), September 22, 1991.

84. Prosecutor John Kiernan, quoted in "Christian Scientists Say Prayer on Trial in Manslaughter Case," *The Atlanta Journal and Constitution*, April 16, 1990.

85. "Christian Scientists Get Probation."

86. Richard N. Ostling, "Tumult in the Reading Rooms," *Time*, October 14, 1991, p. 57.

87. Silberger, *Mary Baker Eddy*, p. 143.

88. Martin Gardner, *Fads & Fallacies in the Name of Science* (New York: Dover, 1957), p. 217.

89. Ibid., p. 218.

90. Ibid., pp. 218–19., P. Philips, ed., *Out of this World*, vol. 7 ([England]: Phoebus, 1978), pp. 13–16.

91. James Randi, *Flim-Flam!* (Buffalo, N.Y.: Prometheus Books, 1986), p. 189.

92. Gardner, *Fads & Fallacies*, p. 219.

93. Randi, *Flim-Flam!* p. 191.

94. Tom Valentine, "U.S. Attorney, TV Newsman Claim Dr. Tony Is a Fraud," *The National Tattler*, September 23, 1973.

95. Ibid.

96. Randi, *Flim-Flam!* pp. 177–87.

97. Valentine, "U.S. Attorney, TV Newsman Claim Dr. Tony Is a Fraud."

98. Francis X. King, *Mind & Magic* (New York: Crescent, 1991), p. 230.

99. Randi, *Flim-Flam!* p. 176.

100. Ibid., pp. 174–76.

101. King, *Mind & Magic*, p. 231.

102. Hines, *Pseudoscience and the Paranormal*, p. 246.

7

Ecstatic Visions

From ancient times, shamans, prophets, and mystics have claimed to see visions of otherworldly figures, from spirits of the dead to angels and other celestial representatives. In the Old Testament, for example, King Saul, seeking advice on how to thwart an encroaching Philistine army, turned to a necromancer, the infamous "witch of Endor," who had a familiar spirit. Saul wished to confer with the deceased Samuel by having the spirit contact Samuel's ghost, and so he donned a disguise and slipped through enemy lines to the town of Endor. "Samuel" prophesied disaster—the most likely outcome, considering Saul's desperation—and the forecast deepened his despair. He and the Israelite army were thus defeated even before the battle began (1 Sam. 28–30).[1]

Most of the Old Testament prophets, of course, communicated not with the underworld but with heavenly entities. Thus Lot conversed with angels (Gen. 19:1–3), and angels saved Elijah from starvation in the wilderness (1 Kings 19:5–8). Similarly, Abraham spoke with God in a dream (Gen. 20:6), and Moses talked with him upon Mount Sinai where he received the stone tablets of the law (Exod. 24:112, 31:18).

In the New Testament, apparitions are central to the story of Jesus. The angel Gabriel announced his conception (Luke 1: 26–31), the "Spirit of God" heralded him at his baptism (Matt. 3:16), and an angel confronted Mary Magdalene at his tomb (Matt. 28).

167

Apparitions in biblical times could take many forms. The angels who were entertained by Abraham (Gen. 18) and Lot (Gen. 19) were indistinguishable from ordinary men. The "angel of the Lord" who spoke to Moses on Mt. Horeb appeared as a burning bush (Exod. 3:2), and at Jesus's baptism,

> lo, the heavens were opened unto him, and he saw the Spirit of God descending like a dove, and lighting upon him: And lo a voice from heaven saying, This is my beloved Son in whom I am well pleased. (Matt. 3:16–17)

Again, at Jesus's tomb, when Mary Magdalene encountered "the angel of the Lord," according to Matthew (28:3), "His countenance was like lightning, and his raiment white as snow."

The guardians at Christ's sepulcher were terrified of the angel, "And for fear of him the keepers did shake" (Matt. 28:4). Responses of others to heavenly visitors ranged from fear to adoration—even, in the case of John, author of the book of Revelation, to falling down at the feet of an angel in worship. However, the angel admonished him, saying:

> See thou do it not: for I am thy fellow servant, and of thy brethren the prophets, and of them which keep the saying of this book: worship God. (Rev. 22:9)

Despite this admonition, the Roman Catholic Church has encouraged the veneration of angels since the late fifth century. Several angels, such as Gabriel and Raphael, have been promoted to sainthood, and churches are sometimes named after those so designated. Although defenders of the practice observe that the veneration of angels is of a lesser form than the veneration of God, bible scholar Gerald Larue states simply: "But worship is worship and angels are worshipped within Catholicism."[2] The same can be said of the veneration of the Virgin Mary.

The status of Mary has been increasingly elevated by the Catholic church. As mentioned in Chapter 2, in relation to the Image of Guadalupe, the ecclesiastical term *hyperdulia* is used to describe the special veneration Mary is accorded—a status in which (as Marcello Craveri pointedly observes in his *The Life of Jesus*), the Virgin eventually "assumed the functions of divinity."[3] Early on, Mary became not merely the mother of Christ, but—much more importantly—the "Mother of God." By the seventh century—although the Gospels clearly refer to the brothers and sisters of Jesus (Matt. 12:46; Mark 3:31, 6:3; Luke 8:19)—Mary's "perpetual virginity" had been declared (i.e., that she avoided sexual relations with Joseph for her entire life). The dogma of the Immaculate Conception eventually proclaimed that Mary was even preserved from original sin at the moment she was conceived in her mother's womb. And in 1950, Pope Pius XII proclaimed the doctrine of Mary's Assumption—that at her death Mary, like Jesus, was assumed bodily into heaven.[4]

Indeed, so much emphasis has been placed on Mary and so many divine attributes conferred on her (such as the ability to produce miracles of her own accord) that some have labeled Marian devotion—especially when expressed before statues and other images—as "Mariolatry."[5] Be that as it may, dramatic illustrations of Mary's special status and supposedly miraculous powers are provided by the Marian apparitions that have come to proliferate throughout the Catholic world.

Marian Apparitions

Although apparitions of the Virgin began to outnumber those of Jesus, saints, and angels in the eleventh and twelfth centuries, when devotion to Mary increased in western Christianity, the early sixteenth century brought a diminution in Marian sightings. This apparently resulted from two factors: first, the Protestant Reformation, which rejected, among many other things, the veneration of the Virgin, and, second, the Inquisition, whose witchhunting proclivities might dampen a seer's desire to claim any sort of experience that might be equated with the occult.[6]

Of the Marian apparitions deemed authentic by the Roman Catholic Church, none occurred for three centuries after that at Guadalupe, Mexico, in 1531 (related in Chapter 2).[7] Then in the nineteenth century—when there flourished such occultish interests as popular mesmerism, spiritualism, Theosophy, and clairvoyance[8]—came a revival in reports of Marian apparitions which drew great crowds to certain sites in Catholic Europe.[9] These interests evidently served as models for such reports and their attendant responses in that century. In her scholarly book *Encountering Mary,* Sandra L. Zimdars-Swartz comments on the phenomenon:

> The peculiar importance that has become attached to some of the Marian apparitions of the past two centuries can be explained, in part, by the

fact that many of these have been both "serial" and "public." A serial apparition is one in which the seers have been led in an initial experience to expect that this experience will be repeated, and when they speak about it to relatives and friends and suggest that it will happen again, word spreads and people gather around the seers at the announced or expected time. The subsequent experiences of the seers, then, occur in the presence of anywhere from a few to several thousand people, giving rise to public events of sometimes immense proportions. A public apparition is simply one in which people surround the seers during their experiences. While those gathered may witness a sign, such as a sun miracle, generally speaking they do not see (or expect to see) the Virgin themselves.[10]

The first nineteenth-century Marian apparition to attract widespread interest was that reported by 24-year-old Catherine Labouré, a peasant-born Sister of Charity in Paris in 1830. Catherine had a penchant for seeing apparitions, notably of St. Vincent de Paul, the founder of her order, and she also claimed to have a personal "angel," a child of about five who was radiant with light. Following a brief appearance of Mary in July, which prompted Catherine to kneel before the apparition, a second vision occurring on November 27 had a specific purpose. Catherine claimed she saw the Virgin in an oval frame on which appeared the words: "O Mary, conceived without sin, pray for us who have recourse to thee." She also heard a voice saying, "Have a a medal struck from this model. Persons who wear it indulgenced will receive great graces, especially if they wear it around the neck; graces will be bestowed abundantly upon those who have confidence." The medallion was produced—after a third "vision"—and became known as the "Miraculous Medal." This apparent holy sanctioning of the concept helped those who were lobbying in favor of the proclamation of Mary's Immaculate Conception to realize their desires in 1854.[11]

St. Catherine (who was canonized in 1947) seems to have been a rather classic example of what psychologists term a "fantasy-prone personality"— a type of person who typically exhibits certain personality characteristics, including having imaginary companions during childhood; spending a considerable amount of time fantasizing; reporting apparitions, or having other mystical experiences; experiencing vivid dreams; and yet being basically a normal, healthy, and socially aware individual.[12]

Given St. Catherine's proneness to fantasy and the rather popular subject matter of the Virgin's alleged message, together with the well-known theological elements contained therein, there seems no reason to give the slightest credence to the apparition.

D. Scott Rogo has suggested otherwise, citing "several accurate predictions" the apparition supposedly made to Catherine.[13] However, these appear to have been Nostradamian in their openness to interpretation, and they concerned events rather obviously foreshadowed by sentiments that had been current for some time across France. Also, some of the prophecies were apparently not revealed until *after* the events they allegedly predicted. According to an authoritative source, "For upwards of forty years Catherine spoke to no one save her confessor of her experience" and "she enjoined silence on him." Indeed, Catherine's role in the alleged prophecies was not made public until shortly before her death in 1876, at which time the events that had supposedly been forecast had already come to pass.[14]

In contrast to St. Catherine's visions, the first modern Marian apparition to occur outside of a cloistered setting, and which drew large crowds, took place in the French Alps in 1846. At La Salette, near Grenoble, two shepherd children claimed a single encounter with a figure described in Marian terms. One was fourteen-year-old Melanie Mathieu, the illiterate daughter of an occasionally employed laborer, described by her own employer as lazy, sullen, and disobedient. Rejected early by her mother and often locked out of the house, Melanie said she was kept company during her isolation by her celestial brother, Jesus. The second child was an eleven-year-old boy named Pierre-Maximin Giraud who was described as "reckless." Maximin's father was often absent, leaving the boy to be raised—as well as reportedly abused—by his stepmother.

The two children had only recently met, and on the morning of September 19, 1846, they took their respective little herds of cattle together up the slope of a nearby mountain. After eating lunch and taking a nap, first Melanie and then Maximin saw a bright light, within which they scarcely discerned the figure of a woman. She began to speak to them, saying: "Come near, my children. Don't be afraid! I am here to tell you great news." The woman then told them that if the populace did not mend their ways, she would cease to be able to restrain her son from wreaking vengeance:

For a long time I have suffered for you; if I do not want my son to abandon you, I am forced to pray to him myself without ceasing. You pay no heed. However much you would do, you could never recompense the pain I have taken for you.

I have given you six days for work; I have reserved the seventh day for myself and no one will grant it to me. It is this which weighs down the hand of my son. Those who drive the carts cannot swear without introducing the name of my son. It is these two things which weigh down the hand of my son.

If the harvest is spoiled, it is your fault. I warned you last year about the potatoes, but you have not heeded it. On the contrary, when you found the potatoes had spoiled you swore and you introduced the name of my son. They will continue this year so that by Christmas there will be none left.

Since Melanie was having a little difficulty in comprehending the lady's French, the apparition switched to the local dialect, continuing:

If you have wheat, it is not good to sow it. All that you will sow, the beasts will eat, and that which remains the beasts will not dare to eat. In the upcoming year it will fall into dust.

A great famine will come. Before the famine comes, the children under seven years of age will be seized by trembling and they will die in the hands of those who hold them.

The others will do their penance in the famine. The walnuts will be worm-eaten and the grapes will rot. If they are converted, the stones and rocks will become heaps of wheat, and the potatoes will sow themselves in the fields (in the year that comes). In the summer only some old women go to Mass on Sunday and the rest work, and in winter the boys only want to go to Mass to mock religion. No one observes Lent; they go to the meat market like dogs.[15]

The figure also instructed the children to pray each evening and morning. "Now, my children," she said, "make this known to my people," whereupon the figure strode up a knoll, rose into the air, and disappeared.[16]

By the following evening, word of the alleged apparition—now identified as the Virgin Mary—had spread throughout the area. Predictably, the site became a focus for local pilgrimages and soon there were the usual reports of miracles. A rock on which the Virgin sat was being broken up for relics when a priest appropriated what was left of it. However, one of the smaller pieces, when later broken in half, was discovered to contain an image of Jesus' face. A spring, which appears to have been near the site all along, became a "miraculous spring" that had magically appeared. Almost immediately, its water was discovered to have healing powers, and many miraculous cures were reported. But as Zimdars-Swartz says in her *Encountering Mary,*

> Many of La Salette's healings, particularly those that were said to have occurred at the site itself, were associated with mass pilgrimages involving very large numbers of people, and this suggests that psychological factors could have played a considerable part in these healings.[17]

A local priest seems to have agreed, writing to the bishop: "Children, old men, old women, pregnant women, all rush up there, arriving sweating and panting, drinking at the spring, and descend again joyous and content. Their prayers and their confidence purify the water; it has harmed no one."[18]

In addition to the reputed healings, divine punishments were also reportedly administered. For example, a man who was said to have declared that "the Virgin was a woman like other women," had his infant daughter taken from him. She died after falling into a pot of boiling water, whereupon the father went with his wife to the mountain site to seek the Virgin's pardon. Let that be a lesson to skeptics, the credulous thought.

Other supposedly miraculous aspects of the affair were the prophecies the children claimed had been given them by the apparition. Although these have been cited as having come true and thus providing proof of the apparition's supernatural powers, the fact is that the "prophecies" about the famine become less than impressive when we consider additional facts: The 1840s had brought a famine to Europe; by the time of the Virgin's alleged visitation, it had already reached the southeastern portion of France (i.e., the Grenoble area), resulting in shortages of food and consequently bringing higher prices. Certain other prophecies—about war and floods, for example—were not in fact contained in any of the early accounts of the children's messages. And as to certain secret messages that the children received, these were obtained by local officials and sent to Pope Pius IX at his specific request. Unfortunately, as even the credulous Rogo admitted, they are "so cryptic that it would be difficult to offer an objective or concise evaluation of them."[19]

The alleged Marian appearance at La Salette is prototypical of certain apparition claims that followed—including those at Lourdes in 1858 (discussed at length in the preceding chapter) and at Pontmain, in northwestern France, in 1871. The latter has been described as "one of the most astonishing of Marian visitations of all time."[20]

In the late nineteenth century, Pontmain (near Le Mans) was a predominantly Roman Catholic village consisting of a town church encircled by homes and farm buildings. On January 17, 1871, while France was at war with Prussia, the Barbadette family was engaged in routine chores. The father and two of his sons, Eugène and Joseph, were working in the barn. At six o'clock, Eugène stepped outside "just to see the weather," when he saw an apparition: in the sky was the figure of a tall, lovely woman wearing a blue robe studded with stars.

Eugène alerted his family, who in turn brought others into the street outside the Barbadette home. His brother and other village children claimed they could see the "apparition," but, try as they would, the adults—Monsieur and Madame Barbadette, and various neighbors, including a beloved and pious nun—were unable to see anything out of the ordinary.[21]

But there is a clue to the selective nature of the vision. Eugène pointedly identified three stars in the sky and explained to the adults how the stars delineated the Blessed Virgin's figure. At least according to some of the accounts of the "miracle," the adults were indeed able to see the triangle of bright stars; they just could not see anything else of significance.[22] This suggests that the apparition was simply an imaginative viewing of a constellation. (Everyone is familiar with constellation charts that depict the figures of Hercules, Andromeda, Perseus, and other mythological beings, creatures, and objects—each supposedly indicated by a patterning of stars but helped along by accompanying white outlines in a sort of connect-the-dots fashion on a blue background. And everyone knows the degree of imagination one must apply to any attempt to visualize a given figure.) The children were less inhibited in being able to "see" (i.e., imagine seeing), in the blue sky and stars, the familiar figure of the Virgin. The children's later explanation of how an "oval frame containing four candles had formed around her"[23] could simply be an extension of the same effect—i.e., inclusion of four additional stars in the constellation picture. That the figure reportedly changed expression, and that words slowly appeared underneath to spell out an innocuous message, could simply be the effect of one or another person's imaginative perception influencing others—in brief, the power of suggestion at work. (The claim that a few children allegedly perceived the figure without prompting is a self-serving one that is obviously included to provide a measure of verisimilitude to the situation. At best, it is a dubious assertion that cannot now be verified.)[24]

The last significant Marian apparition of the nineteenth century was reported in Ireland in 1879. Although Rogo characterizes it (with his usual hyperbole) as "one of the most bizarre incidents in the history of the miraculous,"[25] it scarcely seems so.

The events transpired at the little village of Knock, County Mayo, on August 21, 1879. About seven o'clock in the evening of what had been a dismally rainy day, a young girl named Margaret Beirne was making her daily visit to lock the doors of the village church when she noticed something odd: a strange brightness that illuminated the top of the church. She gave it little thought, but half an hour later Mary McLaughlin was passing by and saw within the glow—which seemed to emanate from the church's southern gable—a "tableau" of immobile figures: Mary, Joseph, and a bishop, standing beside an altar. A crowd of fourteen villagers soon congregated and for some two hours viewed the "apparition" in the falling rain.[26]

Although investigated and deemed authentic by a commission of three priests,[27] the "apparition" seems less akin to the Marian visitations typified by La Salette and Lourdes than to some of the holy illusions we discussed in Chapter 2. Recall the illuminated figure of Jesus, with his hand on the shoulder of a boy, that appeared on a soybean oil tank—an image explained as "a combination of lighting, rust spots, fog, and people's imaginations."

Now it is impossible to recreate the exact conditions that prevailed at that precise place and time, but, considering that the tableau figures were unmoving and unspeaking, the possibility of the ethereal scenes being merely some kind of optical illusion seems likely. Given any potential source for the illumination, such as the moon or a reflection of light from some other source, together with its diffusion by the misty atmosphere, a play of light and shadow could result which would be eminently capable of stimulating the pious imagination of credulous villagers.

Although Rogo implicitly assigned the phenomenon to the realm of the paranormal, some of his observations seem equally applicable to the hypothesis of illusion, imagination, and wishful thinking. Noting that apparitions tend to occur in times of social stress, Rogo continues:

> The country was undergoing one of the worst periods in its history. The potato crop had failed in both 1877 and 1878, and was bound to fail again in 1879. Many who were spared death by the resulting famine were stricken by an epidemic of typhus that swept through the country

that same year. In these hard times, the thoughts of the Knock community no doubt often turned to religion, especially on this special day—for the date of the visitation was the eve of the octave of the Assumption, a feast of special importance in the worship of Mary.[28]

"Miracles" at Fatima

The story of the Marian visitations at Fatima, Portugal, that began in 1917 was also set in a time of trouble. After the fall of the Portuguese monarchy in 1910, there came a wave of anti-clerical sentiment and persecution, followed by various revolutionary conflicts and Portugal's involvement in World War I.[29]

The story properly begins on May 13, 1917, when three shepherd children were tending their flock in a pasture some two miles west of Fatima, a town near Ourém. The children were ten-year-old Lucia de Jesus dos Santos and her two cousins, Francisco Marto, age nine, and his sister Jacinta, seven. A sudden flash of lightning sent the children fleeing down a slope, whereupon the two girls beheld a dazzling apparition: a beautiful woman, radiant in white light, standing among the holly-like leaves of a small holm oak.[30]

Only Lucia talked with the figure, who promised to identify herself at the end of a six-month period—during which the children were to return to the site on the thirteenth of each month. The woman told the children that all of them would go to heaven but that Francisco, who could not see her, would have to recite many rosaries. She then instructed Lucia to have Francisco say the rosary, whereupon the boy became able to see the apparition, although he remained unable to hear it speak. After instructing the children to pray for an end to the war, the figure vanished into the sky.[31]

Although the children agreed that they should keep the matter secret, once home, little Jacinta blurted out to her parents that she had shared in a vision of the Virgin Mary. News soon spread throughout the town, and—when the children revisited the site on June 13—they were accompanied by approximately fifty devout villagers. Kneeling in prayer at the oak, the children presently saw the woman gliding down from heaven and again taking up a position amid the oak's foliage.[32]

Thus began a pattern that was repeated each month of the specified period, although the children were absent on the August 13 date (being detained for questioning by secular authorities who disbelieved their tale and who held them briefly in the public jail at Ourém[33]). On July 13, the children claimed they received a special revelation that the lady forbade them to disclose. Throughout the period the apparition remained invisible to the onlookers, but some reported seeing a little cloud rise from (or from behind?) the tree and a movement of the tree's branches "as if in going away the Lady's dress had trailed over them."[34]

At the end of the six-month period, on a stormy and rainy October 13, an estimated seventy thousand people were in attendance at the site, anticipating the Virgin's final visit and with many fully expecting that she would work a great miracle. As before, the figure appeared, and again only to the children. Identifying herself as "the Lady of the Rosary," she urged repentance and the building of a chapel at the site. After predicting an end to the war and giving the children certain undisclosed visions, the lady lifted her hands to the sky. Thereupon Lucia exclaimed, "The sun!" As everyone gazed upward, and saw that a silvery disc had emerged from behind clouds, they experienced what is known in the terminology of Marian apparitions as a "sun miracle."[35]

This "miracle" was variously described. Some claimed that the sun spun in pinwheel fashion with colored streamers, others that it "danced." One reported, "I saw clearly and distinctly a globe of light advancing from east to west, gliding slowly and majestically through the air." To some, the sun seemed to be falling toward the spectators. Still others saw, before the "dance of the sun" occurred, white flower petals showering down but disintegrating before reaching earth.[36]

Exactly what did happen at Fatima has been the subject of much controversy. Church authorities made inquiries, collected eyewitness testimony, and declared the events worthy of belief as a miracle.[37] Skeptics have countered that people elsewhere in the world, viewing the very same sun, did not see the alleged gyrations; nor did astronomical observatories detect the sun deviating from the norm. Therefore, more tenable explanations for the reports include mass hysteria[38] and local meteorological phenomena such as a sundog (a parhelion or "mock sun"). The latter possibility gains some credence from a researcher's claim that the silver disc's described position seemed to be at the wrong azimuth and elevation to have been the sun.[39] A similar phenomenon occurred in 1988 at an outdoor Catholic service in Los Angeles; according to the *Los Angeles Times,*

... many in the crowd reported seeing a prism effect and brightness in the sky to the north. The reports by some of "another sun" or a "rainbow" or both prompted speculation about a supernatural sign.[40]

But a meteorologist dismissed the phenomenon as a sundog, explaining:

The sun passes through water droplets or ice particles high in the atmosphere or through high, thin clouds, which refract the light in such a way as to have a coloration effect. That area of the sky also looks brighter than the surrounding sky. It actually looks like the sun.[41]

However, several eyewitnesses at the October 13, 1917, gathering at Fatima specifically stated they were looking "fixedly at the sun" or "tried to look straight at it" or otherwise made clear they were gazing directly at the actual sun.[42] If this is so, the "dancing sun" and other phenomena may have been due to optical effects resulting from such factors as temporary retinal distortion caused by staring at the intense light, or by the effect of darting the eyes to and fro so as to avoid fixed gazing (but thus combining image, afterimage, and movement), or other illusory results.

Indeed, there was very likely a combination of factors, including optical effects and meteorological phenomena (e.g., the sun being seen through thin clouds, causing it to appear as a silver disc; an alteration in the density of the passing clouds so that the sun would alternately brighten and dim, thus appearing to advance and recede; dust or moisture droplets in the atmosphere imparting a variety of colors to sunlight; and/or other phenomena[43]). The effects of suggestion were probably also involved, since the people had come to the site fully expecting some miraculous event, had their gaze dramatically directed at the sun by the charismatic Lucia, and excitedly discussed and compared their perceptions[44] in a way almost certain to foster "contagion" (or mass hysteria).

Believers in the Fatima "miracle" also cite certain predictions the apparition allegedly made to Lucia, including the "secret" that Jacinta and Francisco would soon die. Indeed, both soon succumbed to influenza, Francisco in 1919 and Jacinta the following year. Other predicted events included an end to the First World War, the coming of the Second, and the rise of Russia as a major power.[45] However, according to Zimdars-Swartz, "much of what devotees today accept as the content of the apparition comes from four memoirs written by Lucia in the convent [where she later resided] between 1935 and 1941, many years after the series of experiences that constitute the apparition event."[46] Indeed, Lucia's first mention of the "prediction" of the children's deaths was in 1927—several years after the fact![47]

As to the other predictions, they were supposedly part of three "secrets" that had been delivered to Lucia by the apparition on July 13, 1917. Lucia's *Third Memoir* gave the first secret as a vision of hell. The second was a statement that World War I would end, "but if people do not cease offending God, a worse one will break out during the pontificate of Pius XI" (who was pope from 1922 to 1939). The third secret has not been revealed (but is supposedly contained in an envelope kept by the Vatican). However, when we consider that the *Third Memoir* was penned in August 1941, we recognize the after-the-fact nature of the so-called predictions.[48]

To fully comprehend what took place at Fatima in 1917, one must look more closely at its central figure—not the Virgin Mary but Lucia de Jesus dos Santos. Born on March 22, 1907, Lucia was the youngest of seven children born to Antonio and Maria Rosa dos Santos. Five years younger than her next-oldest sibling, Lucia was a petted and spoiled child. Her sisters fostered in her a desire to entertain others and to be the center of attention by teaching her to dance and sing. At festivals, Lucia would be placed on a crate where she would entertain an admiring crowd. Her other talents included a gift for telling stories—fairy tales, biblical narratives, and saints' legends—that made her popular with village children, as well as an ability to persuade others to do her bidding.

Lucia was also overtly religious and competitive, having learned the catechism and made her first communion by age six, although the usual age was ten. Her first confession taught her a lesson about secrecy, for she forgot to close the door and talked so loudly that, when she emerged, everyone laughed at her. However, neither they nor her mother had heard one segment of her confession, and her mother later tried, without success, to get the girl to tell "the secret." This, Lucia would later recall, was the priest's instruction for her to pray before a statue of Our Lady of the Rosary and to ask the Virgin to help her keep her heart for the Lord. As she later knelt before the statue, the imaginative child thought she saw the Virgin smile, and the next day she asked God to make her a saint.[49]

Two years before the famous series of apparitions occurred at Fatima, eight-year-old Lucia was leading three girlfriends in praying the rosary when the children saw an apparition: a figure like "a statue made of snow" that was "rendered almost transparent by the rays of the sun." When news of this spread, Lucia's mother contemptuously exclaimed, "childish non-sense!" Nevertheless, the children "saw" the apparition on two further occasions, and reports of the sightings provoked derisive comments from her sisters and others. Lucia, who had been accustomed to "nothing but caresses," was now stung by the taunts, but perhaps she felt this martyrdom was a path toward her desired goal of becoming a saint.

The following year, Lucia supposedly began to experience supernatural encounters while in the company of her impressionable little cousins, Francisco and Jacinta. They were thrice visited by an "angel"—an apparition of a boy of about fifteen. He materialized suddenly, exhorting the children to pray, and on another occasion he gave them Communion.[50]

Lucia's background is revealing. The seeds of her later visionary encounters were clearly contained in her childhood experiences and in her obviously fantasy-prone personality. Her charismatic ability to influence others drew little Francisco and Jacinta into the fantasy. As Zimdars-Swartz says of Lucia:

> ... it is clear that she played the leading role in the scenario of the apparition itself. All accounts agree that she was the only one of the three seers to interact with both her vision and with the crowd, carrying on conversations with both while her two cousins stood by silently. She has said, moreover, and probably not incorrectly, that Francisco and Jacinta had been accustomed to follow her directives before the apparition began, that they turned to her for guidance afterwards, and that it was she who convinced them that they had to be very careful in their experiences.[51]

Additional evidence that Lucia was the orchestrator of the fantasy and manipulator of the other children is provided by certain incidents. For example, when Jacinta first told the story, she stated that the Virgin had said many things that she was unable to recall but "which Lucia knows." Lucia's own mother was convinced that her precocious daughter was, in her words, "nothing but a fake who is leading half the world astray."[52]

Be that as it may, Lucia had, so to speak, let the genie out of the bottle, and the influence of Fatima on twentieth-century Catholicism has been considerable. Just as the Fatima fantasy borrowed heavily from that of Bernadette Soubirous at Lourdes, later apparitions borrowed from Fatima. Zimdars-Swartz explains:

Many of the apparitions reported in the postwar years repeated the dramatic scenarios that were prominent at Fatima or in these Fatima messages: the dancing sun, Communion from an angel, the promise of a visible sign foreshadowing chastisements, and warnings about Russia. . . . In many of these later apparitions the Virgin is reported to have said that she had returned because people had neglected or forgotten the messages she had conveyed at Fatima. For the many Roman Catholics who believed and found meaning in the Marian apparitions that followed the Second World War, Fatima, along with La Salette and Lourdes, had become a model by which the authenticity of a later apparition might be tested, and those who have seen the later apparitions as authentic have usually understood them as extensions of the mission which the Virgin had inaugurated at Fatima.[53]

Hoax at Garabandal

A truly complex series of alleged Marian visitations began on Sunday, June 18, 1961, at the little village of San Sebastian de Garabandal in the mountains of northwestern Spain. After Mass, four young girls—notably eleven-year-old Maria Concepcion "Conchita" Gonzalez and three companions, Mari Cruz Gonzalez (ten) and Jacinta Gonzalez and Mari Loli Mazon (both twelve)—had been busily engaged in stealing apples from the nearby property of the village schoolmaster. Walking back to town they heard a peal of thunder but, unconcerned, sat down in the lane to eat the purloined fruit and play a game of marbles.

Presently, Conchita noticed that an angelic figure had appeared at the roadside. He was about eight years old, wore a blue robe, and sported pink wings—or so the children soon told the villagefolk. The following day the children held a vigil at the site, accompanied by a small group of largely mocking villagers. When nothing happened, the children returned alone the next day. After another uneventful wait, they started home but were momentarily surrounded by a dazzling light which caused them to scream until it subsided.[54]

The very next day, Wednesday, found the children and an attendant crowd at the site on the rocky lane. After finishing the rosary and reciting a Station of the Cross, the children went into a "deep trance," staring fixedly at a spot at the roadside. Although they reported dejectedly that the angel had been unresponsive to their questions, the crowd was supposed to have been impressed with the performance. Many wept and asked forgiveness for their previous skepticism.

The following evening (June 22), the girls were accompanied by a priest. According to Rogo, who seemed untroubled by the fact, the girls "promptly went into trance";[55] yet this is highly suggestive of what psychologist Robert A. Baker, an expert on trances and trance-like states, terms "the fake trances" that alleged mediums and mystics "exhibit at will."[56] Naively, with the priest looking on, the local rustics "tested" the little visionaries by shining bright lights in their eyes, shaking them, even reportedly pricking them with pins—which actions were, said one witness, "quite incapable of arousing them from their rapture."[57]

Now the "trances" and "visions" were reenacted almost daily at the site from June 23 until July 1 (although the angel failed to visit on June 26, 29, and 30). Increasingly larger crowds were now gathering at the roadside. Then, on July 1, the children (actually their leader, Conchita) made an important announcement: the angel had told them the Holy Virgin herself would appear on the following day! (Pause here to imagine the effect on the piously credulous. . . .)

July 2 inaugurated the second phase of the Garabandal "miracle." Virtually the entire village was emptied as the inhabitants paraded to the site of the anticipated visitation. However, the procession halted when the girls suddenly fell into their rapturous state and immediately saw the Virgin, flanked by twin angels. The four girls supposedly conversed with the figure, telling her at length about their daily lives. She laughed in response and then—after teaching them the proper way to recite the rosary and promising to return the next day—vanished.

Now the children no longer had to seek the Virgin by visiting the site but could receive a "mental command" whenever she wished to talk. Reportedly the four specially favored children all received the "summons" simultaneously and would then go to the roadside (or to a nearby site, a pine grove atop a hill next to the local church). They "usually" arrived at "almost" the same time and then promptly fell into a trance.[58] Supposedly the girls were tested by being deliberately separated, yet they would still meet at the same time. Reports Zimdars-Swartz, "The villagers differ, however, in their recollections of the circumstances under which this was done."[59] And—if the girls were indeed engaged in trickery—all that would be necessary to pull off such a demonstration of their supposedly supernatural communication would be, say, the whisper of a prearranged time at the end of a given rendezvous.

Many other alleged paranormal or supernatural occurrences, which lasted at Garabandal into 1965, cannot now be verified. These include the claim that the girls would sometimes fall to the ground, becoming so heavy that others could not lift them; that from this same position Conchita would sometimes lift her shoulders "as though she were beginning to levitate"; that rosaries and medals given to the entranced girls, so that the Virgin could kiss them, would sometimes be returned smelling of roses; and that the youthful wonderworkers sometimes "seemed able to read minds."[60] Then there is the "little miracle" that supposedly provides "proof" of supernatural intervention at Garabandal. This transpired just after the first anniversary of the original angelic appearance there, when a Communion host (wafer) supposedly materialized on Conchita's tongue.

For weeks Conchita had announced that a miracle would take place on July 18 and, in consequence, a crowd had gathered outside her home. The final "summons" did not come, however, until about one thirty or two o'clock the following morning. Reportedly entranced, Conchita raced outside and led a stampede of the credulous down a lane and into an alley where she stopped abruptly. In the light of the moon and "an infinite number of torches," the onlookers saw Conchita with her tongue outstretched as if to receive Communion. Suddenly the host "appeared" on her tongue. Said an eyewitness, "It did not seem to have been deposited there, but might be described rather as having materialized there, faster than the human eye could see."[61]

All these supernatural effects and supposed miracles come from just such anecdotal reports and were never performed under conditions controlled by competent experts in deception. Moreover, they have (at least to this former professional stage magician) all the earmarks of childish stunts and simple tricks—including, in the latter instance, a possible sleight-of-tongue feat!—coupled with the effects of suggestion. Similar as well as much more impressive "miracles" have been the stock-in-trade of self-styled wizards since ancient times.[62]

There is further evidence that the Garabandal episode—which ended in 1965—was bogus. Although Conchita (who eventually married and moved to New York) continued to publicize the alleged miracles, it is a fact that there were three occasions on which one or all of the Garabandal visionaries retracted some statements they had made about their experiences. For example, all four girls made one somewhat equivocal confession, telling their parents "that they had not seen the Virgin or the angel, but that they had never tried to deceive anyone and that the calls and the miracle of visible Communion were true." Later, according to Conchita, three of them "returned to reality" and reaffirmed the truth of all that had been claimed.[63]

Conchita even maintained that the Virgin had actually *predicted* that the children would deny the visitations and begin to contradict each other. However, it appears that the alleged prediction came only *after the fact* of Conchita's first retraction. According to Zimdars-Swartz, the girl "admitted that her visions might not be 'real' but said that she thought this was not the case with the visions of the other girls." She then reportedly signed a declaration to that effect, in the presence of her aunt and a member of an official diocesan commission that had been created to investigate the affair."[64]

The fourth child, Mari Cruz Gonzalez, who was not yet eleven when the affair began, did not withdraw her retraction. Although her three companions all moved to the United States, "where, to differing degrees, they have remained accessible to Garabandal devotees," Mari Cruz stayed in Spain and continued to deny that the apparition was authentic.[65] She stated that she and her companions had used the trances and apparition claims as a means to get away from the village and play!

One must ask whether it is more likely that one participant in a genuine series of miracles would steadfastly deny their authenticity or that three of four co-conspirators would refuse to admit to perpetrating a hoax. Such is the desire to believe among many that their ability to rationalize knows no bounds, and so they can dismiss all later retractions and evidence of trickery, opting instead for the miraculous. Said one priest, should the children deny the authenticity of the apparition, "they will be in illusion, but not us."[66]

For their part, ecclesiastical authorities ended their investigation by concluding that there had been no apparition and that nothing had occurred that did not have a natural explanation. Claims made by the seers that the pope had actually given them expressions of his affection were denounced as untrue. As a consequence, the diocesan bishop issued a prohibition on pilgrimages or other activities in behalf of what he termed "the alleged apparitions."[67]

A final point remains to be considered. The apparition of the Virgin at Garabandal repeatedly promised that a "great miracle" would occur sometime in the future, and that it would be witnessed by the popular Italian Catholic, Padre Pio, and be accompanied by the discovery of the incorrupt body of Fr. Luis Andreu, a Jesuit who had visited Garabandal.

Alas, Padre Pio died in 1968, and Fr. Luis' remains, disinterred in 1976 (when some seminary burials had to be relocated), were discovered to be skeletonized. The "great miracle" had failed to occur.[68]

Mystery at Zeitoun

A unique series of apparitions that reportedly occurred over a three-year period in Zeitoun, Egypt, provides an interesting contrast to the Marian visitations typified by Lourdes, La Salette, Fatima, and Garabandal.

Zeitoun is a suburb of Cairo, a poor area comprised of both Moslems and Coptic Catholics. The latter represent a sect that separated from the rest of Christianity over a fifth-century doctrinal dispute. The Coptic church has its own pope and ecclesiastical hierarchy, while still retaining many affinities with the Roman church. Such affinities include an emphasis on devotion to Mary (although Copts do not accept the doctrine of Immaculate Conception).[69] According to legend, Zeitoun was the town where Joseph, Mary, and the baby Jesus hid after fleeing Judea in response to Herod's slaughter of all firstborn Jewish children.[70]

It was at the Coptic St. Mary's Church in Zeitoun that the apparitions appeared. On April 2, 1968, two Moslem mechanics left their nearby garage for some fresh air, whereupon they observed a white figure standing atop the church near its central dome. Thinking the figure was a nun, they said, and fearing she intended to jump to her death, the men reacted immediately: One fetched the church's priest while the other phoned the emergency squad. As others gathered, they viewed the figure for some minutes before it eventually disappeared.[71]

The apparition next materialized on April 9, at the same position near the dome, and reappeared thereafter at frequent, if irregular, intervals. On May 5, it reportedly continued in view for several hours. Eventually such large crowds gathered that local officials prepared a place for them to congregate by tearing down some old buildings.

As one source summarizes the observed phenomenon:

> Its arrival was heralded by flashes of light, then the figure would form, human in shape, and white in colour (sometimes bluish-white), wearing flowing robes of light. It was sometimes accompanied by "doves of light" which flew around without flapping their wings. The figure was interpreted as the Blessed Virgin Mary, and that is what people then saw:

they claimed to see her bowing to them, pacing back and forth, hands raised in blessing, garments swaying in the wind.[72]

And so on. Sometimes, during 1969, accoring to Rogo, "a smoky 'fog' would infrequently emanate from the top of the building."[73] Those who saw the phenomenon in one form or another—before it dwindled in 1970 and ceased in 1971—have been estimated to number in the hundreds of thousands.

The available evidence suggests that people did observe some unfamiliar phenomenon, but it appears to have been more in the nature of an illusion than of a holy visitation. After all, the "apparition" never spoke or provided any rationale for its unpredictable manifestations. And it did not so much disappear as peter out, becoming progressively less common, as if, in Rogo's words, "the power that had generated the form was gradually ebbing."[74]

But what could be the nature and source of such a power? Rogo, in his usual credulous fashion, suggested that expectations of the faithful might have caused "an ever-increasing pool of psychic energy created by the thoughts of the Zeitounians which in 1968 became so high-pitched that an image of the Virgin Mary burst into physical reality!"[75]

Unfortunately for such airy speculation, a more likely possibility comes from intriguing geophysical data. This evidence suggests that the phosphorescent display may have been the result of "earthquake lights"—an as yet little-understood phenomenon that is associated with seismic disturbances—being linked with escaping gas, massive frictional effects, and other mechanisms,[76] and that is believed responsible for certain reports of "ghost lights" around the world. For example, an earthquake on the Izu Peninsula of Japan on November 26, 1930, generated in excess of 1,500 reports of mysterious lights described as "auroral streamers," "like . . . fireballs," "a straight row of round masses of light," and so on.[77]

Researchers exploring a possible link between the Zeitoun phenomena and regional seismic disturbances found an impressive set of data: During 1969, and within a radius of less than 500 kilometers from Zeitoun, the seismic activity was determined to have been *ten times greater* than normal, leading the researchers to conclude that the evidence supported the postulated link.[78]

This raises the important question: Did observers of the luminous phenomenon see in it what they expected to see? Or, as the co-authors of one report ask, citing the descriptions of the alleged apparition: "How much of this detail was grafted on to an amorphous luminous shape by the awestruck crowd? Was the Blessed Virgin Mary really present at all?"[79] With one possible exception,[80] the few photographs of the Zeitoun phenomena, obtained and published by Rogo, show just such amorphous shapes.

All evidence considered, therefore, what Rogo represents as "undoubtedly the most spectacular and important series of Marian apparitions documented in modern times" and even "the strongest proof ever obtained demonstrating the existence of the miraculous"[81] is instead revealed as most likely having a quite down-to-earth source.

Medjugorje Mania

The 1980s saw the advent of a new series of Marian apparitions, this time at the remote village of Medjugorje, Yugoslavia. Although the reported visitations soon captured the attention of the world's news media, they also brought in their wake a raging controversy: While many charismatic Catholics believe they are genuine appearances of the Blessed Virgin Mary, the local bishop has branded them a hoax, and a book by a devout Catholic writer concludes they are the handiwork of Satan.

The story of Medjugorje began in 1981 on June 24—the date long celebrated as the birthday of John the Baptist. The scene was Podbrdo Hill, a rocky prominence overlooking the village, which is located in an obscure mountainous region in what was then Communist-controlled Yugoslavia. On the hillside were six children (who were not directly related, although some shared surnames). They included four girls, Ivanka Ivankovic (age 15), Mirija Pavlovic and Mirjana Dragicevic (both 16), and Vicka Ivankovic (17), as well as two boys, Jakov Colo and Ivan Dragicevic (ages 10 and 16, respectively).[82]

The six claimed that at dusk they were suddenly startled by an extremely bright light, at the center of which was a beautiful woman wearing a gray dress with white mantle and veil. She had dark hair and blue eyes, and around her head were a dozen golden stars. The lady, who floated above the ground, carried in her arms an infant whom she alternately revealed and covered, while gesturing for the children to come near. Instead, they ran away in fear.

When the figure appeared the next day, fifteen-year-old Ivanka asked about her mother who had died a few weeks earlier. The reply came that her mother was well and happy and had a message for Ivanka to care for her aging grandmother. The following day, the figure specifically identified herself, saying, "I am the Blessed Virgin Mary." Thereafter, for the next decade, the floating figure appeared almost daily at the same time—about 6:30 P.M.[83]

Events during this ten-year period can only be briefly summarized. The children were initially examined by a psychiatrist, who pronounced them fit, and by several "foreign doctors" who conducted several tests on the children, including the medieval pin-prick test for imperviousness to pain during ecstasy, which supposedly lent credibility to the children's claims. The site of the Virgin's daily visitations changed frequently—from the hill (due to a police prohibition on outdoor gatherings), then from various other locations (on orders from the bishop), and eventually to the St. James Catholic Church in Medjugorje. There the children would stand in a line facing one wall and begin reciting the Lord's Prayer. Suddenly they would kneel in unison and enter their visionary state wherein—their lips moving inaudibly—they allegedly communicated with the Virgin. Their visions were of unpredictable duration, from one to forty-five minutes. Messages received were later recounted to one of the Franciscan priests at the church. In 1984 the Virgin began giving weekly messages to the parish and, in 1987, to the world. The children also claim to have received certain "secrets"—the receipt of ten of which supposedly reduces the frequency of visions from daily to infrequent.[84] By 1991—when civil war in Yugoslavia all but ended the events—most of the children had stopped having daily visions and had begun to make lives for themselves, although "new visionaries" had reportedly "sprung up" in the village.[85]

Whether or not the events will continue at Medjugorje, which the *New York Times* described in the fall of 1991 as resembling "a windblown off-season beach town,"[86] it will long be remembered for the incredible claims attributed to the site. These included, in addition to the daily visitations and messages, sun miracles (like those at Fatima), images of Jesus and Mary that sometimes appeared in the clouds, inexplicable lights on the hill, numerous alleged healings, and other supposedly miraculous occurrences such as rosary beads turning from silver to gold.[87]

Such claims brought huge crowds to the mountain village—more than 50,000 pilgrims on holy days, and an estimated nineteen million over the ten-year period. Yugoslav cynics soon dubbed the apparition "the Madonna of Tourism." The quiet farming village was transformed into a "religious boomtown" with pizza, espresso, and religious-souvenir shops springing up, while villagers built additions onto their homes, or even constructed entire new houses with guest rooms for rent. "Apparition watch" gazebos also cropped up, and the complex of church buildings had a contingent of seven permanent Franciscan priests.[88] Additional priests served on a rotating basis to help with multilingual religious services as well as confession, the latter held in a pavilion of booths adorned with "red and green occupied/unoccupied lights" near the main church.[89]

Until their visionary experiences ended, the teens performed their respective roles in the drama. Vicka regaled the credulous visitors with a tale of how the Virgin once took her—bodily—to heaven, purgatory, and hell. "Heaven is a great space full of a great light, like none on Earth, she said. "Everyone is equal—there are no fat or thin people. They sing and dance together. There are many angels."[90] Vicka, the only one of the six who remained constantly in Medjugorje, cheerfully signed autographs on request and laid her hands on suppliant pilgrims.[91]

The mania spread far and wide. According to *Newsweek,*

From Boston to Barcelona, charismatic Catholics peddle videos of the Yugoslav children in ecstasy and hawk books spreading their prophecies. In the United States, Mary has become a Catholic version of the Pentecostal Protestants' speaking in tongues.[92]

Seven-inch statuettes of Our Lady of Medjugorje, tastefully made of luminous plastic, as well as fifteen-inch models fashioned of "a special wood paste material" with "crystal eyes to give life-like appearance," have taken their place among similar figurines representing the Fatima and other Marian apparitions.[93]

Mindless devotion was not going unchallenged, however. Although the diocese's ecclesiastical leader, Bishop Pavao Zanic, at first accepted the apparition claims as genuine, and reportedly "wept with joy at the possibility of there being another Lourdes in his own diocese,"[94] he soon changed his view. Defenders of Medjugorje have tried to portray the bishop's revised view as a case of sour grapes, the result of friction between him and the Franciscan friars, who had dominated the Roman Catholic Church in that part of Yugoslavia for centuries.[95] Yet the accusation cuts both ways and, in the end, it is the evidence that one must look to.

First of all, the apparitions should be seen in their true context. Due to the "prophecy" of a prominent charismatic—that there would be a great miracle in Yugoslavia and that the Lord had said, "Do not fear, I am sending you my Mother"—the expectation of a Marian visitation was apparently widespread among the emotional charismatics.[96] Moreover, the priest at Medjugorje, Jozo Zovko, had arrived only nine months before and had installed a radically charismatic prayer group in the parish—not merely one that sought the charismatic gifts of praying in tongues, prophecy, and healing, but one that used group motivational techniques, including the use of peer pressure to provoke the public confession of sins and such bizarre practices as (in the words of one critic) "milling 'round, staring into one another's eyes."[97]

In any event, after the apparitions became routine, something happened to trigger suspicion on the part of Bishop Zanic. This was a series of messages allegedly from the Virgin that faulted the bishop and took the Franciscans' side in their clash with him. Since the statements represented the narrow perspective of the Franciscans, Bishop Zanic became understandably suspicious as to the true source of the messages.[98]

When he learned of the messages and of Vicka's "secret diary" in which they were presumably recorded, the bishop sought to obtain the record. However, the children's charismatic spiritual adviser swore on a crucifix that there was no such diary, even though a defender of the children acknowledges that "Vicka did undoubtedly keep a record of some kind."[99]

After his suspicions were aroused, Bishop Zanic found additional grounds for doubting the authenticity of the apparitions, including numerous contradictions in the children's stories. While the charges and countercharges in this regard can become tiresome—as partisans on both sides would doubtless agree—at least one apologist for the miracles concedes that "the children may well have contradicted themselves."[100] To take just one example, when the children were asked why they had gone to Podbrdo Hill on the day they first saw the apparition, they first said they had "gone for a smoke." Later they changed their story, claiming, alternately, that they had gone to round up stray sheep and/or to pick flowers.[101] In addition, some of the alleged messages from the Virgin became progressively elaborated—another indication that they may have been spurious.[102]

Although an additional basis for distrusting the authenticity of the Blessed Virgin's messages—incompatibility with Catholic theology—will be more convincing to Catholics than to non-Catholics, even the latter may appreciate the concern. After all, if long-standing Catholic teachings were in error, it would seem odd for the Virgin to choose such a late date to make that clear. One such point is the Virgin's statement to the effect that all religions are equal. Even one defender of the Medjugorje messages admits that the words seem potentially troubling, "since they suggest the indifferentism which makes no distinction between Christ and the prophet Mohammed."[103]

Other troubling aspects of the apparition's communications include the lady's displeasure at the prospect of children from the crowds trampling on her veil, arguably a vain rather than pious concern. Another, implicit in certain of the lady's communications, is the denial of the truth of the Immaculate Conception. As one commentator observed in this regard, it was as if she were a "Protestant Madonna."[104]

As a consequence of his investigation of the events, Bishop Zanic concluded: "I don't believe that the Madonna is appearing in Medjugorje. Since 1982 I have been certain."[105] He added:

> The phenomenon at Medjugorje will be the greatest shame of the Church in the twentieth century. One can say that these are hallucinations, illusions, hypnosis or lies.[106]

Bishop Zanic promised that if an authentic sign of Mary's presence at Medjugorje ever occurred, he would do penance by traveling there from his residence (about twenty miles) on his knees. Zanic's position was supported by Catholic writer Ivo Sivric, whose *The Hidden Side of Medjugorje* labels the six children "actors" and concludes that the affair was the Devil's handiwork.[107]

In addition to the bishop's criticisms, other problems are apparent. One is the embarrassingly illiterate nature of some of the reputed messages. Admits one defender of their authenticity, it was always "necessary to correct their [the children's] grammar when transcribing the Virgin's messages."[108] Also, during attempts to determine the content of the messages allegedly delivered to Vicka, "the limitations of her own vocabulary became clear. . . ."[109] Defenders suppose this is merely the inability of the children to properly recall the Virgin's exact words and see it as a credible occurrence. It seems, however, rather more akin to some of the alleged communications with departed spirits during the heyday of spiritualism—when the bogus mediums often gave themselves away by using language inappropriate for the deceased persons from whom they were supposedly receiving messages.[110]

Other evidence against authenticity comes from iconographic elements in the children's descriptions of the apparition. Her crown of twelve stars is a motif borrowed from Revelation 12:1 (a passage some believe refers to Mary) and common to traditional representations of the Virgin.[111] As with the Image of Guadalupe (discussed in Chapter 2) such stock motifs say more about iconographic conventions than about authenticity.[112] Finally, the description of the figure as having blue eyes seems less compatible with the racial background of Mary than with the expectations of European children.

But what about scientific tests that supposedly proved that the occurrences at Medjugorje were genuine? These were simply the usual pseudoscientific claims that we have come to expect from miraculists. For example, an Italian professor of electrochemistry and an American associate reported high levels of radiation at the apparition sites that supposedly had no logical explanation and was suggestive of a spiritual rather than a nuclear source, However, other scientists were quick to point out that the primitive means used did not justify such conclusions, and other investigations of radiation levels at Medjugorje offered no evidence of "spiritual energy." As one writer said of the matter, "claims of scientific proof for the existence of the spiritual world seem to have proved short-lived."[113]

As to the medieval pin-prick test, it was carried out not by a physician or scientist but by a priest. The test was performed on Vicka, but it it not true that she "failed to react";[114] rather, her body "moved somewhat to the right but she quickly and gracefully regained balance."[115] A professor of medicine, Henri Joyeux, found the test to be "of little significance." Joyeux performed electroencephalogram, electrocardiogram, and other tests on the children, who were initially most reluctant to allow them. These tests, conducted while the children were supposedly in ecstasy, persuaded Joyeux that they were not merely acting. However, his arguments are unconvincing and equivocal. He and a colleague, René Laurentin (a priest and self-styled "mariologist" who actually wrote their co-authored report) conceded: "The visionaries are evidently not outside themselves; they remain simple and natural. Their identity (consciousness), far from being altered, is merely intensified." As to ecstasy, Laurentin equivocates: while claiming that the word "seems to me to be justified," he launches into various "distinctions" and "clarifications," and finally says of the evidence of the visionaries that "the medical study neither proves nor contradicts their evidence."[116]

Claims for miraculous occurrences did not fare well, either. Despite the predictable claims of "healings," for example, Bishop Zanic stated pointedly:

The majority of the pious public has naively fallen victim to the great propaganda, the talk of the apparitions and the feelings. These people themselves have become the greatest propaganda for the event. They do not even stop to think that the truth has been hidden by deliberate falsehood. They do not know that not one miraculous healing has occurred that could have been verified by competent experts.[117]

As to the supposedly inexplicable lights on the hillside, Sivric's *The Hidden Side of Medjugorje* renders them quite explicable: Some were due, he says, to an illusion produced by atmospheric conditions, others to boys who were known to have lit fires on Podbrdo Hill for fun.[118] Indeed, Laurentin and Joyeux find the phenomena to be "disconcerting in their variety."[119]

A particularly revealing insight into claims of the miraculous at Medjugorje comes from reports of silver rosaries and crucifixes turning into gold—a crassly materialistic concept that speaks volumes about the attitudes of some who have been swept up in Medjugorje mania. The phenomenon was first reported at Medjugorje but later spread to other regions of the world. (See Figures 13 and 14.) Unfortunately for the claims, however, scientific examinations of some allegedly metamorphosed rosaries—including one obtained by Pittsburgh paranormal investigator Richard Busch—did not find evidence of the miraculous. Busch reported on the analysis that was performed on the rosary:

> The results came quickly. The rosary was not gold, nor was it in the past nor likely to be in the future. It was and is brass. The yellowish cast had come from oxidation. There simply was no miracle![120]

The *San Francisco Chronicle* related a similar case.[121] The *Chronicle* also reported that silver-coated rosaries were apparently responsible for some "miraculous" color changes in rosary metal. As the thin coating wore off from handling and the underlying copper was exposed, the metal seemed to be changing physically from silver to gold. According to the *Chronicle:* "Jewelers say the erosion is influenced by body moisture, which changes with exercise and emotion, among other things, and environmental factors such as humidity and climate."[122]

My own encounter with a Medjugorje "miracle" came in Youngstown, Ohio, when I was presented with a photograph and an intriguing tale. Supposedly an Ohio pilgrim to Medjugorje had attempted to take a photograph of the children on the hillside, but when his film was processed he had instead the photograph of the face of Mary![123] I was told by two persons that the picture was supposedly a print from the original negative. Alas, my stereo-microscope revealed the fine screen pattern that results from the "halftone" process of printing color pictures. In other words, the photo was a fake, a copy made by taking a photograph of a likeness of Mary from a printed magazine or book.

In 1986 the Vatican became involved in the Medjugorje affair, taking the matter out of Bishop Zanic's hands and entrusting the question of authenticity to Yugoslavia's national bishops' conference. That group's work is still in progress and could even take years to complete. In the meantime, the bishops' conference issued a warning against any public worship that is directly linked to the alleged apparitions. However, until civil war came to the region and frightened away most pilgrims, Medjugorje seemed unaffected by any such warnings.[124]

Other Apparitions

Numerous other alleged apparitions have been reported, and Medjugorje seems to have inspired several claims of Marian visitations elsewhere: Pescara, Italy (1988); Lubbock, Texas (1988); Conyers, Georgia (1990); and a shrine near Denver, Colorado (1991).

The affair in Pescara, Italy, was mercifully brief. A local woman named Maria Fioritti claimed to have seen a weekly apparition of the Virgin Mary—a claim widely reported in the Italian press. On Sunday, February 28, 1988, more than 10,000 pilgrims flocked to the coastal city and gathered on a hillside at the foot of a sixteen-foot-high cross. Alas, according to state-operated RAI television, the apparition never appeared; worse, many went away complaining that staring into the sun, as Maria Fioritti had directed them to do in anticipation of Fatima-like "sun miracles," had hurt their eyes.[125]

The sun performed better, apparently, for pilgrims at Lubbock, Texas, later the same year. The affair, however, began earlier, just after Monsignor Joseph James, the pastor of St. John Newmann Church, returned from a pilgrimage to Medjugorje. Ten members of the charismatic Roman Catholic congregation had gathered to say the rosary and "felt the strong presence," as one said, "of the Blessed Mother." Only a few days later three parishioners—Mary Constancio, Mike Slate, and Theresa Werner—

allegedly began receiving messages from the Virgin. Mrs. Constancio scribbled the first of her messages in her son's school notebook. It read:

> Go and tell your priest and tell your bishop that Mary your Mother has come to give a message. That they should spread her word throughout radio, throughout television, throughout the newspaper, throughout the pulpit, throughout the world . . . to come and say the rosary with me on Monday nights.[126]

Over the next few months, increasingly during the late summer, pilgrims began to arrive at the church property by car- and busload. On August 15, the Feast of the Assumption, a crowd of some 12,000 religious hopefuls had gathered on St. John Newmann's lawn and began to report "little miracles throughout the day": several believing that their rosaries had turned to gold, one claiming to have "seen a vision of doves flying in formation over the church," another reporting a rumor that the crown atop a statue of Mary "had been seen spinning." According to the *New York Times*:

> Then in the middle of mass, and shortly before dusk, the sun broke dramatically through a gathering curtain of clouds. Shrieks went up from the lawn, and many of those assembled cried, prayed and pointed toward the sky. Some said they saw Jesus in the heavens, some saw the Virgin Mary, some saw the gates of heaven. Others, including a number of priests, stood by, craning their necks but seeing nothing unusual at all.[127]

The *Los Angeles Times* also reported:

> Different people beheld different images, some Jesus and some an eagle and some a serpent with a beady little eye. And some—even a man devout as Joe James—saw nothing at all.
>
> As people peered longer into the brightness, the sun seemed to spin and flip and pulsate, lurching closer, then pulling back. All was spectacle.[128]

The very diversity of the phenomena may illuminate (no pun intended) what really happened at Lubbock as well as at Fatima. The play of light and shadow and the consequences of staring at the sun, coupled with pious imaginations, led people to experience a variety of effects. Thus a ten-year-old cancer victim, Kristy Schoen, cried, "Oh, Mommy, I see her! I see her!" while in contrast, according to one news report, "her parents didn't see what Kristy saw, but they did see colors pulsating around the sun behind the clouds."[129]

In any event, Monsignor James broke into a rendition of "Amazing Grace," and soon church deacons were taking testimony from those who believed they had witnessed an apparition and collecting film from those who might have recorded their visions on camera. Monsignor James said he would keep the evidence in a safe for the present, but eventually would use the materials to persuade the Vatican that a genuine miracle had occurred at Lubbock[130]—"something of a Lone Star Lourdes," as one wag described the site's potential.[131]

In the meantime there were those who were unsure. Deacon Clark Cochrane, head of the political science department at Texas Tech, cautioned the parish not to rely on miracles as a basis of faith. Also, according to the *Los Angeles Times:*

> Skeptics, for the most part, thought the whole thing was something Joe James had imported from Medjugorje.
>
> Nothing deceitful, mind you. But the monsignor had the lyrical tongue of a revivalist. If he was on fire with Our Lady, others naturally would be drawn to the flame for its soul-comforting warmth.
>
> The rosary sessions seemed to them like a seance, the voices born and reborn in the messengers by the powers of suggestion—from Joe James, from their own upbringing, from their longing to know God.
>
> Mary Constancio, after all, spoke of the monsignor as if he preached from some elevated pulpit at the right hand of God. Mike Slate, the burly Vietnam vet, was already a man prone to chatting with angels.
>
> And that batty Theresa. Who knew what went on in her head? She acted as if she had her own burning bush.[132]

Two years later, in 1990, the Virgin allegedly began appearing to a Conyers, Georgia, housewife named Nancy Fowler. Originally from Cambridge, Massachusetts, Mrs. Fowler had begun experiencing visions in the early 1980s when she supposedly saw both heaven and hell. By 1987, Mrs. Fowler was having visions of Jesus and the Virgin, and in July 1990 she and her husband and two sons moved to a thirty-acre site in Georgia—a location directed by yet another vision and purchased by her supporters. In October of that year, Mrs. Fowler began claiming regular visitations from Mary on the thirteenth of each month, accompanied each time by a "Message to the United States." Sitting in the "Apparition Room" of her home, Mrs. Fowler broadcast the heavenly message over a public-address system to crowds of hundreds or even thousands.[133]

Following the message, many pilgrims claimed to experience sun miracles, by now part of the stock-in-trade of Marian-visitation claims. The descriptions varied as usual but, according to paranormal investigator Becky Long, who visited the site,

> Most people said that the sun was either pulsating or dividing into multiple lights. The apparent pulsation did not surprise me, since the eye would certainly rebel at focusing on the sun. From the descriptions of the multiple lights, I concluded that these were afterimages caused by looking toward the sun several times.[134]

She and some fellow members of Georgia Skeptics—an innovative paranormal-investigation group—were using a telescope with solar filters, which provoked some curiosity. People soon swarmed about the telescope saying they wanted a close-up look at the miraculous things they had just witnessed. Reports Long: "I estimate that well over two hundred people viewed the sun through one of our solar filters, and without exception they saw nothing unusual when looking through the mylar."[135]

One type of sun miracle was especially intriguing, and several people at Conyers claimed to have documented it in photographs. It appears to be indistinguishable from a phenomenon recorded by Polaroid photos at Lubbock. As described in that case, the pictures "showed the outline of what could be an entrance superimposed on the sun." Miraculists dubbed the phenomenon "the doorway to heaven."[136] Others called it the "Golden Door"[137] mentioned in Revelation 4:1, which states:

> After this I looked, and, behold, a door was opened in heaven: and the first voice which I heard was as it were of a trumpet talking with me; which said, Come up hither, and I will shew the things which must be hereafter.

It is to the excellent investigative work of Georgia Skeptic Dale Heatherington that we have an explanation for this "miracle." He noticed that—just as at Lubbock—the allegedly supernatural pattern was only seen on Polaroid "instant" photographs. States Heatherington, after purchasing an inexpensive Polaroid One Step camera:

I took it to my home several miles northwest of Roswell and took a few pictures of the sun. In spite of the fact that I'm a skeptic, I was 40 miles from Conyers, the date was February 29th (not the 13th) and the camera had never been blessed by Nancy Fowler, I got excellent photos of the "Golden Door." I took several pictures in an effort to find out what conditions cause the Golden Door to appear. I even produced a Golden Door picture by photographing a 50 watt halogen spot light in a dark room.[138]

Heatherington immediately realized that the phenomenon was an effect produced by the camera and soon discovered that the Polaroid's iris had the exact same shape (straight vertical sides, curved top and bottom) as the Golden Door. He then calculated the height-to-width ratio of both the Golden Door in the photos and the camera's iris opening and discovered they were the same. Heatherington states: "It seems that through some quirk in the Polaroid One Step camera optics, an image of the iris is projected onto the film when a bright point source of light is centered in the field of view." As he concluded, the Golden Door is "actually the doorway into the camera, not heaven."[139] (See Figures 15 and 16.)

Thus the Golden Door phenomenon went the way of another claim of the miraculists at Conyers. As related in Chapter 6, the well water at the site—supposedly blessed when Jesus appeared to Mrs. Fowler—was found to be contaminated and "unsatisfactory for drinking."[140]

Yet another American woman was claiming to see apparitions of the Blessed Virgin in late 1991, at the Mother Cabrini Shrine near Denver. Theresa Lopez, an attractive woman of about thirty, had recently pleaded guilty to a felony charge of check fraud and suffered other troubles.[141] She had her first vision, she claimed, on March 17 at Medjugorje, then at other locations: in the reflection of a Colorado lake on June 25, for example, and on December 7, at the Cabrini Shrine, where the message was as follows:

Mass must be the center of life. The holy sacraments of Eucharist and reconciliation are vital to spiritual growth. I desire my children to gather together and [God's] heart shall be softened. Save the West from the wrath.[142]

Mrs. Lopez described the Virgin as "wearing a golden gown. . . . And she was surrounded by pink sparkling lights. . . . Her voice [was like] thousands of wind chimes. . . . She has dark brown hair. She has blue eyes that draw you in. . . ."

Mrs. Lopez's "visions" continued through 1992—supposedly the Virgin found it convenient to appear on the second Sunday of each month. On December 8, the feast day of the Immaculate Conception, an estimated five to six thousand pilgrims were drawn to the mountaintop shrine and people looked to the sky in expectation of a sun miracle. There were some serious physical consequences, as reported by Al Galipeau of the Rocky Mountain Skeptics:

One of the most significant physical results of the event of December eighth was retinal burning caused by staring directly at the sun. We had talked with people who said the sun was "dancing" and that it changed color. We had suspected that this could be caused by their looking directly at the sun and receiving temporary, and possibly permanent, damage to their retinas. Most people were shielding their eyes from direct sunlight with their hands or pieces of paper when they looked into the sky for a sign, but some were not, and they must have been damaging their eyes.

Sure enough; the very next day Denver area opthalmologists began seeing patients suffering from solar retinopathy—patients who admitted they had looked into the sun for signs of a vision at Mother Cabrini Shrine. Newspaper reporters began calling the opthalmologists, and the newspaper articles showed up on Wednesday, Thursday, and Friday following the event. Dr. Douglas Pechette of Evergreen treated two such patients and heard of two more who were treated by another ophthalmologist. Porter Memorial Hospital's Center for Sight had two more referred. One was a 29-year-old woman. The *Rocky Mountain News* reported on the twelfth that they had located fourteen people who hurt their eyes at the shrine on Sunday. Dr. Lawrence A. Winograd of Denver saw two of them and estimated that with 100 opthalmologists in the Denver area there were potentially hundreds of people being treated. By Friday, the *Denver Post* reported that the known toll was "at least two dozen." But, as Dr. Winograd had said, the actual number of persons being treated was likely much greater. And many would not seek treatment.

Galipeau reported that one woman, who was at the shrine to pray for her crippled child, probably suffered permanent eye damage. Ironically, she was the wife of a physician.[143]

In May 1993, an eighteen-month investigation concluded. As the archbishop said of Mrs. Lopez's visions: "There does not appear to be evidence which would indicate a supernatural origin for these alleged events."[144]

Soon, no doubt, visionaries similar to Theresa Lopez will spring up elsewhere if we read the trend correctly. But there have been non-Catholic visionaries, too, although rarely have they drawn great crowds or created a public spectacle.

Oral Roberts did grab headlines with his claim, in 1980, that he had had a vision of a 900-foot Jesus. As he described it, the giant figure lifted the steel structure of Roberts' 60-story hospital center. In 1987, Roberts claimed God told him that unless he raised a "quick" $4.5 million, God was going to take his life. His son, Richard, sent letters to previous contributors, pleading, "Let's not let this be my dad's last birthday." Within a month, Roberts' public relations officer claimed that his followers had already pledged $1.6 million.[145]

The "Mormon" church—that is, the Church of Jesus Christ of Latter Day Saints—was actually founded by a man who allegedly had been visited by an angel. In 1823 Joseph Smith claimed that a heavenly visitor named Moroni had revealed the existence of a new gospel—the Book of Mormon—which was engraved on gold plates hidden in a hill near Palmyra, New York, together with a pair of jeweled spectacles for their decipherment. After he "translated" the plates, Smith claimed, he returned them to the angel, thus thwarting critics who wished to examine them. A follower of Smith, Martin Harris, was permitted to show a partial "transcript" of the writing to some experts, including Columbia University Professor Charles Anthon. Anthon's opinion was that the language was bogus and the tale of the gold plates a hoax. But Smith persuaded the gullible Harris that because of the difficulty in engraving the plates the scribe had switched to a "shorthand" form of Egyptian writing unknown to the professor. Before the *Book of Mormon* was even printed, Smith was convicted of fraud. Years later, when Smith ran out of money buying up land surrounding his Kirtland, Ohio, Mormon community, he decided to open his own bank.[146] According to one source:

There was just one problem: you had to have money to open a bank. Never a stickler for details, Smith went out and borrowed the money to open the Kirtland Safety Society Bank and have plates made up for printing the currency the bank would issue. To assure depositors that their money would be secure, he filled several strong boxes with sand, lead, old iron, and stones, then covered them with a single layer of bright fifty-cent silver coins. Prospective customers were brought into the vault and shown the heaping chests of silver. "The effect of those boxes was like magic," claimed one witness. "They created general confidence in the solidity of the bank, and that beautiful paper money went like hot cakes. For about a month it was the best money in the country."[147]

Eventually, of course, the bubble burst, the bank failed, and in 1838 Smith "declared bankruptcy with his feet," fleeing the community along with his followers.[148] In 1844, following a newspaper attack on him, Smith ordered its press destroyed and its editor expelled. As a result, he and his brother were arrested and put in jail in Carthage, Illinois, but a mob broke in and shot them to death.[149] Thus the prophet of Mormonism—who repeatedly claimed that he was visited by angels or given revelations directly from God—was apparently, at last, on his own.

Select Bibliography

Arvey, Michael. "Miracles and the Virgin Mary—Urgent Messages from Heaven?" Chapter 4 of *Miracles: Opposing Viewpoints*. San Diego: Greenhaven Press, 1990. An account of the Fatima and Zeitoun apparitions, taken largely from Rogo.

Ashton, Joan. *The People's Madonna: An Account of the Visions of Mary at Medjugorje*. London: Fount, 1991. A book-length treatment of the alleged miracles at Medjugorje by one who (according to the Foreword) "writes as an Anglican Christian deeply committed to the authenticity of the visions."

Laurentin, René, and Henri Joyeux. *Scientific and Medical Studies on the Apparitions at Medjugorje*. Dublin: Veritas, 1987. A study of the Medjugorje claims from the perspective of "a world renowned mariologist" (who actually wrote the text) and a French medical professor; an indication of their approach comes from their statement that "the visionaries agreed to ask the Virgin's permission to allow this test and it is with her consent and theirs that we proceeded with these unprecedented experiments" (p. 130).

Rogo, Scott. "Miraculous Interventions." Part three of *Miracles: A Parascientific Inquiry into Wondrous Phenomena*. New York: Dial Press, 1982. A typically Rogovian approach, attempting to portray Marian apparitions—at most of the famous sites—as "psychic" phenomena.

Zimdars-Swartz, Sandra L. *Encountering Mary: From La Salette to Medjugorje*. Princeton, N.J.: Princeton University Press, 1991. A scholarly treatment of several major apparitions, including Lourdes, Fatima, and Medjugorje. Taking a phenomenological approach, and attempting to be "neither apologetic nor antagonistic," it is necessarily skeptical given the weight of the evidence.

Notes

1. For a discussion, see Isaac Asimov, *Asimov's Guide to the Bible,* vol. 2: *The Old Testament* (New York: Avon, 1968), pp. 293–94.

2. Gerald A. Larue, *The Supernatural, the Occult, and the Bible* (Buffalo, N.Y.: Prometheus Books, 1990), p. 63.

3. Marcello Craveri, *The Life of Jesus,* trans. Charles Lam Markmann (New York: Grove, 1967), pp. 27–28.

4. Alan Schreck, *Catholic and Christian: An Explanation of Commonly Misunderstood Catholic Beliefs* (Ann Arbor, Mich.: Servant Books, 1984), pp. 173–81.

5. Joan Ashton, *The People's Madonna: An Account of the Visions of Mary at Medjugorje* (London: Fount, 1991), p. 29.

6. Sandra L. Zimdars-Swartz, *Encountering Mary: From La Salette to Medjugorje* (Princeton, N.J.: Princeton University Press, 1991), p. 4.

7. Rosemary Ellen Guiley, *Harper's Encyclopedia of Mystical and Paranormal Experience* (San Francisco: Harper Collins, 1991), p. 343.

8. Richard Cavendish, ed., *Encyclopedia of the Unexplained: Magic, Occultism, and Parapsychology* (London: Routledge & Kegan Paul, 1974), pp. 114–21, 181, 205, 230–35, 248–54.

9. Zimdars-Swartz, *Encountering Mary,* pp. 4–5; Guiley, *Harper's Encyclopedia,* p. 343.

10. Zimdars-Swartz, *Encountering Mary,* p. 5.

11. Ibid., pp. 26–27; John Coulson, ed., *The Saints: A Concise Biographical Dictionary* (New York: Hawthorn Books, 1958), p. 104.

12. Robert A. Baker, *They Call It Hypnosis* (Buffalo, N.Y.: Prometheus Books, 1990), pp. 245–50. Baker cites S. C. Wilson and T. X. Barber, "The Fantasy-Prone Personality: Implications for Understanding Imagery, Hypnosis, and Parapsychological Phenomena," in A. A. Sheikh, ed., *Imagery: Current Theory, Research and Application* (New York: John Wiley and Sons, 1983).

13. D. Scott Rogo, *Miracles: A Parascientific Inquiry into Wondrous Phenomena* (New York: Dial Press, 1982), p. 208.

14. Coulson, *The Saints,* p. 104.

15. Quoted in Zimdars-Swartz, *Encountering Mary,* p. 30.

16. Ibid., p. 31.

17. Ibid., p. 37.

18. Abbé Pierre Melin, curé of Corps, letter to the bishop of Grenoble, Mgr. Philbert de Bruillard, quoted in Zimdars-Swartz, *Encountering Mary,* p. 38.

19. Rogo, *Miracles,* p. 210 n.; Zimdars-Swartz, *Encountering Mary,* pp. 40–41.

20. Rogo, *Miracles,* p. 214.

21. Ibid., pp. 214–16. Zimdars-Swartz gives 1870 as the year of the Pontmain apparition.

22. Rogo, *Miracles,* p. 216. (including footnote).

23. Ibid.

24. Ibid.

25. Ibid., p. 218.

26. Ibid., pp. 218–20.

27. Guiley, *Harper's Encyclopedia,* p. 343; Rogo, *Miracles,* p. 219.

28. Rogo, *Miracles,* p. 219. Rogo also relates a claim that the spot where the figures appeared remained dry despite the rain, but, again, the exact conditions are unknown—for instance, the area might have been sheltered, say, by a tree. Also, people excited by an alleged apparition may not be particularly credible reporters of such details.

29. "Portugal," *Encyclopaedia Britannica,* 1960 ed.

30. Michael Arvey, *Miracles: Opposing Viewpoints,* Great Mysteries Series (San Diego, Calif.: Greenhaven Press, 1990), p. 66; Rogo, *Miracles,* pp. 222–23. The holm oak (or holly oak) is a variety of evergreen, *Quercus ilex.*

31. Arvey, *Miracles: Opposing Viewpoints,* p. 66; Rogo, *Miracles,* pp. 221–23.

32. Arvey, *Miracles: Opposing Viewpoints,* pp. 66–67; Rogo, *Miracles,* pp. 222–23.

33. Zimdars-Swartz, *Encountering Mary,* pp. 192–93.

34. Rev. V. Dacruz, quoted by Rogo, *Miracles,* pp. 224–25. (Rogo's source is given as "V. Montes de Oca. *More About Fatima.* No publisher listed, 1945.")

35. Arvey, *Miracles: Opposing Viewpoints,* pp. 69–71. (For more on "sun miracles," see Zimdars-Swartz, *Encountering Mary,* pp. 5, 15, 82–83, 162, 213.)

36. Gerald A. Larue, *The Supernatural, the Occult, and the Bible* (Buffalo, N.Y.: Prometheus Books, 1990), pp. 195–96; Arvey, *Miracles: Opposing Viewpoints,* pp. 70–71; Rogo, *Miracles,* pp. 227, 230–32.

37. Zimdars-Swartz, *Encountering Mary,* p. 90.

38. Larue, *The Supernatural, The Occult, and the Bible,* p. 195.

39. Rogo, *Miracles,* p. 229n.

40. John Dart, "Surprises Mark Revival of Mary's Hour Bowl Service," *The Los Angeles Times,* May 21, 1988.

41. Dan Bowman, operations director of Weather Data, Inc., Wichita, Kansas, quoted by Dart, "Surprises Mark Revival of Mary's Hour Bowl Service."

42. Quoted in Rogo, *Miracles,* pp. 230, 231.

43. Larue, *The Supernatural, The Occult, and the Bible,* p. 195, mentions

the silver-disc and color-effect possibilities, but not the advancing/receding illusion, which is my own hypothesis.

44. See Rogo, *Miracles,* pp. 229–30.

45. Zimdars-Swartz, *Encountering Mary,* pp. 194, 218.

46. Ibid., p. 68.

47. Ibid., p. 197

48. Ibid., pp. 198–99.

49. Ibid., pp. 69–72.

50. Rogo, *Miracles,* p. 222; Zimdars-Swartz, *Encountering Mary,* pp. 73–74.

51. Zimdars-Swartz, *Encountering Mary,* p. 68.

52. Quoted in Zimdars-Swartz, *Encountering Mary,* pp. 71, 86.

53. Zimdars-Swartz, *Encountering Mary,* pp. 90–91.

54. My account is taken largely from Rogo, *Miracles,* pp. 238–50, and Zimdars-Swartz, *Encountering Mary,* pp. 124–56. Some details disagree: for example, whereas Rogo says the girls were "blocked" by "an intense screen of light" (p. 240), Zimdars-Swartz states that "they seemed to be surrounded by a dazzling light that momentarily hid them from one another" (p. 126).

55. Rogo, *Miracles,* p. 240.

56. Baker, *They Call It Hypnosis,* p. 162.

57. Quoted in Baker, *They Call It Hypnosis,* citing F. Sanchez-Ventura y Pascual, *The Apparitions of Garabandal* (Detroit: San Miguel Publishing Co., 1966). I say the tests were naive because, although the ability to resist distracting stimuli can be a characteristic of genuine trance states, there is no objective, verifiable criteria by which the authenticity of a trance can be determined; see Baker, pp. 162–66.

58. Rogo, *Miracles,* pp. 241–42.

59. Zimdars-Swartz, *Encountering Mary,* p. 133.

60. Rogo, *Miracles,* pp. 242–43.

61. Alejandro Damiens, a Barcelonan photographer, quoted in Rogo, *Miracles,* p. 248.

62. See, for example, Milbourne Christopher, *Panorama of Magic* (New York: Dove, 1962), and Joe Nickell, *Wonder-workers: How They Perform the Impossible* (Buffalo, N.Y.: Prometheus Books, 1991).

63. Zimdars-Swartz, *Encountering Mary,* pp. 130–31, 146–50.

64. Ibid., pp. 130–31.

65. Ibid., pp. 148, 301 (n. 104).

66. Quoted in Zimdars-Swartz, *Encountering Mary,* p. 150.

67. Ibid., p. 153.

68. Rogo, *Miracles,* p. 249; Zimdars-Swartz, *Encountering Mary,* pp. 225–30.

69. Richard Kennedy, *The Dictionary of Beliefs* (East Grinstead, Sussex, England: Ward Lock Educational/BLA Publishing Ltd., 1984), p. 55; "Copts," *Encyclopaedia Britannica,* 1960 ed.

70. Arvey, *Miracles: Opposing Viewpoints,* p. 81.

71. Rogo, *Miracles,* pp. 250–52.

72. Janet Bord and Colin Bord, *Unexplained Mysteries of the 20th Century* (Chicago: Contemporary Books, 1989), pp. 257–58. Rogo, *Miracles,* pp. 252–56, provides more extensive descriptions of the phenomenon.

73. Rogo, *Miracles,* p. 255.

74. Ibid., p. 257.

75. Ibid., pp. 256–57.

76. *Bulletin of the Seismological Society of America* 63 (December 1977): 2177–78, cited in Carroll C. Calkins, ed., *Mysteries of the Unexplained* (Pleasantville, N.Y.: Readers' Digest Association, 1982), p. 253. For more on earthquake lights, see Calkins, pp. 237, 238, 249, 253.

77. Calkins, *Mysteries of the Unexplained,* p. 253.

78. John S. Derr and Michael A. Persinger, "Temporal Association between the Zeitoun Luminous Phenomena and Regional Seismic Activity," *The Explorer* 4 (October 1987): 15, summarized in *Science Frontiers* 55:4 (cited by Bord and Bord, *Unexplained Mysteries,* p. 258).

79. Bord and Bord, *Unexplained Mysteries,* p. 258.

80. This is a photo of a luminous form on the church's roof that does look distinctly figural, resembling a robed man or woman with a disc-like "halo," similar to depictions of holy personages in traditional Christian art. Given the photo's stylized, artificial look, however, Rogo's failure to mention whether the negative was properly examined leaves the authenticity of this particular piece of evidence in question.

81. Rogo, *Miracles,* pp. 250, 256.

82. Ashton, *The People's Madonna,* pp. 20–21; John Thavis, "Girls Who Say They See Visions Interviewed," *The Tidings* (Los Angeles), March 25, 1988.

83. Ashton, *The People's Madonna,* pp. 20–22.

84. Ibid., pp. 47, 86, 96–102.

85. Thavis, "Girls Who Say They See Visions Interviewed."

86. Chuck Sudetic, "In Shrine to Virgin, Threat of War Darkens Streets," *The New York Times,* September 27, 1991.

87. Jeffrey L. Sheler et al., "What's in a Vision?" *U.S. News & World Report,* March 12, 1990.

88. Kenneth L. Woodward with Andrew Nagorski, "Visitations of the Virgin," *Newsweek,* July 20, 1987; Sura Rubenstein, "Reported Apparitions by the Virgin Mary Put a Yugoslav Village on Map," *The Sunday Star-Ledger* (Newark, N.J.), December 13, 1987; Dusko Doder, "Religious Boomtown Rakes in Cash," *Rocky Mountain News,* June 20, 1991.

89. Doder, "Religious Boomtown Rakes in Cash."

90. Thavis, "Girls Who Say They See Visions Interviewed."

91. Ashton, *The People's Madonna,* pp. 79, 81.

92. Woodward with Nagorski, "Visitations of the Virgin."

93. *Religious Articles Catalog,* 1989–1990 (St. Paul, Minn.: Leaflet Missal Co., 1989), pp. 14, 19.

94. Ashton, *The People's Madonna,* p. 52.

95. Ibid., pp. 51–61.

96. Rev. Father Gerard Dunn, "Medjugorje: Reasons for the Bishop's Condemnation," a recorded audio program distributed by Keep the Faith, 810 Belmont Avenue, North Haledon, N.J. 07508. See also Ashton, *The People's Madonna,* pp. 34–36.

97. Dunn, "Medjugorje: Reasons for the Bishop's Condemnation."

98. Ashton, *The People's Madonna,* pp. 51–61.

99. Ibid., p. 56.

100. Ibid.

101. Dunn, "Medjugorje: Reasons for the Bishop's Condemnation."

102. Ibid.

103. Ashton, *The People's Madonna,* p. 30. (See also pp. 30–39 for a contrary view.) Cf. Dunn, "Medjugorje: Reasons for the Bishop's Condemnation."

104. Dunn, "Medjugorje: Reasons for the Bishop's Condemnation."

105. Quoted in Rubenstein, "Reported Apparitions by the Virgin Mary . . ."

106. Quoted in Woodward with Nagorski, "Visitations of the Virgin."

107. Ashton, *The People's Madonna,* pp. 52, 67–70. See also Hilary Evans, "More Light on Medjugorje," *The Skeptic* (United Kingdom), July/August 1991.

108. Ashton, *The People's Madonna,* p. 72.

109. Ibid., p. 56.

110. For an example, see Lady Conan Doyle's supposed communication with the spirit of Harry Houdini's mother (in Milbourne Christopher, *Houdini: The Untold Story* (New York: Thomas Y. Crowell, 1969), pp. 168–70.

111. *Religious Articles Catalog,* p. 18.

112. See Joe Nickell and John F. Fischer, "The Image of Guadalupe: A Folkloristic and Iconographic Investigation," *Skeptical Inquirer* 8.4 (Spring 1985): 243–55

113. Ashton, *The People's Madonna,* p. 103. For a discussion see pp. 103–104.

114. Ibid., p. 101.

115. René Laurentin and Henri Joyeux, *Scientific and Medieval Studies on the Apparitions at Medjugorje* (Dublin: Veritas Publications, 1987), p. 18.

116. Ibid., pp. 8, 126. As indicated, these authors are not skeptics.

117. Chuck Sudetic, "Do 4 Behold the Virgin? Bishop Is Not a Believer," *New York Times International,* September 28, 1990.

118. Ashton, *The People's Madonna,* p. 69.

119. Laurentin and Joyeux, *Scientific and Medieval Studies on the Apparitions at Medjugorje*, p. 196.

120. Richard Bush (Chair, Paranormal Investigating Committee of Pittsburgh), typescript report, "The Non-Miracle of Medjugorje," May 1988.

121. Torri Minton, " 'Miracle' Changes in Rosary Beads," *San Francisco Chronicle*, May 13, 1988.

122. Ibid.

123. The image is identical (except for facing in the opposite direction) to one accompanying an article on Medjugorje (Sheler et al., "What's in a Vision?"). It is attributed to "Anonymous."

124. Sheler et al., "What's in a Vision?"; Sudetic, "In Shrine to Virgin . . ."

125. "No Vision for Believers," *Pensacola News Journal*, February 29, 1988.

126. Quoted in Lisa Belkin, "Reports of Miracles Draw Throngs," *New York Times*, August 17, 1988.

127. Belkin, "Reports of Miracles Draw Throngs."

128. "VISIONS: Messages from the Virgin Mary or Delusions?" *Los Angeles Times*, April 9, 1989.

129. Theresa Churchill, "Ill Girl, 10, Believes in Vision," *Decatur Herald & Review* (Decatur, Ill.), August 19, 1988.

130. Belkin, "Reports of Miracles Draw Throngs."

131. Paul Weingarten, *Chicago Tribune*, reprinted as "Thousands Gather in Texas to Await Miracles," *Washington Post*, August 16, 1988.

132. "VISIONS: Messages from the Virgin Mary or Delusions?"

133. Becky Long, "The Conyers Apparitions," *The Georgia Skeptic* (newsletter of the Georgia Skeptics) 5.2 (March/April 1992): 3.

134. Ibid., pp. 3, 8.

135. Ibid., p. 8.

136. "VISIONS: Messages from the Virgin Mary or Delusions?"

137. Dale Heatherington, "The Mystery of the Golden Door," *The Georgia Skeptic* 5.3 (May/June 1992): 1.

138. Ibid.

139. Ibid., p. 3.

140. Bill Osinski, "Woman Asked to Post Warning About Water at Apparition Site," *Atlanta Constitution*, February 15, 1992.

141. Al Galipeau, "A Holy Vision Reported in the Rocky Mountains," part I, *Rocky Mountain Skeptic* (newsletter of the Rocky Mountain Skeptics) 9.4 (Nov./Dec. 1991): 1.

142. Quoted in Galipeau, "A Holy Vision Reported in the Rocky Mountains," part I.

143. Al Galipeau, "A Holy Vision Reported in the Rocky Mountains," part II, *Rocky Mountain Skeptic* 9.5 (Jan./Feb. 1992): 4.

144. Gary Massaro, "Apparitions Case Still up in Air," *Rocky Mountain News*, May 12, 1993.

145. John Omicinski, "Preacher Draws Fire for Give-or-I-Die Appeal," *The Courier-News*, February 12, 1987.

146. Steven Naifeh and Gregory White Smith, *The Mormon Murders* (New York: Weidenfeld & Nicolson, 1988), *passim;* "Latter Day Saints, Church of Jesus Christ of," *Encyclopaedia Britannica*, 1960 ed.; "Smith, Joseph," *Encyclopedia Americana*, 1990 ed.

147. Naifeh and Smith, *The Mormon Murders*, pp. 25–26.

148. Ibid.

149. "Smith, Joseph."

8

Sanctified Powers

Are saints and other holy persons imbued with certain mystical powers? Stressing that "we still have no real idea of the outer limits of human physical potential," Patricia Treece suggests in *The Sanctified Body* that the answer is yes. As she claims, "The human body in sanctity"—i.e., the body of someone possessing "authentic holiness"—"will inevitably reflect its mystical life by unusual energies."[1] In addition to such special powers as incorruptibility and psychic abilities, including clairvoyance (already discussed in Chapters 4 and 5 respectively), mystics may exhibit luminosity, levitation, bilocation, stigmata, inedia, the ability to exorcise demons, and the production of "apports."

Luminosity

Throughout history, sacred personages have often been depicted, in word or image, as exhibiting a special radiance: either surrounding the entire body (and known as an *aureole*) or around the head (and termed a *nimbus,* or more popularly, a halo). A combination of the two constitutes a *glory.*[2] Today, many promoters of allegedly paranormal or supernatural phenomena use the term *aura* to describe a multicolored aureole or "human rainbow" that consists of "bands of colored light allegedly radiating from and surrounding the bodies of human beings, animals and plants, and visible to clairvoyants and sensitives."[3]

Just as people commonly speak of a bride's "radiance," an expectant mother's "glow," or of someone "beaming" with satisfaction, the countenance of a pious person may appear to possess a special sheen that seems to reflect his or her inner holiness. The effect may be magnified by expectation, since in the symbolism of many religions—including Hinduism, Judaism, Christianity, and Islam—God is associated with light.[4] Thus St. Bonaventure (1221–1274) said of St. Francis of Assisi (1181–1226) that "the extraordinary illumination" which was alleged to have occasionally appeared around St. Francis's body "was witness to the wonderful light that shone within his soul."[5]

This statement, typical of many of the reports of saintly luminosity, points up the problems one faces in attempting to evaluate such phenomena: the reports are at second hand (St. Bonaventure, for example, could not have witnessed St. Francis' illumination, having been just four years old at the latter's death), or they in any case represent purely anecdotal evidence. It is, therefore, difficult to determine to what extent the observations were the result of pious imaginations or attributable to some illusion of reflected light (such as those discussed in Chapter 2)—or even to other causes.

One wonders, for instance, why anyone should give credence to a report, prominently cited by Patricia Treece, concerning Father Maximilian Kolbe's alleged luminosity. At Assisi in 1930, Kolbe was supposedly "transfigured in a diaphanous form, almost transparent, and surrounded by a halo of light," yet the report dates from almost twenty years later, and derives from a single observer—one who casually stated that he had "problems with my eyes."[6]

Treece admits that "not all saints become luminous," and that "those who do are certainly not luminous all the time." She alternately claims that the luminosity is a function of the saint's "moments of ecstasy or rapture" and that only certain people may be able to view the light.[7] In short, the alleged phenomenon is so elusive and unpredictable as to suggest its fictitiousness.

Looked at scientifically, claims for the existence of auras have fared poorly. As pseudoscience, however, they have thrived. For instance, in 1911 Dr. Walter J. Kilner published his *The Human Atmosphere,* in which he not only claimed to see the aura and to use it to make medical diagnoses, but also uncritically accepted the validity of nonexistent "N-rays" and clairvoyant powers.[8] Kilner's peers rightly scoffed. *The British Medical Journal* stated, "Dr. Kilner has failed to convince us that his aura is more real than Macbeth's visionary dagger."[9]

Interest in the aura was boosted in the 1970s by the popularity of a technique known as Kirlian photography, in which a high-voltage, high-frequency electrical discharge is applied across a grounded object. This yields an air-glow or "aura" that can be recorded directly onto photographic paper, film, or plates. Supposedly, the auras of living things contain information about their "life-force," those of people indicating their psychic state. In fact, the Kirlian aura is really only "a visual or photographic image of a corona discharge in a gas, in most cases the ambient air." Experiments yield "no evidence as yet" that any property of the aura pattern "is related to the physiological, psychological, or psychic condition of the sample," with the probable exception of moisture due to sweating.[10]

Not surprisingly, controlled tests of alleged psychics' abilities to see auras have met with failure. One involved placing either one or two persons in a completely dark room and asking the psychic to state how many auras she saw; only chance results were obtained.[11] James Randi conducted another test on his two-hour television special, "Exploring Psychic Powers—Live." Anyone who could detect auras or otherwise demonstrate psychic ability would win $100,000, and Barbara Martin was the challenger in the aura-reading category. She had selected ten people she maintained had clearly visible auras, each of whom was asked to stand behind a screen. Martin agreed that the auras would extend above the screens and that she would therefore be able to tell which screens had people standing behind them. Alas, she got only four out of ten correct guesses—fewer than the five that chance allowed.[12]

Miraculists and New Age devotees may not be convinced by such evidence, or by any evidence that fails to substantiate the existence of the imagined auras. One awaits controlled tests of the certifiably sanctified. In the meantime, evidence for auras in general—if not saintly luminosity in particular—appears to be dim indeed.

Levitation

In his book, *Comparative Miracles,* the Rev. Robert D. Smith, a Catholic writer, asks this question: "Is it a fact that some mystics, when in a state of ecstatic trance, have been lifted from the ground and have remained suspended for a notable time in mid-air, without the interference of any human agency?"[13]

Skeptics may reply that the law of gravity directs a negative answer, but miraculists are rarely persuaded by science. After all, they say, by definition a miracle occurs in defiance of natural laws. The question then, like others concerning allegedly miraculous phenomena, must be answered on the basis of the evidence—the burden of which lies, of course, on levitation's defenders.

Proponents certainly have a number of alleged levitators to present, but since we are concerned with not the quantity but the quality of the evidence, we must hasten to underscore the word *alleged*. The majority of such claims come from three major traditions: legends of Catholic saints, claims of certain spiritualistic mediums, and reports of feats by the Hindu fakirs of India.

Regarding the last, for example, in the late 1820s self-levitation was reported in Madras, India. An old Brahmin mystic was able to sit cross-legged some four feet above the ground, while his hand grasped an upright cane that fitted into a bench. After his death in 1830, a fakir by the name of Sheshal, known as "the Brahmin of the Air," performed the same feat. And in 1866, Louis Jacolliot, Chief Justice of Chandenagur, witnessed the great fakir Covindasamy perform the so-called cane levitation.[14]

Actually, the feat is not truly a *levitation*. In stage magicians' parlance that term is reserved for effects in which the person appears to float freely in air. For example, in "The Floating Lady" illusion, a hoop is passed over the lady's body to "prove" that there are no hidden wires or supports. (For the secret, see standard texts on conjuring.[15]) Quasi-levitations like those the fakirs performed—in which there is some visible connection between the person's body and the ground, floor, or stage beneath—are properly called *suspensions*.

By the time of Covindasamy's performances, European magicians had perfected the much more convincing levitation effect, but over the years exaggerated tales of the fakirs' powers of "levitation" persisted. Then, in the late 1930s, the trick that had originated in Madras more than a century before was brought to London where it was finally photographed. The pictures, according to magician Walter B. Gibson, "indicated what had been suspected all along."[16]

In actuality, the bamboo cane was a metal rod which was securely attached to the bench. It connected with a curved rod that extended under the fakir's loose sleeve and continued down his back. There it terminated in a seat, hidden beneath his flowing garments, that comfortably supported the "levitating" fakir—or, in this case, faker. Says Gibson:

> Yet despite the obvious trickery involved, many people still believe that Hindu yogis possess the power of levitation. Stories are told of adepts who cross ravines by striding boldly through the air. Others are said to sit in Himalayan caves and gradually float upward through the aid of breathing exercises that render their bodies weightless.[17]

It is this legendary tradition, obviously, that lies behind the claim of Transcendental Meditation (TM) founder Maharishi Mahesh Yogi that he could teach his credulous disciples to levitate. His Ministry of Information even issued a photograph depicting a TM student sitting in the lotus position and apparently levitating several inches in the air. However, her scarf was blown upward, revealing that the photo did not depict her in tranquil levitation but rather caught her in the act of *bouncing*. Skeptics quickly duplicated the obviously fake photograph.[18]

Spiritualist mediums have likewise claimed the ability to levitate, but the alleged instances range from suspected to proven fakes.[19] One such performer was the notorious Daniel Dunglas Home (1833–1886), who produced a variety of supposedly paranormal effects, including pretended imperviousness to fire and such spiritualistic phenomena as the production of "spirit" forms and levitation. On one occasion in 1852, when Home was nineteen, he floated so high—allegedly lifted by a spirit—that his head touched the ceiling. One spectator who had been holding his hand felt his feet and noted they were well off the floor.[20] However, the event took place in complete darkness. As magician Milbourne Christopher writes:

> One method used then, and later, by mediums is most convincing. In the dark the psychic slips off his shoes as he tells the sitters his body is becoming weightless. The sitter to the medium's left grasps his left hand, the one to the right puts a hand on the mystic's shoes, near the toes. Holding his shoes together with his right hand pressing the inner sides, the medium slowly raises them in the air as he first squats then stands on his chair. The man holding his hand reports the medium is ascending; so does the sitter who touches the shoes. Until I tried this myself, it was hard to believe that spectators in a dark room could be convinced an ascension was being made.[21]

Home's most famous levitation occurred at a London house in 1868. The medium reportedly floated out one upstairs window and glided through another into an adjacent room. Again, however, the rooms were dark,[22] and the witnesses gave different versions of what actually happened. Also, no one actually *saw* Home levitating. All we really know is that they were *told* he went out the one window and then saw him *appear* to come in the other. The great magician Harry Houdini thought Home might have had a wire dangling outside which he used to swing from one window balcony to another. Another researcher suggested a plank could have been placed between the balconies, while yet another postulated that the balconies were close enough (about four feet) that Home could simply have stepped from one to another.

Still other researchers have suggested that after noisily opening the first window, Home slipped quietly in the dark to the other which he then opened and pretended to enter. It would have been difficult to tell whether his dimly silhouetted form was actually outside or inside the window. And people often "see" what they expect to see. Whatever actually happened, the dark room and other circumstances suggest trickery. Home specifically instructed the witnesses to remain seated. "On no account leave your places," he insisted.[23] What did he have to fear from their moving about? Probably detection of his trick!

The third group of alleged levitations, those of Catholic saints, are quite numerous, some of the reported miracle-workers being St. Arey (d. 304), St. Francis of Assisi (c. 1181–1226), St. Ignatius (c. 1491–1556), St. Teresa of Avila (1515–1582), St. Joseph of Copertino (1603–1663), and St. John Joseph of the Cross (1654–1734).[24] But there are problems. As Smith says in *Comparative Miracles:*

Many of these non-biblical instances of levitation both early and late are poorly attested, e.g., only one witness saw the phenomenon, or the ecstatic did not leave the ground completely (during prayer the body appearing to rise into the air several inches while his garments still touched the floor concealing whether there still was bodily contact with the floor, or the ecstatic is on tiptoe for a long time in such a way that natural support seems impossible), or the light was dim, or the reports of levitation crept in only fifty years or more after the death of the ecstatic while being absent from the earliest biographies.[25]

The Rev. Herbert Thurston, the often skeptical English priest who wrote several treatises on miracles, reached the conclusion that "the evidence for levitation in the case of some very eminent saints is far from satisfactory."[26]

The most astonishing claims of levitation concern St. Joseph of Copertino, dubbed "the flying friar." One report has Joseph uttering a shriek, springing into the air, and "coming to rest on the top of an olive tree where he remained in a kneeling position for half an hour."[27] Such reports seem to have embarrassed Thurston, who glossed over them, but Robert D. Smith takes a more analytical tack. He states that "St. Joseph appears to have been a gymnast," citing "certain natural feats performed by St. Joseph which parallel levitation" (for example, sometimes standing on tiptoe for long periods). Smith adds:

> This opens up the possibility that at least in some of the alleged cases of levitation (many of which did, it can be noticed, originate from a leap, and not from a prone or a simple standing or kneeling position) the witnesses mistook a leap of a very agile man for levitation.[28]

Other reports of St. Joseph's alleged levitations may be attributed, Smith says, to the "gross exaggeration" of biographies published more than half a century after the saint's death. The original records of inquiry that led to Joseph's canonization are no longer available for study.[29] Even so, the canonization process itself—requiring, as it does, evidence of miracle-working—could well foster some pious exaggeration on the part of a beloved friar's brethren, not to mention trickery on the part of the friar himself, who might covet as his legacy the special status of sainthood.

Thurston felt that "the most satisfactory example" of the phenomenon was St. Teresa of Avila (1515–1582), but even that example is dubious in the extreme. Smith dismissed the claims on various grounds, summarized below:

> 1) None of Teresa's levitations occurred in public, but only before her own order and friends.

> 2) While individual witnesses testified to seeing the levitations, we have no documented examples of levitations seen by more than one person at any given time.

> 3) St. Teresa's passion for secrecy would indicate that her levitations were not well known and thus could not have been well witnessed.

4) The Church officials who transcribed eyewitness reports about the levitations kept their records confidential and presumably did not allow their informants to check over the accounts for accuracy.

5) Many accounts of St. Teresa's levitations are contradictory, and some of the witnesses altered their accounts at various times when they retold their stories.

6) St. Teresa's own accounts are suspect, because the saint experienced her levitations while in an altered state of consciousness brought on by ecstasy. She may not, therefore, have been aware of exactly what was happening to her.[30]

Although it is claimed that St. Teresa levitated in view of multiple witnesses, the source is Teresa's own autobiography, which existed only in a manuscript that was long kept from the view of outsiders. States Smith:

> Thus, St. Teresa's report that she levitated before many witnesses has no greater strength than her reports of private levitations. They both rely entirely on her own personal acceptability as a witness. Verification from others is not at hand.[31]

Smith concludes that with St. Teresa—as with all reported claims of levitation—the evidence is simply insufficient. Stating that some day the matter may be resolved, Smith concludes, "But as of now the doubt remains."[32]

Bilocation

If the evidence for levitation remains doubtful, that for bilocation—the supposed supernatural ability of being in two places simultaneously—is even more so. States Rogo:

> Evidence documenting the existence of bilocation can be found in two different bodies of literature—the autobiographic accounts of those saints and ascetics who could produce the miracle, and the testimony of witnesses who were present at the scenes of those visitations. Both sources, however, present unusual problems for the investigator. Self-delusion may well be a factor in the former, and eyewitness accounts by witnesses to miracles are hard to come by.[33]

An example of the first possibility, potential self-delusion, may be found in the case of Suor Maria Coronel (1602–1665), the abbess of a Franciscan convent at Agreda, Spain. From childhood Maria exhibited—or imitated—virtually every form of religious state known to Catholicism: She had visions; suffered demonic attacks and their attendant illnesses; practiced fasting, sleep deprivation, and self-flagellation; experienced ecstasies and saw visions; read others' minds; levitated; and allegedly bilocated. Typically, while praying alone Suor Maria would be mystically transported to Mexico where she provided religious instruction to the natives. Fearing that her bilocations might really be hallucinations, she claimed to have tested her experiences: After one such remote visit in which she recalled giving rosaries to the Mexicans, Suor Maria supposedly discovered that her supply of rosaries was depleted.[34]

As to the testimonials of eyewitnesses to bilocation, the case of St. Martin de Porres (1579–1639) supposedly provides some of the "better documented" instances, according to Rogo. For example, when Martin's fellow friars would mentally call him to their sickbeds, he would visit in the form of an "apparition" and reportedly utter consoling words or even bring medicines.[35] Yet how many of the sick were feverishly imagining the astral visits, or were remembering actual visits paid them when they were delirious? The answer cannot now be known, just as the individual anecdotal reports cannot now be verified.

As with levitation, bilocation is not an exclusive claim of saints. Many people experience a related phenomenon known as an "out-of-body experience" (OBE) in which one's "astral body" (or spirit) seems able to leave the physical body and visit other locations. (It is usually distinguished from bilocation by the lack of any physical link like that in the Suor Maria Coronel case).[36] The OBE is also termed "astral travel" or "astral projection." Skeptical parapsychologists like Susan Blackmore, however, attribute the experience to a psychological illusion,[37] and Robert A. Baker in his superb book *Hidden Memories,* states: "As for the experimental evidence, what little there is, is methodologically poor, lacking adequate controls, and the conclusions drawn are based upon inadequate data."[38]

Bilocation and astral projection are also among the feats claimed by swamis and yogis of the Orient.[39] One such case was reported in the Surat district of India, when a fakir promised that, while being "buried alive" for a month, his "astral body" would appear at a town some two hundred miles away on the fifteenth day. In this case the local governor was skeptical that the Yogi could accomplish the double miracle, so he ordered guards to apprehend the man's confederates immediately following the burial and to search for the expected secret tunnel. This was uncovered beneath a huge water jar in the men's nearby camp, and the fakir was apprehended on his way out of the tunnel.[40]

More recently, in 1965, the Indian wonder-worker Satya Sai Baba—dubbed the "Man of Miracles"[41]—supposedly added bilocation to his repertoire. This includes materializing small objects and "holy ash" (discussed later in this chapter), reading minds, and performing other magical feats that even Rogo admits are often accomplished by sleight-of-hand.[42]

Sai Baba's alleged bilocation took place at the home of Ram Rao, a technical school director in Manjeree, Kerala, many miles from the Hindu magician's residence at the time. On the day in question, Sai Baba reportedly appeared at the man's door and asked him to invite his neighbors to visit while he sang "some Sai Baba songs," produced holy ash in the manner of Sai Baba, and performed other feats in common with him. Later, eight witnesses supposedly confirmed Sai Baba's presence at the director's home while investigators reportedly established that—at the time of the alleged visitation—the miracle worker had been on the opposite side of the Indian peninsula, at Venkatagiri palace, where records established his visit.[43]

For once, Scott Rogo was a skeptic, noting that the investigation was conducted ten years after the incident and that witnesses' accounts were "somewhat inconsistent." Moreover, given Sai Baba's known penchant for trickery and illusion, Rogo concluded:

> It therefore seems possible that Sai Baba may have hired a confederate to pose as himself in Kerala. Since none of Rao's neighbors had previously seen or met Baba, such a stunt could have come off rather easily, and the Hindu miracle worker could count on it to generate added publicity and new converts.[44]

Indeed, the investigators conceded that at least two of the reported witnesses did not believe the mysterious visitor was actually Sai Baba.[45]

Although Rogo's skepticism was not unbounded, and he gave credence to many reports of the alleged phenomenon, he did acknowledge that "conventional science has no explanation for human duplication" and that "of all the miracles performed by both holy men and psychics, bilocation is perhaps the most enigmatic."[46] It may also, of course, be the most bogus.

Stigmata

Perhaps no miraculous power is more equated with sanctity in the popular mind than stigmata, the spontaneously duplicated wounds of Christ's crucifixion upon the body of a Christian. I say Christian because, as the Rev. Smith observes:

> The major non-Christian religions do not seem to have anything parallel to stigmata; their ascetics and even their mystics do not seem to claim to receive wounds which are not inflicted by external instruments, wounds produced either by human suggestion or by divine action. This is not surprising since none of the great founders of the non-Christian religions and philosophies (Buddha, Confucius, Mohammed, Socrates, Plato, etc.) died violent deaths. Stigmata are also absent in both the major separated branches of Christianity. Even the separated Christians who accept the full significance of the crucifixion of Christ have developed no "crucifixion complex" in their piety, either before or since the time of St. Francis of Assisi.[47]

Stigmata typically take the form of wounds in the hands (as in John 20:25); less commonly in the feet,[48] the side (as from the lance wound in John 19:34), and brow (as from the crown of thorns, Matt. 27:29). In rare cases, stigmatics have supposedly believed that the heart was wounded also or that its tissue had miraculously formed into the semblance of some Christian object such as a cross or chalice. A related phenomenon is the appearance on the finger of certain "brides of Christ" of a "mystical ring" which may take the form of a reddish band, a thickening of the skin, or the like.[49]

History's first recorded stigmatic was St. Francis of Assisi, the founder of the Franciscan Order, whose alleged ability to levitate was noted earlier. He supposedly exhibited the stigmata in 1224, two years before his death. Francis had gone with some of his "disciples" up Mount Alverno in the Apennines where—on September 14 (then celebrated as Holy Cross Day), after forty days of fasting and prayer—he had a vision. As described in the *Fioretti* (an early work of Francis's acts and sayings):

> He began to contemplate the Passion of Christ . . . and his fervor grew so strong within him that he became wholly transformed into Jesus through love and compassion.
>
> And on this same morning, while he was thus inflamed by this con-

templation, he saw a seraph with six shining, fiery wings descend from heaven. This seraph drew near to Saint Francis in swift flight, so that he could see him clearly and recognize that he had the form of a man crucified. . . .

As Saint Francis gazed on him he was filled with great fear, and at the same time with great joy, sorrow and wonder. He felt great joy at the gracious face of Christ, who appeared to him so familiarly and looked on him so kindly; but seeing him nailed to the cross, he felt infinite sorrow and compassion. . . . Then after a long period of secret converse this marvelous vision faded, leaving . . . in his body a wonderful image and imprint of the Passion of Christ. For in the hands and feet of Saint Francis forthwith began to appear the marks of the nails in the same manner as he had seen them in the body of Jesus crucified. . . .[50]

While this account dates from nearly a century after the event, Francis's successor, Brother Leo, sent out this message to Franciscans on the death of the future saint:

I announce to you great joy, even a new miracle. From the beginning of ages there has not been heard so great a wonder, save only in the Son of God. . . . For, a long while before his death, our Father and Brother [Francis] appeared crucified, bearing in his body the five wounds which are verily the stigmata of the Christ. For his hands and feet had as it were piercings made by nails fixed in from above and below, which laid open the scars and had the black appearance of nails; while his side appeared to have been lanced, and blood often trickled therefrom.[51]

(See Figure 17.)

It should be pointed out that Francis's stigmata occurred in a medieval climate of morbid fascination with the physical effects of crucifixion—depicted in art, shown in miracle plays, and expressed in acts of self-mutilation. For example, just two years before Francis exhibited the stigmata a young man was tried on a charge that he "made himself out to be Christ and . . . perforated his hands and feet," apparently deliberately, so as to enable him to be repeatedly nailed to a cross for exhibitionistic purposes.[52] Although Ian Wilson ultimately comes to the opposite conclusion, he concedes, in his *The Bleeding Mind,* the possibility that given such fascination with crucifixion at the time, St. Francis, "not necessarily with any conscious deception on his part, might in some hunger-crazed state have similarly inflicted crucifixion wounds upon himself."[53]

Certainly there have been fake stigmatics. In a rare moment of skepticism, Michael Freze, author of *They Bore the Wounds of Christ: The Mystery of the Sacred Stigmata,* admits that "there have been cases where some overly fanatic souls have so desired the Sacred Stigmata that they have intentionally wounded themselves with knives, picks, etc., in order to produce false impressions to others that they were extraordinary saints!"[54] Despite this all-too-brief acknowledgment of deliberately faked stigmata—as if they were uncommon—Freze does admit there are other types of "false Stigmata" which he attributes to such "possible causes" as "diabolical origins; mental disease or sickness; hysteria; self-hypnotic suggestion; and nervous conditions that can cause the skin to redden, break and even bleed."[55] By contrast, in *Comparative Miracles* the Rev. Smith freely admits that since St. Francis, a great many impostors have attempted to simulate true stigmata.[56]

Ian Wilson catalogs several cases of such fakery. For example, Magdalena de la Cruz (1487–1560) underwent ecstasies, abstained from food, performed mortifications (self-punishment), and finally exhibited the stigmata—practices that impressed the Spanish nobility, including Queen Isabella herself, and led expectant mothers to seek Magdalena's blessing on their awaited infants' clothing and nursery furniture. Then, becoming seriously ill in 1543 and fearing she would die a sinner, Magdalena suddenly confessed, admitting that for many years she had been practicing deceptions. She was tried by the Inquisition and received a severe sentence.[57] Such a case should give the miraculists pause, since Magdalena's deception went undetected and, had she not confessed of her own volition, she might now be venerated as St. Magdalena—her "ecstasies" and other alleged experiences and manifestations being cited by the credulous as confirmation of her sanctity. (As it is, Freze consigns her fake stigmata to the "diabolical" category, explaining that "the devil" has produced stigmatic marks "many times in the course of Christian history."[58])

Another fake stigmatic was Maria de la Visitacion (b. 1556) who exhibited a stock set of stigmata, including an inch-long wound in the side and crown-of-thorns puncture marks on the forehead. Maria was exposed by a sister nun who saw her painting a stigma onto her hand, but was defended by doctors in 1587. (Apparently her ploy—that her wounds were unbearably painful to the touch—restricted the examination to mere visual scrutiny.) Eventually Maria was investigated by the Inquisition, whose examiners scrubbed away the "wounds" to reveal unblemished flesh.[59] According to a contemporary report:

The nun of Portugal who was universally held for a saint has been found out at last. The stigmata are proved to be artificial and the whole trick invented to gain credit in the world. She was induced to act thus by two friars of her Order of St. Dominic, with a view to being able some day to tell the King that unless he handed Portugal over to Don Antonio he would be damned forever, and with the further object of raising a rebellion against the King. The friars are in the prisons of the Inquisition, the nun in a convent awaiting sentence. . . .[60]

The case is instructive in showing that medical authorities can be deceived even by imitation stigmata—not to mention real but self-inflicted wounds—and that confreres of a bogus wonder-worker may be co-conspirators in the imposture.

Yet another fake stigmatic was Palma Maria Matarelli (1825–1888), an illiterate Italian peasant whose tricks included "miraculously" producing Communion hosts on her tongue. (Recall the same stunt performed by Conchita Gonzales, discussed in "Hoax at Garabandal" in the previous chapter.) She also claimed that fire appeared spontaneously beneath her clothing, afterward showing burns in her flesh. Also, cloths which she pressed to her heart were reportedly "marked with extraordinary patterns when they were removed." Her stigmata were studied by a French medical professor, Dr. A. Imbert-Goubeyre. Fancying himself an expert on stigmatics, whose wounds he delighted in studying with a magnifying glass, the professor wrote enthusiastically of the young widow's phenomena in the 1873 edition of his *Les Stigmatisées*.[61] Yet, only two years later a singularly unimpressed Pope Pius IX stated privately:

I have had an investigation made concerning Palma. In consequence of the report which was then drawn up . . . take good heed. . . . What Palma is doing is the work of the devil, and her pretended miraculous Communions with hosts taken from St Peter's are a pure piece of trickery. It is all imposture, and I have the proofs here in the drawer of my bureau. She has befooled a whole crowd of pious and credulous souls. One of your fellow-countrymen has written a book about her which has been delated to the Holy Office. Out of consideration for the author, who is a good Catholic, and whose intentions are excellent, the Holy Office decided not to condemn him publicly, but has begged him to withdraw the book from circulation.[62]

Interestingly, Dr. Imbert-Goubeyre did not reprint his book, and his later references to Palma Matarelli were much more subdued.[63]

More recently, Gigliola Giorgini (b. 1933), an Italian whose stigmata appeared in her hands as linear scars, was discredited by church authorities, and in 1984 she was convicted of fraud by an Italian court.[64]

The genuineness of some stigmatics' wounds and other phenomena may be questioned in view of the mystic's general character. For example, Englishwoman Teresa Helena Higginson (1844–1905)—whose claims included ecstasies, mortifications, and stigmata—was once dismissed from school for "apparent poltergeist phenomena" and later accused of theft, drunkenness, and unseemly conduct: accusations that led to her dismissal as a teacher.[65] Berthe Mrazek, a Brussels-born circus performer who claimed a miracle cure in 1920 and who later received the stigmata, was first regarded seriously; but then (as Wilson explains) "doubts began to be expressed and late in 1924 she was arrested for obtaining money by deception and committed to an asylum as insane."[66]

Other stigmatics must be viewed in light of their propensity for self-punishment and self-mutilation. They include Lukardis of Oberweimar (c. 1276–1309) who, for two years before allegedly receiving the stigmata, "had the habit of driving her fingernails into her palms"(!); St. Maria Maddalena de' Pazzi (1556–1607), who, before the age of ten, "adopted the habit of hiding herself in 'the most secret part of the house,' and there whipping and mortifying herself with an improvised crown of thorns and prickly belt"; St. Margaret Maria Alacoque (1647–1690), who had a "particularly strong penchant for inflicting injuries upon herself" and who also "apparently burnt or carved the name of Jesus on her breast"; Domenica Lazzari (1815–1848), who "beat herself mercilessly with her fists"; and so on.[67] Would such people also be willing to inflict stigmata upon themselves? The answer seems obvious.

Then there are those like Therese Neumann, Padre Pio, and many others, who arouse suspicion by the sheer variety of their allegedly miraculous abilities. Neumann (1898–1962) not only exhibited the stigmata, including weeping bloody tears, but she also claimed to experience visions of Mary, undergo miraculous cures, and avoid all food and drink except daily Communion (the last claim being analyzed in the following section of this chapter).[68] Padre Pio (1887–1968) added to his exhibition of stigmata the claim that he was often physically assailed by evil spirits and that he had performed a variety of alleged "miracles." (His many reported bilocations, however, seem to be best characterized as anecdotal reports similar to Elvis Presley sightings.)[69]

Herbert Thurston attributes the phenomenon of stigmatization to the effects of suggestion:

First of all we have the striking fact that not a single case of stigmatization was heard of before the beginning of the thirteenth century. No
sooner, however, was the extraordinary phenomenon which marked the
last days of St. Francis published throughout the world, than other unques-
tionable cases of stigmata began to occur even among people who were
much lower than St. Francis in religious stature, and have continued
to occur without intermission ever since.

Therefore, Thurston states:

What I infer is that the example of St. Francis created what I have
called the "crucifixion complex." Once it had been brought home to
contemplatives that it was possible to be physically conformed to the
sufferings of Christ by bearing His wound-marks in the hands, feet and
side, then the idea of this form of union with their Divine Master took
shape in the minds of many. It became in fact a pious obsession; so
much so that in a few exceptionally sensitive individuals the idea conceived
in the mind was realized in the flesh.

Thurston continues:

If the suggestion just made were well founded, we should expect to find
that the exteriorization of the "crucifixion complex" would vary much
in degree according to the suggestibility of the particular subject. But
this is in fact what happens. It is noteworthy that in a good many cases
the development never goes any further than a certain deep reddening
of the skin or the formation of something resembling a blood blister
in the site of each of the wounds. It is equally noteworthy that the form
and position of these wounds or markings vary greatly. In some instances
the wound in the side is on the right, in others on the left. Sometimes
we have a round puncture, sometimes a straight cut, sometimes a crescent-
shaped wound.[70]

In brief, Thurston concludes: "All these things seem to point to an auto-suggested effect rather than to the operation of an external cause whatever its nature."[71] However, experimental attempts to duplicate the phenomenon, as with hypnosis, have been ultimately unsuccessful[72]—except for one instance cited by Wilson involving incredible claims which were attributed to an anonymous subject and which I suspect of having been an elaborate hoax.[73]

Indeed, I feel that hoaxing—the proven explanation in numerous cases —provides the most credible overall solution to the mystery of stigmata. Since Thurston has found "no satisfactory case of stigmatization since St. Francis of Assisi,"[74] it is well to consider whether St. Francis's own stigmata could have been faked. Smith admits that knowledge of their miraculous nature "is gained not directly and exclusively from a study of the records of his stigmata" but rather "from a consideration of his preeminent sanctity and character."[75] But what was that character? According to John Coulson's *The Saints:*

> [Francis] had only one aim, to love Christ and to imitate him and his life perfectly, even literally, and he followed this aim ever more completely from his conversion to his death. He was by nature impulsive and sensitive, with an immense capacity for self-sacrifice. . . . Above all, he was a son of the church to the marrow of his bones; her sacraments, her teaching and her priesthood were all manifestations of Christ, and his simple faith ultimately became a mystical contemplation of the incarnate word, the crucified Jesus.[76]

While this personality profile would seem inconsistent with a willingness to perpetrate deception for crass motives, it would appear entirely compatible with a desire to foster a pious hoax—one that would, to Francis's mind, promote the example of Christ to others.

Inedia

Some mystics claim to practice *inedia,* the alleged ability to forgo nourishment by suspending all eating and, sometimes, drinking—except usually the taking of Communion. In this way they supposedly fulfill Jesus' promise to the chosen:

> Verily, verily, I say unto you, Except ye eat the flesh of the Son of man, and drink his blood, ye have no life in you. Whoso eateth my flesh and drinketh my blood, hath eternal life; and I will raise him up at the last day. For my flesh is meat indeed, and my blood is drink

indeed. He that eateth my flesh, and drinketh my blood, dwelleth in me, and I in him. As the living Father hath sent me, and I live by the Father: so he that eateth me, even he shall live by me. This is the bread which came down from heaven: not as your fathers did eat manna, and are dead: he that eateth of this bread shall live for ever. (John 6: 53–58)

Of course by taking this figurative passage literally, the inedics reveal themselves as intellectually challenged, and, indeed, many have been poorly educated villagers.

Take St. Catherine of Siena (1347–1380), for example. Although her father was a prosperous tradesman, she was the youngest child of an extremely large family and in adolescence began to eschew intellectual life for prayer and solitude. At sixteen, Catherine joined a Dominican order. "Thenceforward for three years she never left her room, except to go to mass and confession, and spoke to no one except her confessor."[77]

Catherine also practiced flagellation, thought herself tortured by demons, experienced visions, and showed other symptoms of severe mental disturbance. She believed she wore a "mystical ring" that was placed on her finger by Jesus himself. Adding to this vainglory, as shown by contemporary paintings, she permitted her hand to be kissed by devotees. Catherine supposedly became stigmatized at the age of twenty-eight, but the marks disappeared so that she was left only with the pain of her five "invisible" wounds.[78] In the meantime she had begun to restrict her diet. According to Ian Wilson, Catherine "declined all food from the age of twenty, and would be sick when any was forced on her"—a condition that supposedly continued until her death thirteen years later.[79] However, in his book *Holy Anorexia,* Professor Rudolph M. Bell attributes Catherine's suffering to "an eating/vomiting pattern typical of acute anorexia," i.e., *anorexia nervosa,* a psychological condition characterized by a loathing of food. Eventually, says Bell:

Exhausted by her austerities and broken emotionally by her failure to reform the Church, Catherine's will to live gave way to an active readiness for death. She contributed directly to that outcome by not drinking water for nearly a month. The self-imposed dehydration had its effect, and Catherine entered her deathbed. She lingered on for three months, suffering greatly and experiencing only brief periods of full lucidity. During this time her adolescent uncertainties returned, and she was tormented by fear that all her work had been for naught. In semidelirious states she shouted out "Vainglory no, but the true glory and praise of God, yes," denying to herself a truth revealed by the very passion with which she refused it. In the end she had committed the sin of vainglory and had starved herself to death. It had been her will, not His, that had triumphed all these years and that now lay vanquished.[80]

Maria Maddalena de' Pazzi, discussed earlier as an alleged stigmatic who whipped herself with a crown of thorns, was also reputed to abstain from nourishment. Actually she was given to "vomiting any food except bread and water," a situation that sounds remarkably like anorexia. She also began wearing nothing but a tunic. As Wilson says, "This was somewhat skimpy for her various antics, which included . . . writhing on the floor and being hit by invisible blows." He adds: "But even this single remaining garment she would sometimes tear off in order to roll herself on thorns, or give herself another savage whipping." Wilson observes that Maria had obviously become "a florid, sadomachochistic neurotic," and he cites the opinion of one investigator that the seventeenth-century criteria by which she was elevated to sainthood would not be acceptable today.[81]

Citing the "great likelihood of imposture" in claims of inedia, Smith writes in *Comparative Miracles:*

> As with all prodigies, even apart from whether money is sought, there are many other motives by which men can be driven to great lengths in perpetrating a fraud. And inedia lends itself especially to such a purpose because of the very great difficulty in observing the phenomenon completely. Whereas most other alleged prodigies require only a short period of concentrated observation, inedia, by definition, requires a long time. And the more extraordinary the fast, the longer must the observation extend.[82]

The very problem Smith describes is well illustrated by Therese Neumann, whose surprising variety of claims was briefly mentioned in the discussion of stigmata. Therese was a peasant who spent her entire life in the Bavarian village of Konnersreuth. Her poor, Catholic family farmed and she, the eldest of nine children, helped with chores. Therese thought of becoming a missionary, but in 1918 (at the age of twenty), supposedly as the result of an injury, she began a period of confinement as an invalid. For several years Therese experienced alternate bouts of convulsions, blindness, deafness in one ear, inability to speak, paralysis in different parts of the body, and so on. The effects seem to have been due to hysterical hypochondria or, more likely, outright fakery since the alleged conditions evaded diagnosis. For example, when Therese was "blind," examination revealed that her pupils responded normally to light. Not surprisingly, therefore, are the attendant miracle "cures," notably those of her blindness in 1923 and her paralysis in May 1925. Soon, however, Therese was experiencing additional ailments and by the following year had begun to exhibit stigmata. Two years later she was also claiming inedia.[83]

Controversy began to attend Therese Neumann's various claims, particularly those of stigmata and inedia. By 1928, investigations were begun by church authorities but were received unenthusiastically by the Neumann family. A Professor Martini, who conducted a surveillance of Therese, observed that blood would flow from her wounds only on those occasions when he was persuaded to leave the room. He reported that this "arouses the suspicion" that something "needed to be hidden from observation." He added: "It was for the same reason that I disliked her frequent manipulations behind the raised coverings."[84]

As to her alleged inedia, Wilson declares that these claims also arouse "suspicion." As he says, "Therese had a vigorous, stocky build throughout most of this time, and all reason tells us that it would be impossible to survive so long without food or drink." The local bishop instigated a surveillance in 1927 that purportedly produced definitive evidence in favor of her claims, but the observations were only for fifteen days. Therese's urine was monitored during this time and for the following fortnight. A study of the results, says Wilson, is as expected for the period of observation; however, the post-observation data were indicative of "a return to normal, suggesting that once Therese was no longer subject to round-the-clock observation, she went back to normal food and drink intake." Magnifying the suspicion was Therese's subsequent refusal to undergo further surveillance.[85]

A more recent case, with even clearer evidence of fraud, was that of one Alfonsina Cottini who lived in a little Alpine village in northern Italy. When in her late fifties, Signorina Cottini took to bed, announcing that she had forsaken all food and drink and that, consequently, she no longer had any bowel or bladder functions. For ten years, she succeeded in gulling credulous pilgrims who arrived by busloads to see the pious, reclining inedic surrounded by mementos of the publicity she had generated. Eventually church authorities were alerted by stories that circulated in the area, alleging that Alfonsina was surreptitiously eating and that her sister was amassing large sums of money. Investigation by a special commission revealed that the suspicions were correct. At night Alfonsina left her bed, ate her fill, and performed other bodily functions. Among the investigators' discoveries was that the beatific Alfonsina's eliminations were "of a remarkable potency."[86]

A more modern and comic example of inedia is described in the delightful book, *High Weirdness by Mail* (1988). Under the heading "Breatharians," followed by a post box address in Larkspur, California, is this amusing entry:

> Eating is merely an acquired habit. Wiley Brooks, the guru of breatharianism, espouses a system of physical vitality by which one may stop eating and drinking entirely, and live, lichenlike, off light and air. "Modern man is the degenerate descendant of the Breatharian, and has descended through five states: Breatharianism, Liquidarianism, Fruitarianism, Vegetarianism, and Carnivorism." This health cult's faith was severely shaken when Brooks was discovered to have been sneaking out at night and buying junk food at convenience stores for all these years. Presumably, his followers have forgiven this serious backsliding, but it's left them on shaky ground so don't send money until you ascertain that they're still there.[87]

Exorcism

Still another power frequently claimed by holy persons is the ability to exorcise "demons." Curiously, alleged demon possession is a condition that often afflicts those individuals who are supposedly the most sanctified.

Belief in demon or spirit possession flourishes in societies where ignorance about mental states prevails. Such societies include relatively primitive cultures like those that may be found in the villages of Ethiopia or India, or among the voodoo practitioners of the Caribbean.

The medieval Church held that demons were able to take over an individual and control his or her behavior; by the sixteenth century, demonic behavior had become rather stereotyped: it included convulsions, unusual strength, temporary deafness or blindness, insensitivity to pain, and other abnormal characteristics such as clairvoyance. Some early notions of possession may have been fomented by three brain syndromes: epilepsy, Tourette's syndrome, and migraine,[88] but psychiatric historians have long attributed the manifestations to such aberrant mental conditions as schizophrenia and hysteria, noting that—as mental illness began to be recognized as such after the seventeenth century—demonic superstitions declined.[89]

However, Nicholas Spanos, an expert in abnormal psychology, has observed that such diagnoses do little more than label the behavior. Spanos rejects the interpretation of demon possession as mental illness; it is instead a learned role that fulfills certain important functions for those claiming it. Agreeing with Spanos, Robert A. Baker explains:

> In France, for example, during the sixteenth and seventeenth centuries the most celebrated possession cases occurred among the nuns. Becoming a nun wasn't usually highly desired, and families would place their adolescent daughters in convents to avoid the financial burden involved in providing a dowry. Unless one was truly devout, being a nun left a lot to be desired. The life was hard, dull, filled with chores, frequent prayer, rigid rules, loneliness, no men, boredom, and monotony. The unwilling nun had no means of protesting against her predicament. If she adopted the demoniac role—and the script for this role was well known by all of the nuns—this was a relatively safe way to protest. The nun could take out her frustrations on her family, her superiors, and the Church, and act out her sexual frustrations on the exorcist and other males and blame it all on the nasty, possessing demon! Other advantages of being possessed included escape from unpleasant duties and responsibilities, being the center of attention, flaunting constrictive rules and regulations, as well as getting sympathetic attention from the higher ups, priests, physicians, and others. Moreover, the possessed nun instantly became a seer who possessed strange, magical powers—one who was due awe and respect. Once a nun was possessed, and her advantages were made apparent to other nuns—epidemics of possession would often sweep across the convents. Adoption of the possession role frequently led to a dramatic rise in social status. Moreover, the demonically possessed, despite their invective against God and Church, were more the unwitting servants of the clerical establishment than they were rebels against it.[90]

Such a bout of possession was effected by a French prioress and her nuns at Loudun. Soeur Jeanne des Anges (1602–1665), developing what Ian Wilson terms "a love-hate infatuation" for Urbain Grandier, the Protestant parson of Loudun, sparked the outbreak which resulted in Grandier's being burned at the stake in 1634. Soeur Jeanne and the nuns were given to writhings and convulsions, and the prioress herself exhibited stigmatic-like designs and lettering on her skin. A bloody cross "appeared" on her forehead, and various names—including those of Jesus, Joseph, and Mary—were found on her hand. Interestingly, these never appeared on her right hand but were clustered on her left—just as a right-handed person would find it convenient to mark them.

In the late 1630s the prioress went on tour as a "walking relic" and was seen by the French king and queen as well as other notables. She was exhibited in Paris to thousands of credulous sightseers who lined up to view her remarkable hand, which she dangled out of a hotel window from four o'clock in the morning to ten o'clock at night. There were a few skeptics, but only a few, and Cardinal Richelieu rejected a proposed test that would have had Soeur Jeanne's hand enclosed in a sealed glove. He felt that such an approach would amount to testing God.[91]

As we have seen, many others who have claimed stigmata, inedia, and other powers have also supposedly exhibited demonic possession—a condition that is childishly simple to fake, as shown by a case which was the subject of a televised "exorcism" in 1991. ABC's "20/20" broadcast the segment, featuring a sixteen-year-old girl whose family claimed was possessed by no fewer than ten demonic spirits. These allegedly caused her to levitate and speak in tongues. Although psychiatrists had diagnosed the girl as actively psychotic, Catholic church authorities decided that she was indeed possessed and required an exorcism to free her of the diabolical entities.

Exhibiting what looked to me like poor acting, the girl stole glances at the camera before affecting convulsions and other "demonic" behavior. The levitations? A priest claimed that had she not been held down she *would have been* levitating! As for the speaking in tongues? The girl merely chanted "Sanka dali. Booga, booga." Although she was reportedly much improved after the exorcism and had resumed attending school, it was also reported that the teenager continued to be "on medication."[92]

What was most astonishing in this case was not the sixteen-year-old's behavior, but instead the credulity and foolishness of the adult men and women who participated in this farce. One Catholic scholar subsequently denounced the entire affair as an embarrassing carry-over from the Middle Ages, decrying such Catholic "fundamentalists." He said that exorcism "holds the faith up to ridicule."[93]

Apport Production

Certain mediums and adepts claim to produce "apports"—objects such as coins, pebbles, etc., that are allegedly materialized out of thin air or "teleported" through walls or other solid matter. (Paranormalists claim teleportation is a type of psychokinesis or mind-over-matter phenomenon.)[94]

During the heyday of spiritualism, mediums usually claimed spirits delivered the apports which sometimes consisted of flowers, live doves, or showers of semiprecious stones. However, many mediums were exposed as tricksters when investigation revealed that their productions—which typically occurred in the dark—had been hidden on their persons or in another location, such as a secret compartment of their chair.[95]

In his confessional exposé of fraudulent séance mediums, *The Psychic Mafia,* M. Lamar Keene tells how he and fellow mediums "apported" lost objects during séances. Actually an accomplice would have stolen the object on an earlier visit to the sitter's home (made on a pretext such as delivering flowers purportedly sent by an anonymous admirer). As the unsuspecting person looked for a vase for the flowers, the accomplice would quickly purloin a small object such as a piece of jewelry. Then, when the victim kept his or her next appointment with the phony medium, the object was "apported" to the séance table.[96]

Other apport producers may be found among the Sufis of Islam and the holy men of the Hindus. Among the latter is Sathya Sai Baba, the "man of miracles" whose alleged feat of bilocation was described earlier. His apports include *vibuti* (or "holy ash"), gold jewelry, religious statuettes, business cards, even dishes of food! One source asserts that although some adepts have been caught performing magic tricks, "others, such as Sai Baba of India, have never been exposed as frauds."[97]

Actually, as Scott Rogo has pointed out, there is evidence that Sai Baba "often deliberately fakes his purported miracles." According to Rogo, "When films taken of some of his exhibitions are slowed down, it is clear that he is quite an expert at sleight-of-hand."[98]

A crusader against Sai Baba and his ilk is the Indian conjurer B. Premanand, whose feats—including the production of "holy ash" from thin air—the author has been pleased to observe. A charming conjurer, Premanand differs from the Indian godmen only in his ready admission that his wonder-workings are the result of simple tricks.[99] According to one source, "Sai Baba, it appears, has often actually changed his itinerary on hearing that Premanand was going to examine his performance. Today, claims Premananad, Sai Baba only performs within the hallowed and 'safe' precincts of his own *ashram,* helped by almost 5,000 devotees."[101] As for himself, Premanand states:

> When I was 12, I was a great believer in miracles and wanted to possess "miracle" powers. At 19, I left home in search of God, and miracles. No one could give me a real definition of God, but I did see several miracles! Six months later, I returned, convinced that all miracles are fraudulent.[102]

Select Bibliography

Gibson, Walter B. *Secrets of Magic: Ancient and Modern.* New York: Grosset & Dunlap, 1967. Illustrated explanations of secrets behind many feats performed by alleged miracle workers, such as levitation, "suspended animation," spirit communication, and the like.

Rogo, D. Scott. "Miraculous Talents." Part One of *Miracles: A Parascientific Inquiry into Wondrous Phenomena.* New York: Dial Press, 1982. A discussion of levitation, stigmata, and bilocation (each at chapter length) as putatively paranormal phenomena.

Smith, Robert D. *Comparative Miracles.* St. Louis, Mo.: B. Herder Book Co., 1965. A rather skeptical look at levitation, stigmata, inedia, and similar phenomena by a Catholic writer who nevertheless believes that genuine miracles do occur; also includes a critical look at the supposedly miraculous production of the Koran.

Treece, Patricia. *The Sanctified Body.* New York: Doubleday, 1989. A credulous look at such alleged phenomena as luminosity, inedia, levitation, and bilocations, written by a Catholic convert.

Watkins, A. J., and W. S. Brickel. "A Study of the Kirlian Effect." *The Skeptical Inquirer* 10.3 (Spring 1986): 244–57. A demystification of the so-called Kirlian effect, alleged by paranormalists to represent photos of the human "aura."

Wilson, Ian. *The Bleeding Mind: An Investigation into the Mysterious Phenomenon of Stigmata.* London: Weidenfeld and Nicholson, 1988. An extended discussion of stigmata, suggesting that it has a "mind over matter" origin, while acknowledging that in many cases the wounds have been self-inflicted or otherwise faked.

Notes

1. Patricia Treece, *The Sanctified Body* (New York: Doubleday, 1989), pp. 2, 10.

2. "Aureola, Aureole," *Encyclopaedia Britannica,* 1960 ed.

3. Richard Cavendish, ed., *Encyclopedia of the Unexplained: Magic, Occultism and Parapsychology* (London: Routledge & Kegan Paul, 1974), p. 48.

4. Treece, *The Sanctified Body,* pp. 30–31.

5. Quoted in Treece, *The Sanctified Body,* p. 33.

6. Ibid., p. 29.

7. Ibid., pp. 42, 43.

8. W. J. Kilner, *The Human Atmosphere,* 1911; reprinted as *The Aura* (York Beach, Maine: Samuel Weiser, 1984).

9. *The British Medical Journal,* January 6, 1912; quoted in the foreword to the 1984 edition of Kilner, *The Human Atmosphere,* p. iii.

10. A. J. Watkins and W. S. Bickel, "A Study of the Kirlian Effect," *The Skeptical Inquirer* 10.3 (Spring 1986): 244–57. See also Terence Hines, *Pseudoscience and the Paranormal* (Buffalo, N.Y.: Prometheus Books, 1988), p. 302.

11. R. W. Loftin, "Auras: Searching for the Light, *The Skeptical Inquirer* 14.4 (Summer 1990): 403–409.

12. Robert Steiner, "Live TV Special Explores, Tests Psychic Powers," *The Skeptical Inquirer* 14.1 (Fall 1989): 3.

13. Robert D. Smith, *Comparative Miracles* (St. Louis, Mo.: B. Herder Book Co., 1965), p. 35.

14. Walter B. Gibson, *Secrets of Magic: Ancient and Modern* (New York: Grosset & Dunlap, 1967), p. 81.

15. See ibid., pp. 114–16, for example. See also Henry Hay, ed., *Cyclopedia of Magic* (Philadelphia: David McKay, 1949), pp. 291–92.

16. Gibson, *Secrets of Magic,* p. 82.

17. Ibid., p. 83.

18. James Randi, *Flim-Flam! Psychics, ESP, Unicorns and Other Delusions* (Buffalo, N.Y.: Prometheus Books, 1982), pp. 99–108. Other fake levitation photos have been made. For example, one of British medium Colin Evans in 1937 shows him in a hunched position with his hair mussed and his feet and hands blurred—obvious indicators that he jumped into the air as the photo was being snapped. The photograph is reproduced in Joyce Robbins, *The World's Greatest Mysteries* (New York: Gallery Books, 1989), p. 56. A 1934 photo of Brazilian medium Carlos Mirabelli "levitating" was examined by Gordon Stein ("Famous Levitation Photo Is a Fake," *Skeptical Inquirer* 15 [Winter 1991]: 119–20) and found to have been chemically retouched to remove the stepladder that Mirabelli was standing on.

19. See, for example, the following: John Mulholland, *Beware Familiar Spirits* (1938; reprint New York: Scribners, 1979), pp. 50–51; Milbourne Christopher, *ESP, Seers & Psychics* (New York: Thomas Y. Crowell, 1970), pp. 176, 185–86; and Gordon Stein, "The Lore of Levitation," *The Skeptical Inquirer* 13.3 (Spring 1989): 277–78.

20. This discussion is adapted from the author's biography of Home in his *Wonder-workers! How They Perform the Impossible* (Buffalo, N.Y.: Prometheus Books, 1991), pp. 26–33.

21. Quoted in *Wonder-workers*, p. 31.

22. Although the rooms were dark, the men claimed to have witnessed the feat by moonlight. However, an 1868 almanac shows there would have been a new moon which—according to historian Trevor Hall—"therefore could not even faintly have illuminated the room" (quoted in *Wonder-workers*, p. 31).

23. Ibid., p. 33.

24. Additional saints who allegedly levitated are listed in Smith, *Comparative Miracles*, pp. 37–38.

25. Ibid., p. 38.

26. Herbert Thurston, *The Physical Phenomena of Mysticism* (Chicago: H. Regnery Co., 1952), p. 9 (quoted in Smith, *Comparative Miracles*, p. 38).

27. Eric Dingwall, *Some Human Oddities* (1947), quoted in D. Scott Rogo, *Miracles: A Parascientific Inquiry into Wondrous Phenomena* (New York: Dial Press, 1982), p. 24.

28. Smith, *Comparative Miracles*, pp. 48–49.

29. Ibid., p. 48.

30. Summarized in Rogo, *Miracles*, p. 19; cf. Smith, *Comparative Miracles*, pp. 41–43.

31. Smith, *Comparative Miracles*, p. 44.

32. Ibid., p. 52.

33. Rogo, *Miracles*, p. 82.

34. Ibid., pp. 85–86.

35. Ibid., pp. 82–84.

36. See "Bilocation" and "Out-of-body experience" in Rosemary Ellen Guiley, *Harper's Encyclopedia of Mystical and Paranormal Experience* (New York: Harper Collins, 1991), pp. 57, 419–23.

37. Susan J. Blackmore, *Beyond the Body* (London: Granada, 1982); *Adventures of a Parapsychologist* (Buffalo, N.Y.: Prometheus Books, 1986); and "Visions from the Dying Brain," *New Scientist*, May 1988, pp. 43–46.

38. Robert A. Baker, *Hidden Memories: Voices and Visions from Within* (Buffalo, N.Y.: Prometheus Books, 1992), p. 267.

39. Rogo, *Miracles*, p. 89.

40. Gibson, *Secrets of Magic: Ancient and Modern*, p. 106.

41. Howard Murphet, *Sai Baba: Man of Miracles* (York Beach, Maine: Samuel Weiser, 1973).

42. Rogo, *Miracles,* p. 90.

43. Ibid., pp. 89–90. Rogo cites Karlis Osis and Erlendur Haraldsson, "OOBE's in Indian Swamis: Satya Sai Baba and Dadaji," in *Research in Parapsychology 1975,* ed. by Joanna Morris, Robert Morris, and W. G. Roll (Metuchen, N.J.: Scarecrow Press, 1976).

44. Rogo, *Miracles,* p. 90.

45. Ibid.

46. Ibid., p. 109.

47. Smith, *Comparative Miracles,* p. 29. Protestant stigmatics are exceedingly rare but not nonexistent.

48. The gospels do not mention the nailing of Jesus' feet, and the only reference to the nail wounds in the hands is the post-resurrection statement of Thomas, "Except I shall see in his hands the print of the nails. . . ." (John 20:25). Many Christians cite a passage in Psalms which they believe foretold the crucifixion: "they pierced my hands and my feet" (Psalms 22:16).

49. Smith, *Comparative Miracles,* p. 23.

50. From the *Fioretti* or "Little Flowers," comprised almost a century after the saint's death. This quote is in *The Little Flowers of St. Francis,* trans. L. Sherley-Price (1959), quoted in Ian Wilson, *The Bleeding Mind: An Investigation into the Mysterious Phenomenon of Stigmata* (London: Weidenfeld and Nicolson, 1988), pp. 11–12. See also "Francis of Assisi, St.," *Encyclopaedia Britannica,* 1960 ed.

51. Brother Leo, from his message of 1226, translated by Reginald Balfour, *Seraphic Keepsake,* quoted in Wilson, *The Bleeding Mind,* p. 13.

52. Wilson, *The Bleeding Mind,* p. 18.

53. Ibid.

54. Michael Freze, *They Bore the Wounds of Christ: The Mystery of the Sacred Stigmata* (Huntington, Ind.: Our Sunday Visitor, 1989), p. 216.

55. Ibid., p. 13.

56. Smith, *Comparative Miracles,* p. 24.

57. Wilson, *The Bleeding Mind,* pp. 25–26, 135.

58. Freze, *They Bore the Wounds of Christ,* p. 216.

59. Wilson, *The Bleeding Mind,* pp. 26–27, 136.

60. Quoted in Wilson, *The Bleeding Mind,* pp. 26–27.

61. Wilson, *The Bleeding Mind,* pp. 10, 37, 41–42, 141, 142.

62. Mgr. Barbier de Montault, quoted in Wilson, *The Bleeding Mind,* p. 42.

63. Wilson, *The Bleeding Mind,* p. 42.

64. Ibid., p. 147.

65. Ibid., p. 142.

66. Ibid., pp. 144-45.

67. Ibid., pp. 24, 132, 139, 141.

68. Ibid., pp. 47-53, 77, 145.

69. Ibid.; see also John McCaffery, *Tales of Padre Pio* (Kansas City, Kan.: Andrews and McMeel, 1978).

70. Thurston, *The Physical Phenomena of Mysticism*, pp. 122-23.

71. Ibid., p. 123.

72. Smith, *Comparative Miracles*, p. 25.

73. See Wilson, *The Bleeding Mind*, pp. 93-99, 112, 117. The psychiatrist, Dr. Alfred Lechler, reported that bloody tears welled inside her eyelids, then poured down her cheeks; however, a photograph of the subject—"Elizabeth K"—shows rivulets originating outside the eyes. (See photo in Wilson, *The Bleeding Mind*, the thirteenth unnumbered page of photographs following p. 86.)

74. Thurston, *The Physical Phenomena of Mysticism*, p. 100.

75. Smith, *Comparative Miracles*, p. 28.

76. John Coulson, ed., *The Saints: A Concise Biographical Dictionary* (New York: Hawthorn Books, 1958), p. 188.

77. Ibid., p. 106.

78. Rudolph M. Bell, "Holy Anorexics: Seeking God through Self-Starvation," *Rutgers Alumni Magazine*, February 1986, pp. 10-13, consisting of excerpts from Bell's *Holy Anorexia* (Chicago: University of Chicago Press, 1985),

79. Wilson, *The Bleeding Mind*, p. 133.

80. Bell, *Holy Anorexics*, p. 13.

81. Wilson, *The Bleeding Mind*, pp. 24-25, 136. Wilson refers to the late Eric Dingwall, *Very Peculiar People* (1950).

82. Smith, *Comparative Miracles*, p. 33.

83. Rogo, *Miracles*, pp. 47-50; Wilson, *The Bleeding Mind*, pp. 65-68.

84. Quoted in Wilson, *The Bleeding Mind*, p. 53.

85. Ibid., pp. 114-15.

86. Dalbert Hallenstein, "Saints," *Sunday Times* (London), November 9, 1980, cited in Wilson, *The Bleeding Mind*, pp. 115-16.

87. Rev Ivan Stang, *High Weirdness by Mail* (New York: Simon & Schuster, 1988), p. 33.

88. Barry L. Beyerstein, "Neuropathology and the Legacy of Spiritual Possession," *The Skeptical Inquirer* 12.3 (Spring 1988): 248-62.

89. Baker, *Hidden Memories*, p. 192.

90. Ibid., pp. 194-95.

91. Wilson, *The Bleeding Mind*, pp. 27-28, 137-38. (Wilson seems unsure as to whether or not Soeur Jeanne was faking.) For the secret to one method of "blood writing" see Gibson, *Secrets of Magic: Ancient and Modern*, pp. 143-44.

92. *The Exorcism,* "20/20" (ABC network), April 5, 1991. See also "ABC

to Televise an Exorcism in Florida," *USA Today,* April 5, 1991, and "Real-life Exorcism Hits Prime-Time Television," *Newark Star-Ledger,* April 5, 1991.

93. An interview with Rev. Richard McBrien, on ABC's "Nightline," April 5, 1991.

94. Rosemary Ellen Guiley, *Harper's Encyclopedia of Mystical & Paranormal Experience* (New York: HarperCollins, 1991), pp. 30, 609.

95. Ibid., p. 30. See also John Mulholland, *Beware Familiar Spirits* (1938; reprint New York: Scribner, 1979), and Milbourne Christopher, *ESP, Seers and Psychics* (New York: Thomas Y. Crowell, 1970).

96. M. Lamar Keene, *The Psychic Mafia* (New York: St. Martin's Press, 1976), pp. 95–114. Keene explains other fake séance trappings such as floating trumpets, "ectoplasm" production, etc.

97. Guiley, *Harper's Encyclopedia of Mystical & Paranormal Experience,* p. 30.

98. Rogo, *Miracles,* p. 90.

99. Minnie Vaid-Fera, "On the Trail of the Godmen," *Imprint,* October 1987, pp. 59–64.

100. Ibid., p. 64.

101. Quoted in Vaid-Fera, "On the Trail of the Godmen."

102. Ibid., p. 61.

9

Afterword

Do miracles exist? The foregoing chapters illustrate the lack of compelling evidence for the existence of "miraculous" phenomena beyond the range of nature and man's natural capabilities. Those who would assert otherwise necessarily bear the burden of proof, and it appears to be one that is incapable of being met.

Nevertheless, claims of the miraculous continue to pour in. For example, a mere *photograph* of the spurious Image of Guadalupe (discussed in Chapter 2) was "attracting attention and amazement" from some pilgrims. Thousands flocked to Kentucky churches to see the photo, which has been on tour since 1991 and has been frequently tied to anti-abortion activities. Newspaper articles have described reports of "healings and other signs," including alleged "visions of rose petals seeming to fall from the photo," and "the feel of a heartbeat on the image." The Associated Press, however, labeled the reports "unsubstantiated."[1]

Then there was the "Jesus tree" in a park adjoining St. Michael's church in New Haven, Connecticut. A large, shaggy sycamore, the tree drew sizable crowds of pilgrims, many of whom described what they perceived as the face of Jesus in a sunken area of the tree between two of its outstretched limbs. Flowers, prayer cards, and similar offerings were heaped at the foot of the tree, but not everyone reacted piously. One man said to his wife: "Let's get out of here. You have to use your imagination."[2]

According to a news report, even some who finally "see" the face "know that they have pulled a shape out of the clouds; know that the face is muddy, put together by the mind, not particularly Jesus' face in aspect . . . and knowing that they look a little weary, a bit disappointed."[3]

A deacon at another parish, who is also director of psychological services to the homeless, was critical of the affair. He said that whereas visions of Mary appeared in times of hope, those of Jesus seemed to occur in times of despair and were accompanied by an expectation and desire for punishment. As he explained, "It's a Christian form of voyeurism: Now, God's gonna come and get all you bad people and beat you up—and I get to watch!" He though the "Jesus tree" was largely attributable to hysteria. He said that after his brother died, at the funeral his mother saw her dead son in the clouds, waving to her. "Well," said the deacon, "it must've been a pretty short wave because when I looked up, there was nothing there. But I wasn't about to tell her it was phenomenological wish fulfillment."[4]

Claims of Marian visitations continue as well. At Marlboro Township, New Jersey, Joseph Januszkiewicz, a middle-aged draftsman, claimed that the Virgin Mary had begun appearing to him. This occurred in March 1989, six months after he had visited Medjugorje and was allegedly healed of an old back injury and hearing loss. Januszkiewicz built a shrine in his back yard where, predictably, credulous folk began to arrive by the thousands. By the end of 1992, the once-a-month affair had become such a health and safety problem that township officials asked the draftsman/visionary to install "No Trespassing" signs. He refused, and subsequently the officials amended the local zoning ordinance to define a place of worship and to require Januszkiewicz to apply for a permit. Meanwhile, the Trenton diocese appointed a commission to investigate the claims, asking the faithful to avoid the site until the investigation was completed. According to newspaper reports, however, more than 2,000 people turned up anyway.[5]

On August 31, 1992, national attention shifted briefly to Cold Spring, Kentucky, where the Virgin was supposed to appear at St. Joseph's Catholic Church. Its pastor, the Rev. Leroy Smith, following his ninth visit to Medjugorje, claimed an anonymous "visionary" had told him of the visitation, which was supposed to occur inside the church at midnight. With huge throngs being forecast, the city adopted several ordinances to protect both individuals and residential property. The local police also called in the National Guard, and souvenir hawkers readied their wares—one replacing his best-selling goose figures with religious statuettes.

I joined the estimated 7,000 visitors in St. Joseph's parking lot, which began to fill in the afternoon. Although the original prediction had been for a message, not "signs" or an apparition, and although the diocesan bishop later officially concluded—after conferring with Rev. Smith—that "nothing of a miraculous nature" had occurred at the site, many of the charismatic Catholics who gathered there clearly believed otherwise.

During the afternoon there were reports of sun miracles. Some religious hopefuls exhibited instant-camera snapshots with wispy shapes that they interpreted as the visage of Mary. Instead, they were obviously due to lens flares (i.e., the result of interreflection between lens surfaces) or other artifacts. There were also the familiar pictures of the "Golden Door," as well as claims that rosaries were turning from silver to gold (both discussed in Chapter 7). (See Figures 13–16.)

Later, around midnight, came reports of "bright lights" and related "apparitions" which also seemed to fall short of the miraculous. Described as "almost like a lightning flash," or collectively, "almost . . . as if there were a light show," the effects were exactly what I, too, experienced: At midnight, countless spectators and news photographers tripped their electronic flashes—ironically in hopes of capturing the expected visitation on film.[6]

Almost two months later, in Korea, came another religious non-event. It was supposed to be "Rapture," the ascent of the faithful to heaven. This would occur at midnight, October 28, 1992, and usher in seven years of apocalypse, culminating in the annihilation of the earth and the Second Coming of Christ. The alleged prophecy—launched by the Seoul-based Mission for the Coming Days church and advertised in many newspapers across the United States—had a far different outcome, however. Some followers quit their jobs, sold their homes, and burned their furniture and other worldly possessions, and a few committed suicide before the appointed day; thousands more were left to experience nothing more than disillusionment.

Although the Christian cultists should have been forewarned by an obvious sign—the earlier arrest of the mission's pastor on charges of bilking his followers—they were obviously guided not by reason but by emotion. And when the day came and went like any other Wednesday, their emotions turned to rage: One preacher had hymnals thrown at him, another was cornered and slapped, and still another was pulled from his pulpit and beaten. Nor did the Christians turn only on their own: A cult expert who had leafleted against the doomsday leaders, calling for their prosecution on grounds they had caused social unrest, was hospitalized with serious stab wounds.[7]

These events underscore the words of Martin Gardner:

> Because no century of the Christian era has been free of believers insisting fervently that the Second Coming was just around the corner, one might suppose that today's evangelists would be uncomfortable about warning their flock to prepare for the Rapture—being lifted into the clouds to meet Jesus. But few fundamentalists have any sense of history, although they have finally learned the folly of specifying the year of the Lord's return.[8]

Of course, as the events in Seoul illustrate, not all have learned even that. However, in the wake of the failed doomsday prophecy and subsequent violence, the church disbanded the following Monday and apologized to the people of South Korea for "misinterpreting the Bible."[9]

Quite different from this contrition was the response of a Hindu "holy man" to those who doubted the genuineness of his late-1992 feat: staying submerged in a sealed tank of water for four days. At the end of the period, while some 5,000 followers chanted hymns, a tarpaulin was rolled back to reveal a 2.74-meter-deep pit that was filled with water. There, floating face down near the surface but unharmed, was Kapil Adwait, a former air force pilot known popularly as "Pilot Baba." He told the crowed: "I have mastered the art of surviving in conditions akin to that in the womb." But instead of discoursing on Hindu spiritualism, Adwait raised suspicions that his feat was merely a stunt when he quickly turned to politics and used the occasion to endorse a local candidate for prime minister.

Naturally, the Indian Rationalist Association—well aware of the "burial alive" tricks of the past (as explained in Chapter 8)—was skeptical. Association members investigated and discovered, at the bottom of the pit, two pipes that they said could have been used to drain the water. The association then challenged "Pilot Baba" to a test: repeat his feat for a mere two hours in a glass tank under properly controlled conditions. His response to the challenge? He simply ignored the skeptics.[10]

Faith healing also continues to attract the hopeful, but two newsworthy incidents provided interesting sidelights on the subject. One suggested that country music might have as great a healing power as any religion could offer. The mother of an eighteen-month-old Tennessee girl who, doctors said, would never walk because she was born with cerebral palsy, made an interesting claim. She reported that her daughter was prompted to take her first steps by the popular music video "Achy Breaky Heart" by Billy Ray Cyrus. (The possibility that the doctors might simply have been mistakenly pessimistic was apparently not considered.) Now, says the mother, "anytime [Cyrus's] music comes on, she stops what she's doing and starts dancing around and singing."[11]

Another incident concerned the operator of a faith-healing center in the Philippines who demonstrated the supposed efficacy of faith by being *crucified*. As it happens, the crucifixion was not the first endured by the woman, known as Mother Paring. Rather, it was the fifth in a projected annual series of fifteen, allegedly requested by the Virgin Mary. As might be expected, however, the "crucifixion" requires no special powers to be endured. As is typically the case, the nails are aluminum ones, soaked for a year in alcohol, then driven into the hands and feet in such a way as to miss the bones and major blood vessels. To prevent the flesh tearing from the weight of the body, the arms are supported by brackets and bandages, and the duration of the crucifixion is limited to two or three minutes. Nevertheless, following the ceremony, Mother Paring stated: "What I did was not a show; God made me do it."[12] Be that as it may, although the Catholic Church discourages such rituals, nevertheless "they have become fixtures and attract throngs of tourists, much to the delight of the impoverished local community."[13]

As such reports demonstrate, around the world miraculous claims persist, and outright miracle-mongering continues to attract the ignorant and superstitious. It has ever been so, of course, but we may hope that, eventually, the situation will improve. Perhaps this offering will enhance that possibility by making people more aware of how easy it is to be deceived—not only by pious frauds but by their own wish-fulfilling natures.

Notes

1. "Photo Draws Believers in Power of Cloak" (Associated Press), *Lexington Herald-Leader* (Lexington, Ky.), December 26, 1992.

2. Kathie Dobie, "Lord of the Trees: Jesus Appears in New Haven," *Voice*, December 29, 1992.

3. Ibid.

4. Ibid.

5. Sue Epstein, "Marlboro Girding for Crowds from 'Apparition,' " *The Star-Ledger* (Newark, N.J.), December 3, 1992.

6. This brief report is abridged from Joe Nickell, "Miraculous Signs in Cold Spring?" *Skeptical Inquirer* 17.2 (Winter 1993): 120–22.

7. J. Michael Parker, "Group Believers Rapture Scheduled Today," San Antonio *Express-News,* October 28, 1992; "Worshippers Attack Ministers in Doomsday Debacle," *Rocky Mountain News,* October 30, 1992; "Thousands of Rapture Believers in Despair," *Courier-News,* October 29, 1992.

8. Martin Gardner, "Waiting for the Last Judgment," *Washington Post* ("Book World"), November 8, 1992.

9. "World Ends for Doomsday Church in Korea, as It Disbands, Apologizes," *Rocky Mountain News,* November 3, 1992.

10. "All Politics in Mystic 'Womb,' " *The Sydney* (Australia) *Morning Herald,* undated clipping received December 1992.

11. "Achy Breaky Miracle," *Lexington Herald-Leader* (Lexington, Ky.), December 9, 1992.

12. Harry Edwards, "Crucifixion," *The Skeptic* (Australia), Spring 1992: 43.

13. Ibid.

Index